RXpert SERIES
Student's Companion

Novel Drug Delivery Systems

RXpert SERIES
Student's Companion

Novel Drug Delivery Systems

Satyanarayan Pattnaik
M. Pharm, Ph. D., FIC
Professor & Principal,
Faculty of Pharmacy
Sanskriti University, Mathura, Uttar Pradesh.

Kamla Pathak
M. Pharm, Ph. D.
Professor & Dean, Faculty of Pharmacy,
Uttar Pradesh University of Medical Sciences,
Saifai, Uttar Pradesh.

Kalpana Swain
M. Pharm, Ph. D., FIC
Professor, Faculty of Pharmacy,
Sanskriti University, Mathura, Uttar Pradesh.

PharmaMed Press™
An imprint of BSP Books Pvt. Ltd
4-4-309/316, Giriraj Lane,
Sultan Bazar, Hyderabad - 500 095.

Novel Drug Delivery Systems

***by* Satyanarayan Pattnaik, Kamla Pathak and Kalpana Swain**

Published by:

™ **PharmaMed Press**

An imprint of BSP Books Pvt. Ltd.

4-4-309/316, Giriraj Lane, Sultan Bazar, Hyderabad - 500 095.

Phone: 040-23445688; Fax: 91+40-23445611

E-mail: info@pharmamedpress.net

www.bspbooks.net/www.pharmamedpress.net

ISBN: 978-93-49562-86-8 (Hardback)

PREFACE

Novel Drug Delivery Systems (NDDS) play a crucial role in enhancing therapeutic efficacy and improving patient outcomes. This field represents a cutting-edge area of pharmaceutical science that combines principles from various disciplines to revolutionize the way drugs are administered and utilized in the body. Understanding these advanced delivery mechanisms is essential for pharmacy students as they prepare for careers in pharmaceutical sciences and healthcare.

This book has been meticulously designed to align with the syllabus prescribed by the Pharmacy Council of India (PCI), ensuring that students receive relevant and comprehensive knowledge. While primarily intended for undergraduate pharmacy students, it may also serve as a valuable resource for postgraduate students seeking deeper insights into NDDS.

I express my heartfelt gratitude to all those who have supported and encouraged me throughout this journey. Their unwavering guidance and blessings have been instrumental in bringing this book to fruition.

I sincerely hope that this book proves to be a useful companion in your academic and professional endeavors.

-Authors

Contents

Chapter 3

Microencapsulation

Chapter 4

Mucosal Drug Delivery

Chapter 1

CONTROLLED DRUG DELIVERY SYSTEMS

♦ LEARNING OBJECTIVES ♦

***After completing this lesson, the Reader should be able to understand*:**

- **The need for controlled drug delivery**
- **Various advantages and disadvantages of controlled drug delivery systems**
- **How to select drug candidates for designing controlled drug delivery systems**
- **Various principles exploited to design controlled drug delivery systems**

1.1 INTRODUCTION

The purpose of drug dosing in any disease is to achieve the desired therapeutic concentration of drug at the site of action or at least in plasma for a stated period of time, usually for the entire duration of treatment. Hence, drugs are administered at a particular amount (dose) and at a definite time interval (frequency). The frequency of drug administration usually depends on its elimination half-life or mean residence time (MRT). Better medical treatments do not always require stronger medicines. The effectiveness of drug substances depends on the method of administration. Hence, the treatment outcomes can be improved by choosing suitable drug formulations or drug delivery systems and delivering through a proper route. If the duration of therapy offered by a single administration of a dosage form is insufficient, re-administration (multiple dosing) of the dosage form is needed so as to maintain the steady-state therapeutic drug concentration in the plasma. When a drug is delivered as a conventional dosage form such as a tablet, the dosing interval is usually shorter than the half-life of the drug resulting in a number of drawbacks:

1. Multiple dosing needed for drugs with short half-lives leading to possible poor patient compliance.
2. A typical peak-valley plasma concentration-time profile is obtained which makes attainment of the steady-state condition difficult (*see* Fig 1.1).
3. The unavoidable fluctuations in the drug concentration may lead to under-medication or over-medication.
4. The fluctuating drug levels may lead to precipitation of adverse effects especially of a drug with a narrow therapeutic index whenever over-medication occurs.

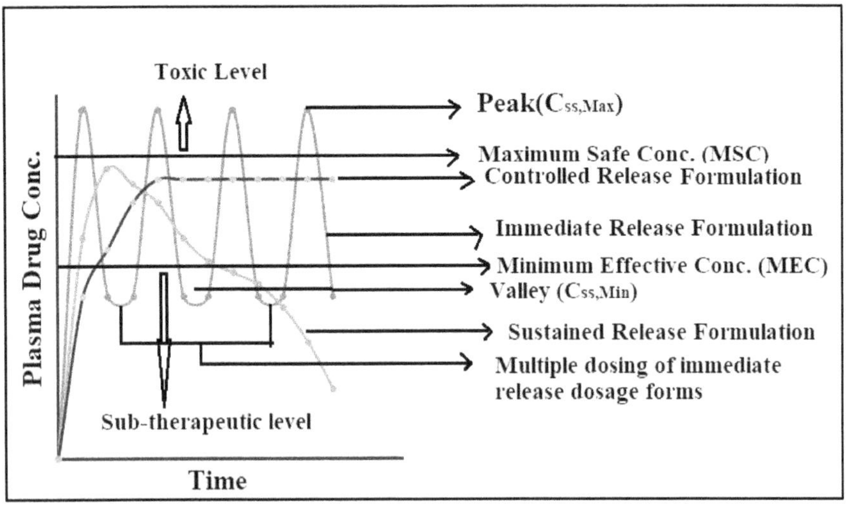

Fig.1.1 Schematic plasma drug concentration vs time profile of immediate release and controlled release drug products.

There are two ways to overcome such a situation:

1. Accelerate drug discovery strategies to develop new, better and safer drugs with longer half-lives and large therapeutic indices.
2. Re-designing of existing drugs through concepts of controlled and targeted delivery systems for effective and safer use.

Though the first approach seems very attractive, it is not a cost-effective method and therefore resulted in increased interest in the second approach. The second approach, owing to several technical advancements, has resulted in the development of drug delivery systems capable of controlling the rate of drug delivery, sustaining the duration of therapeutic action and/or targeting the delivery of drugs to a particular tissue. An ideal controlled release drug delivery system (CDDS) should deliver the drug at a rate dictated by the needs of the body over a specified period of treatment. The two basic modalities of controlled drug delivery are:

- **Spatial drug delivery:** It relates to targeting a drug to a specific organ, tissue or cell. Such precise control over the distribution of the drug is of great significance when the natural distribution causes drug molecules to encounter normal and healthy tissues (non-targets) causing damage and/or major side effects that prohibit further treatment. This situation is often the cause of non-adherence to chemotherapy regimens leading to therapeutic failure. Moreover, in certain instances, the natural distribution of the drug does not allow drug molecules to reach their molecular site of action or receptors due to various pathophysiological barriers (e.g. blood-brain barrier). In such cases controlling the drug distribution through the targeting approach could improve the treatment outcomes.
- **Temporal drug delivery:** It refers to the delivery of a drug over an extended period of time or for a specific duration during treatment. This type of control is highly beneficial for drugs having fast elimination after administration.

An appropriately designed controlled-release drug-delivery system can improve the therapeutic efficacy and safety of a drug by precise temporal and spatial placement in the body, thereby reducing both the size (dose) and the number of doses (frequency) required. Controlled drug delivery may be achieved through oral or non-oral administration.

1.2 ADVANTAGES & DISADVANTAGES OF CONTROLLED DRUG DELIVERY

***The various advantages of controlled drug delivery systems include*:**

1. Improved patient convenience and compliance due to less frequent drug administration.
2. Reduction in fluctuation in steady-state levels and therefore –
   - Better control of disease condition, and
   - Reduced-intensity of local or systemic side-effects.
3. Increased safety margin of high potency drugs due to better control of plasma levels.
4. Maximum utilization of drug enabling reduction in the total amount of dose administered.
5. Reduction in health care costs through –
   - Improved therapy
   - Shorter treatment period

- Lower frequency of dosing, and
- Reduction in personnel time to dispense, administer and monitor patients.

The various disadvantages associated with controlled drug delivery systems include:

1. Decreased systemic availability in comparison to immediate-release conventional dosage forms. This may be due to:
   - Partial or incomplete release
   - First-pass hepatic metabolism
   - Insufficient gastrointestinal residence time
   - Site-specific absorption of drugs having narrow absorption windows
   - pH-dependent solubility.
2. Poor *in vitro–in vivo* correlation.
3. Possibility of dose dumping due to food, physiologic or formulation variables or chewing or grinding of oral formulations by the patient and thus, increased risk of toxicity.
4. Treatment withdrawal is difficult in case of toxicity, poisoning or hypersensitivity reactions.
5. Limited or no flexibility for dosage adjustment of drugs normally administered in varying strengths.
6. Formulation cost is too high.

1.3 SELECTION OF DRUG CANDIDATES

All drugs are not candidates for controlled delivery. Hence, developmental strategies for oral controlled drug delivery warrant for a rational selection of drug candidates. Various physicochemical, pharmacokinetic and pharmacodynamic factors related to the drug candidates dictate their suitability for controlled delivery. The selection criteria are outlined as follows:

A. Physicochemical factors

The acronym LADME refers to liberation, absorption, distribution, metabolism, and excretion of drugs. Each of these LADME processes potentially affects the performance of a drug presented as a controlled-release system. The first step upon administration of a dosage form is release (liberation) of the drug (s) from the dosage form and subsequent to this is the migration to the site of action. The liberation or release of drugs from the drug delivery system (dosage form) depends upon the fabrication of the formulation and the physicochemical properties of the drug whereas the migration of the drug to the site of action depends on the pharmacokinetics of the drug. In comparison to conventional dosage form where the rate-limiting step in drug bioavailability is usually absorption through the biomembrane, the rate-determining step in the availability of a drug from the controlled delivery system is the rate of release of drug from the dosage form which is much smaller than the intrinsic absorption rate for the drug. The desired physicochemical properties of a drug to be used in a controlled-release drug delivery system are discussed below.

1. **Molecular Weight:** Lower the molecular weight, faster and more complete the absorption. For drugs absorbed by the pore transport mechanism, the molecular size threshold is 150 Daltons for spherical compounds and 400 Daltons for linear compounds. However, more than 95% of drugs are absorbed by passive diffusion. Drugs with large molecular size are poor candidates for oral controlled-release systems e.g. peptides and proteins.
2. **Aqueous Solubility:** A drug with good aqueous solubility, especially if pH-independent, serves as a good candidate for controlled-release dosage forms e.g. pentoxifylline. The lower limit of solubility of a drug to be formulated as CDDS is 0.1mg/ml. Drugs with pH-dependent aqueous solubility e.g. phenytoin, or drugs with solubility in non-aqueous solvents e.g. steroids, are suitable for parenteral (e.g. i.m. depots) controlled-release dosage forms; the drug precipitates at the injection site and thus, its release is slowed down due to change in pH or contact with aqueous body fluids. The solubility of drugs can limit the choice of mechanism to be employed in CDDS, for example, diffusional systems are not suitable for poorly soluble drugs. Absorption of poorly soluble drugs is dissolution rate-limited which means that the controlled-release device does not control the absorption process; hence, they are poor candidates for such systems.
3. **Lipophilicity:** Greater the apparent partition coefficient of a drug, greater its lipophilicity and thus, greater is its rate and extent of absorption. Such drugs have increased tendency to cross even the more selective barriers like BBB. The apparent volume of distribution of such drugs also increases due to increased partitioning into the fatty tissues and since the blood flow rate to such tissues is always lower than that to an aqueous tissue like liver, they may exhibit characteristics of models having two or more compartments. The parameter is also important in determining the release rate of a drug from lipophilic matrix or device.
4. **Drug pK_a and Ionisation at Physiological pH:** The pK_a range for acidic drugs whose ionisation is pH-sensitive is 3.0 to 7.5 and that for basic drugs is 7.0 to 11.0. For optimum passive absorption, the drugs should be non-ionised at that site at least to an extent 0.1 to 5%. Drugs existing largely in ionised forms are poor candidates for controlled delivery.

5. **Drug Stability:** Drugs that are unstable in GI environment cannot be administered as oral controlled-release formulation because of bioavailability problems e.g. nitroglycerine. A different route of administration should then be selected such as the transdermal route or buccal route. Drugs unstable in gastric pH, e.g. propantheline can be designed for sustained delivery in intestine with limited or no delivery in stomach. On the other hand, a drug unstable in intestine, e.g. probanthine, can be formulated as gastroretentive dosage form.
6. **Mechanism and Site of Absorption:** Drugs absorbed by carrier-mediated transport processes and those absorbed through a *window* are poor candidates for controlled-release systems e.g. several B vitamins.
7. **Biopharmaceutic Aspects of Route of Administration:** Oral and parenteral (i.m.) routes are the most popular followed by transdermal application. Routes of minor importance in controlled drug delivery are buccal/sublingual, rectal, nasal, ocular, pulmonary, vaginal and intrauterinal. The features desirable for a drug to be given by a particular route are discussed below.
   (a) **Oral Route:** For a drug to be successful as oral controlled-release formulation, it must get absorbed through the entire length of GIT. Since the main limitation of this route is the transit time (a mean of 14 hours), the duration of action can be extended for 12 to 24 hours. The route is suitable for drugs given in dose as high as 1000 mg. A drug, whose absorption is pH-dependent, destabilized by GI fluids/enzymes, undergoes extensive presystemic metabolism (e.g. nitroglycerine), influenced by gut motility, has an absorption window and/or absorbed actively (e.g. riboflavin), is a poor candidate for oral controlled-release formulations.

   (b) **Intramuscular/Subcutaneous Routes:** These routes are suitable when the duration of action is to be prolonged from 24 hours to 12 months. Only a small amount of drug, about 2 ml or 2 grams, can be administered by these routes. Factors important in drug release by such routes are solubility of drug in the surrounding tissues, molecular weight, partition coefficient and pK_a of the drug and contact surface between the drug and the surrounding tissues.

   (c) **Transdermal Route:** The route is best suited for drugs showing extensive first-pass metabolism upon oral administration or drugs with low dose such as nitroglycerine. Important factors to be considered for percutaneous drug absorption are partition coefficient of drug, contact area, skin condition, skin permeability of drug, skin perfusion rate, etc.

In short, the main determinants in deciding a route for administration of a controlled-release system are physicochemical properties of the drug, dose size, absorption efficiency and desired duration of action.

B. Pharmacokinetic Characteristics of Drug

A detailed knowledge of the ADME characteristics of a drug is essential in the design of a controlled-release product. An optimum range of a given pharmacokinetic parameter of a drug is necessary beyond which controlled delivery is difficult or impossible.

1. **Absorption Rate:** For a drug to be administered as controlled-release formulation, its absorption must be efficient since the desired rate-limiting step is rate of drug release K_r i.e. $K_r << K_a$. A drug with slow absorption is a poor candidate for such dosage forms since continuous release will result in a pool of unabsorbed drug e.g. iron. Aqueous soluble but poorly absorbed potent drugs like decamethonium are also unsuitable candidates since a slight variation in the absorption may precipitate potential toxicity.
2. **Elimination Half-Life:** An ideal CRDDS is the one from which rate of drug of absorption (for extended period of time) is equal to the rate of elimination. Smaller the $t_{½}$, larger the amount of drug to be incorporated in the controlled-release dosage form. For drugs with $t_{½}$ less than 2 hours, a very large dose may be required to maintain the high release rate. Drugs with half-life in the range 2 to 4 hours make good candidates for such a system e.g. propranolol. Drugs with long half-life need not be presented in such a formulation e.g. amlodipine. For some drugs e.g. MAO inhibitors, the duration of action is longer than that predicted by their half-lives. A candidate drug must have $t_{½}$ that can be correlated with its pharmacological response. In terms of MRT, a drug administered as controlled-release dosage form should have MRT significantly longer than that from conventional dosage forms.
3. **Rate of Metabolism:** A drug which is extensively metabolized is suitable for controlled-release system as long as the rate of metabolism is not too rapid. The extent of metabolism should be identical and predictable when the drug is administered by different routes. A drug capable of inducing or inhibiting metabolism is a poor candidate for such a product since steady-state blood levels would be difficult to maintain.
4. **Dosage Form Index (DI):** It is defined as the ratio of $C_{ss,max}$ to $C_{ss,min}$. Since the goal of controlled-release formulation is to improve therapy by reducing the dosage form index while maintaining the plasma drug levels within the therapeutic window, ideally its value should be as close to *one* as possible.

C. Pharmacodynamic Characteristics of Drug

1. **Drug Dose:** In general, dose strength of 1.0 g is considered maximum for a CDDS.
2. **Therapeutic Range:** A candidate drug for controlled-release drug delivery system should have a therapeutic range wide enough such that variations in the release rate do not result in a concentration beyond this level.
3. **Therapeutic Index (TI):** The release rate of a drug with narrow therapeutic index should be such that the plasma concentration attained is within the therapeutically safe and effective range. This is necessary because such drugs have toxic concentration nearer to their therapeutic range. Precise control of release rate of a potent drug with narrow margin of safety is difficult. A drug with short half-life and narrow therapeutic index should be administered more frequently than twice a day. One must also consider the activity of drug metabolites since controlled delivery system controls only the release of parent drug but not its metabolism.
4. **Plasma Concentration-Response (PK/PD) Relationship:** Drugs such as reserpine whose pharmacological activity is independent of its concentration are poor candidates for controlled-release systems.

A summary of desired biopharmaceutic, pharmacokinetic and pharmacodynamic properties of a drug is given in table 1.1.

Table 1.1 Factors affecting the Design of Controlled Release Systems.

	Properties of Candidate Drug	**Desired Features**
A.	***Biopharmaceutic Properties***	
	1. Molecular size	< 600 Daltons
	2. Aqueous solubility	> 0.1 mg/ml
	3. Partition coefficient $K_{o/w}$	Within 1 – 2
	4. Dissociation constant pK_a	Acidic drugs, $pK_a > 2.5$ Basic drugs, $pK_a < 11.0$
	5. Ionisation at physiological pH	Not more than 95%
	6. Stability in GI environment	Stable at both gastric and intestinal pH
	7. Absorption mechanism	Passive, no absorption window
B.	***Pharmacokinetic Properties***	
	1. Absorption rate constant K_a	High
	2. Elimination half-life $t_{½}$	2 – 4 hours
	3. Metabolism rate	Not too high
	4. Dosage form index	One

Table contd...

C.	*Pharmacodynamic Properties*	
	1. Dose	Not beyond 1.0 g
	2. Therapeutic range	Broad
	3. Therapeutic index	Broad
	4. PK/PD relationship	Good

1.4 DESIGN OF CONTROLLED DRUG DELIVERY SYSTEMS

The release of drug from the drug delivery device may be controlled by various principles i.e. diffusion, dissolution, etc. The optimal control on the drug release often achieved by combination of principles. The delivery can be either systemically or locally. The controlled release formulations may be classified based on the principle(s) of drug release as follows:

A. Diffusion-controlled drug delivery systems

In these types of systems, the rate of drug release from the controlled release product depends on the diffusion of dissolved drug molecules through the polymeric barriers. The rate determining step (slowest step) in these systems is diffusion. The rate-controlling element (usually polymers) in such a system is thus not soluble, not erodible nor degradable but is water-swellable or water-insoluble. Water-swellable materials include hydrophilic polymers and gums such as xanthan gum, guar gum, high viscosity grades of HPMC and HPC, alginates, etc. Water-insoluble polymers most commonly used in such systems are ethyl cellulose and polymethacrylates.

B. Dissolution-controlled drug delivery systems

In these systems the rate-limiting phenomenon responsible for imparting the controlled-release characteristics to the drug delivery device is either of the two:

(a) **Slow dissolution rate of the drug:** The drug present in such a system may have inherently slow dissolution rate e.g. griseofulvin, digoxin and nifedipine. Such drugs act as natural prolonged-release products. The systems may also include drugs that convert to slow dissolving forms on contact with GI fluids e.g. ferrous sulphate.

(b) **Slow dissolution rate of the reservoir membrane or matrix:** The drug present in such a system may be the one having high aqueous solubility and dissolution rate e.g. pentoxifylline and metformin. The challenge in designing such systems lies in controlling the drug dissolution rate by employing either or combination of following techniques:

   i. Embedment in slowly dissolving or erodible matrix. The matrix in addition may have low porosity or poor wettability.

ii. Encapsulation or coating with slow-dissolving or erodible substances. In this approach, the rate of dissolution fluid penetration and/or wettability of the reservoir system are controlled.

Slowly soluble and erodible materials commonly employed to achieve these objectives include hydrophobic substances such as ethyl cellulose, polymethacrylates with pH independent solubility (e.g. Eudragit RS and RL 100) and waxes such as glyceryl monostearate, and hydrophilic materials like sodium carboxy methylcellulose.

C. Diffusion and Dissolution-controlled drug delivery systems

The rate of drug release from these systems is controlled by both diffusion of drug and dissolution of drug and/or release modifying polymer(s). Since, dual control is available, there exist more possibilities to fine tune the drug release characteristics as per the requirements in varied situations.

D. Ion-Exchange Resin based systems

Controlled delivery of ionizable acidic and basic drugs can be obtained by complexing them with insoluble non-toxic anion exchange and cation exchange resins respectively. The drug is released slowly by diffusion through the resin particle structure. The following equation represents the release of a basic drug, NH2R', from a cation exchange resin RSO_3H when in contact with GI fluid containing an ionic compound A^+B^- (either gastric HCl or intestinal NaCl):

$$RSO_3^-NH_3^+R' + A^+B^- \longrightarrow RSO_3^-A^+ + NH3{+}R'B^-$$

A number of basic drugs like noscapine, phenylpropanolamine and phentermine have been retarded by such an approach. The complex can be prepared by incubating the drug-resin solution or passing the drug solution through a column containing ion-exchange resin. The drug-resin complex can be coated with cellulose or hard paraffin and formulated as ion free suspension for paediatric use.

The principles mentioned above are exploited while designing of controlled drug delivery systems in broad categories like reservoir type systems and matrix type systems. Both types of systems contain appropriate type and amount of release modifying agent or polymer(s) to control the release rate of drug.

A. Reservoir type systems

In these systems, the drug is present as a core compartment encapsulated by release controlling polymeric membrane (see Fig 1.2). Hence, these systems are also called as membrane-controlled delivery systems. The drug in the core must dissolve in the micro-environment fluid, partition and diffuse through the membrane for successful drug delivery. Upon administration of the drug delivery device, the body fluid (e.g. gastrointestinal fluid in case of oral administration) comes in contact with the system and permeate through the membrane/film to enter inside the device to reach the drug core and dissolve the drug. The dissolved drug, then, partitions and diffuses through the membrane/film. The physicochemical nature and the thickness of the membrane control the rate of fluid permeation into the drug delivery device and rate of diffusion of dissolved drug from the device. These systems include coated drug particles, crystals, granules, pellets, minitablets and tablets.

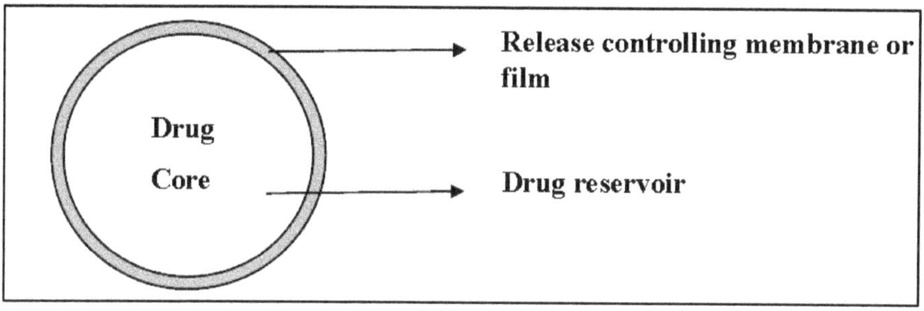

Fig.1.2 Schematic representation of Reservoir type-CDDS.

B. Matrix type systems

In these systems, the drug is uniformly distributed or dispersed in the release retarding polymeric material (see Fig 1.3). These systems are otherwise called as monolithic drug delivery systems. The matrix systems may be either hydrophilic or hydrophobic depending on the nature of release retarding materials used in the design of the drug delivery devices. The release retarding polymeric materials are water soluble/swellable or erodible in hydrophilic matrix systems and are insoluble or very slowly soluble/erodible in hydrophobic matrix systems. The hydrophilic matrix materials include HPMCs, HPC, HEC, xanthan gum, sodium alginate, guar gum, locust bean gum, PEO (polyethylene oxide) and cross-linked polymers of acrylic acid. The hydrophobic matrix materials include glyceryl monostearate, cetyl alcohol, hydrogenated vegetable oils, beeswax, carnauba wax, ethyl cellulose, polymethacrylates, etc.

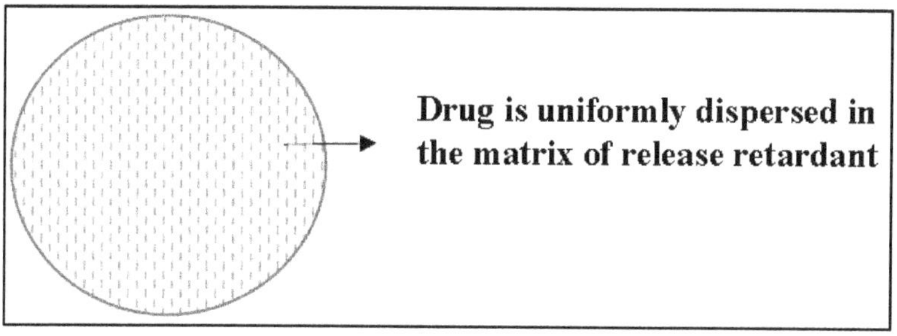

Fig.1.3 Schematic representation of Matrix type-CDDS.

C. Hybrid type systems

These systems are those where the drug in matrix of release-retarding material is further coated with a release-controlling polymer membrane. Such a device thus combines the constant release kinetics of reservoir system with the mechanical robustness of matrix system.

1.5 TIME LINE

1900	Paul Ehrlich hypothesized Magic Bullet concept
1952	First controlled release system was introduced by Smith Klein Beecham.
1953	Introduction of Eudragit
1964	Silicone based subcutaneous implants were developed
1970s	Drug eluting stents
1982	First elementary osmotic pump for indomethacin delivery.

1.6 CHAPTER AT A GLANCE

Term	Description
Conventional or immediate release dosage forms	The dosage forms in which no attempts are made to modify or control the rate of release of drugs.
Controlled release drug delivery systems (CDDS)	These are the dosage forms (more appropriately drug delivery systems) in which the release of the drug is modified or controlled by adopting suitable formulation or engineering strategies.
Spatial drug delivery	It refers to targeting a drug to a specific organ, tissue or cell.
Temporal drug delivery	It refers to the delivery of a drug over an extended period of time or for a specific duration during treatment.
Selection of drug candidates for CDDS	Physicochemical properties of the drug; Pharmacokinetic properties of the drug; Pharmacodynamic properties of the drug
Principles of CDDS	Diffusion controlled; Dissolution controlled; Hybrid control; Ion-exchange
Types of CDDS	Reservoir type; Matrix type; Hybrid type

EXERCISES

Multiple choice Questions

1. When a drug is delivered as a conventional dosage form-
   (a) the dosing interval is usually higher than the half -life of the drug
   (b) the dosing interval is usually shorter than the half-life of the drug
   (c) the dosing interval is usually equal to the half-life of the drug
   (d) none of the above
2. Fluctuations in drug levels are characteristics of-
   (a) Controlled drug delivery
   (b) Sustained drug delivery
   (c) Immediate release dosage forms
   (d) Targeted drug delivery
3. Targeting a drug to a specific organ or tissue/cell is achieved by-
   (a) Spatial delivery (b) Temporal delivery
   (c) Sustained drug delivery (d) None of the above
4. Which of the following is not an advantage of controlled drug delivery.
   (a) Fluctuating steady-state levels
   (b) Better patient compliance
   (c) Reduced dosing frequency
   (d) Better control of disease condition
5. Which of the following statement is correct?
   (a) Drugs having high molecular weight are good candidates for CDDS.
   (b) Drugs showing pH independent solubility are better candidates for CDDS.
   (c) Drugs having longer elimination half-lives are suitable for CDDS.
   (d) Drugs having narrow therapeutic window are ideal candidates for CDDS.
6. In matrix type systems, the drug release is controlled by-
   (a) The release controlling polymeric film/membrane.
   (b) Fickian diffusion
   (c) The nature of polymer matrix
   (d) All of the above
7. Fluctuation of plasma drug concentration is sometimes dangerous for-
   (a) Poorly soluble drugs (b) Lipophilic drugs
   (c) Drugs with narrow therapeutic window (d) Protein/peptide drugs

8. Which of the following is a suitable drug candidate for buccal drug delivery?
   (a) Metformin HCl (b) Nitroglycerine
   (c) Niclosamide (d) Lamivudine
9. Why a drug with slow absorption is poor candidate for CDDS?
   (a) They will form a pool of unabsorbed drug
   (b) They eliminate fast
   (c) Their bioavailability is already high
   (d) None
10. The drug release in reservoir type systems are mainly controlled by-
   (a) The nature and thickness of encapsulating membrane
   (b) Lipophilicity of drug core
   (c) o/w partition coefficient
   (d) None of the above

Short Answer Questions

1. What are the various advantages of CDDS over conventional drug delivery?
2. Explain how solubility of drugs is important while designing CDDS.
3. Why pharmacokinetic properties of drugs are considered while designing CDDS?
4. What are the key disadvantages of CDDS?
5. Explain matrix type CDDS.

Long Answer Questions

1. Discuss the various factors which influence selection of drug candidates for CDDS.
2. What are the limitations of immediate release dosage forms? Present an account of various principles adopted for designing CDDS.
3. With the help of neat diagrams explain matrix and reservoir type CDDS.
4. What are the advantages of controlled drug delivery? Explain the difference between matrix and reservoir type of devices.
5. What are the major limitations of controlled drug delivery. Add a note on diffusion and dissolution controlled systems.

Answer Key MCQs

(1) (b), (2) (c), (3) – (a), (4) – (a), (5) – (b), (6) – (c), (7) – (c), (8) – (b), (9) – (a), (10) – (a)

BIBLIOGRAPHY

1. Hopfenberg, H. B.; In Paul, D. R.; Harris, F. W. Eds. Controlled Release of Polymeric Formulations. ACS Symposium Series 33, Washington, DC: American Chemical Society, 1976; pp 26–31
2. Yeon Hee Yun, Byung Kook Lee, Kinam Park. Controlled Drug Delivery: Historical perspective for the next generation. J Control Release. 2015; 219: 2–7.

Chapter

2

POLYMERS

♦ LEARNING OBJECTIVES ♦

***After completing this lesson, the Reader should be able to understand*:**

- **Types of polymers used in drug delivery.**
- **Properties of polymers relevant to drug delivery applications.**
- **Applications of polymers in controlled release drug product development**

2.1 INTRODUCTION

The word polymer is derived from the Greek words "polus" for "many" and "meros" for "part" which means "consisting of many parts". Hence, polymers are large molecules or macromolecules consisting of many repeated sub-units or "monomers". Polymeric materials are widely used in a broad range of pharmaceutical products, and constitute essential components of many dosage forms. Therefore, it is important to understand the function of polymeric materials in the design and development of pharmaceutical products and manufacturing processes. Usually, the small molecules have a distinct molecular weight with each molecule having the same nominal mass. Polymers, on the other hand, are characterized by a diverse population in which there is a broad distribution of molar masses across the entire chain population. Polymers are simply chains of many monomeric residues covalently linked together.

Since drawing a complete structure of a polymer is almost impossible, the structure of a polymer is displayed by showing the repeating unit (the monomer residue) and an "n" number that shows how many monomers are participating in the reaction. From the structural prospective, monomers are generally classified as olefinic (containing double bond) and functional (containing reactive functional groups) for which different polymerization methods are utilized. If two, three, four, or five monomers are attached to each other, the product is known as a dimer, trimer, tetramer, or pentamer, respectively. An oligomer contains from 30 to 100 monomeric units. Products containing more than 200 monomers are simply called a polymer. From a thermodynamic perspective, polymers cannot exist in the gaseous state because of their high molecular weight. They exist only as liquids, semisolids and solid materials.

2.2 CLASSIFICATION

Since Polymers are numerous in number with different behaviours and can be naturally found or synthetically created, they can be classified in various ways. The following below are some basic ways in which they are classified.

A. Based on source of availability: The polymers may be classified on the basis of the source of availability.

(i) ***Natural Polymers:*** They occur naturally and are found in plants and animals. For example, proteins, starch, cellulose, and rubber.

(ii) ***Semi-synthetic Polymers:*** They are derived from naturally occurring polymers and undergo further chemical modification. For example, cellulose nitrate, cellulose acetate, hydroxypropyl methylcellulose.

(iii) ***Synthetic Polymers:*** These are man-made polymers. Plastic is the most common and widely used synthetic polymer. For example, Carbopol, Eudragits, Polyesters, etc.

B. Based on structure of monomer unit: The polymers may be classified on the basis of the structure of monomer units as follows.

(i) ***Linear Polymers:*** The structure of polymers containing long and straight chains fall into this category. Foe example, Polyvinyl chloride (PVC), etc.

(ii) ***Branch chain Polymers:*** The structure of these polymers is like branches originating at random points from a single linear chain. Monomers join together to form a long straight chain with some branched chains of different lengths. As a result of these branches, the polymers are not closely packed together. They are of low density having low melting points. For example, Low-density polyethene (LDPE), etc.

(iii) ***Cross-linked Polymers:*** In this type of polymers, monomers are linked together to form a three-dimensional network. The monomers contain strong covalent bonds as they are composed of bi-functional and tri-functional in nature. These polymers are brittle and hard. They have a stronger covalent bond in comparison to other linear polymers. Bakelite and melamine are examples in this category.

C. Based on type of monomer units: The polymers may be classified on the basis of the types of its constituent monomer units as follows.

(i) ***Homopolymer:*** In this type, a single type of monomer unit is present. For example, Polyethene.

(ii) ***Heteropolymer or co-polymer:*** It consists of different type of monomer units. For example, nylon. Depending on their structure, monomers display different reactivities during the polymerization reaction. If the reactivities of two monomers are similar, there will be no preference for which monomer is added next, so the polymer that is formed is called a random copolymer. When one monomer is preferentially added to another monomer, the monomers are added to each other alternatively and the polymer product is called an alternate copolymer. Sometimes, monomers preferentially add onto themselves and a block copolymer is formed. This happens when one monomer has a very high reactivity toward itself. Once more reactive monomers have participated in the reaction, the macroradical of the first monomer will attack the second monomer with the lower activity, and the second monomer will then grow as a block. Pluronic surfactants are composed of block units of ethylene oxide and propylene oxides attached to each other. The major difference between graft copolymer and the other copolymer types is the nature of their building blocks. Other copolymer types are made of two or more monomer types, while a monomer and a polymer are generally used to make graft copolymers. For example, the physical chemical properties of carboxymethyl cellulose (CMC) can be changed by grafting various monomers such as acrylic acid, acrylamide, and acrylonitrile onto the cellulose backbone.

D. Based on Molecular Forces: The polymers may also be classified on the basis of molecular forces as follows.

(i) ***Elastomers:*** These are rubber-like solids weak interaction forces are present. For example, Rubber.

(ii) ***Fibres:*** Strong, tough, high tensile strength and strong forces of interaction are present. For example, nylon.

(iii) ***Thermoplastics:*** These have intermediate forces of attraction. Polymers with a linear or branched structure generally behave as thermoplastics. Thermoplastic polymers can undergo melting, which is potentially useful in processes such as compression molding, injection molding, and thermoforming. In other words, a polymer that is originally a solid can flow upon application of heat. The process of thermo-melting and solidification can be repeated indefinitely with thermoplastic polymers. Examples include polystyrene, polyethylene, and poly (vinyl chloride).

(iv) ***Thermosetting Polymers:*** thermosetting polymers are cross-linked polymers, which are formed upon combined application of a cross-linker and heat or combined application of heat and reaction of internal functional groups. These polymers greatly improve the material's mechanical properties. It provides enhanced chemical and heat resistance. For example, phenolics, epoxies, and silicones.

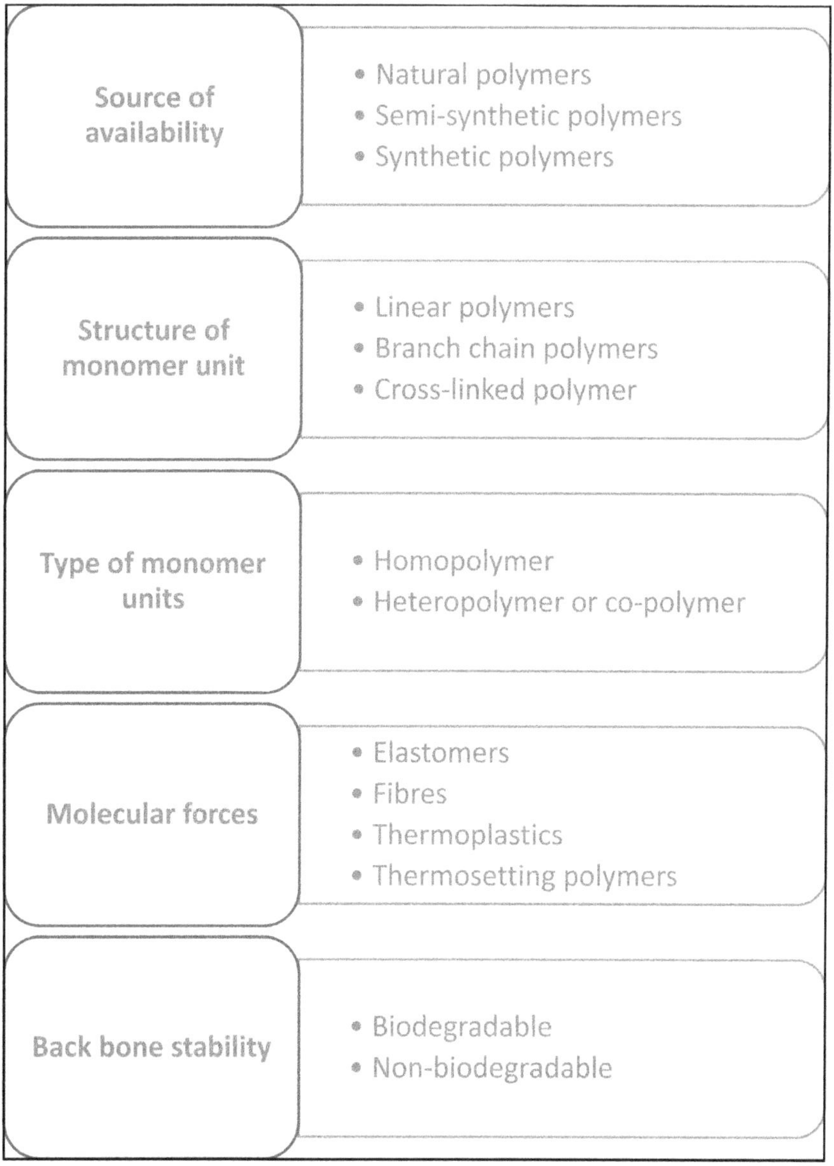

Fig.2.1 Summary of classification of Polymers.

E. Based on backbone stability: The polymers may be classified based on the stability of the backbone as follows.

(i) ***Biodegradable:*** The polymers, either of synthetic or natural origin, which are degraded and decayed by microorganisms like bacteria are known as biodegradable polymers. Natural biodegradable polymers are also called as biopolymers. The biodegradability of polymers can be manipulated by incorporating a variety of labile groups such as ester, orthoester, anhydride, carbonate, amide, urea and urethane in their backbone. These types of polymers are used in surgical bandages, capsule coatings and in surgery. For example, (lactide-co-glycolide) copolymer, Polyglycolide (PGA), Polyvinyl alcohol (PVA), Polysaccharides, etc.

(ii) ***Non-Biodegradable:*** These polymers are biostable and they usually do not degrade or decay. A variety of non-degradable polymers are used in drug delivery. For example, carboxymethyl cellulose, ethyl cellulose, cellulose acetate, cellulose acetate propionate, hydroxypropyl methyl cellulose, polydimethylsiloxane, polyvinyl pyrrolidone (PVP), etc.

2.3 PROPERTIES

The properties of polymers are usually studied under physical, thermal and mechanical properties. The properties are discussed in detail as follows.

A. Physical Properties:

Physical properties of polymers include molecular weight, molar volume, density, degree of polymerization, crystallinity of material, and so on. Important properties are discussed herewith in the following sections.

(i) ***Degree of Polymerization and Molecular Weight:*** The degree of polymerization $(DP)_{-n}$ in a polymer molecule is defined as the number of repeating units in the polymer chain. For example,

$$-(-CH_2 - CH_2-)-_n$$

The molecular weight of a polymer molecule is the product of the degree of polymerization and the molecular weight of the repeating unit. The polymer molecules are not identical but are a mixture of many species with different degrees of polymerization, that is, with different molecular weights. Therefore, in the case of polymers we talk about the average values of molecular weights. In general, a given polymer cannot be identified as a molecule with a specific molecular weight. Since chains are different, the molecular weight of all chains should be considered and must be averaged to have a more realistic figure for molecular weight of a given polymer. There are different ways that molecular weights of a polymer can be expressed; by the number of the chains, by the weight of the chains (the chain size), or by viscosity. However, the two most common ways are number (Mn) and weight (Mw) average calculations. If all polymer chains are similar in size, then the number and weight average values will be equivalent. If chains are of different sizes, then weight average is distancing itself from the number average value. The term polydispersity (PD) indicates how far the weight average can distance itself from the number average. A PD value closer to 1 (one) means the polymer system is close to monodispersed and all of the polymer chains are almost similar in size. The farther the value from 1 indicates that the polymer system is polydispersed and chains are different in size.

(ii) ***Polymer Crystallinity:*** In linear polymers, the polymer chains can pack together in regular lattice or crystalline state. In certain cases, the structure of a polymer is so irregular that crystal formation is thermodynamically infeasible. Such polymers form glass instead of crystal domains. A glass is a solid material existing in a non-crystalline (i.e., amorphous) state. With increased crystallinity, the polymer strength and stiffness increases. With an increase in crystallinity, the optical properties of a polymer are changed from transparent (amorphous) to opaque (semicrystalline). The increased crystallinity increases the barrier properties of the polymer which is exploited during coating of dosage forms or when used as packaging materials. The level of crystallinity also influences diffusion and solubility of drugs in drug delivery systems. A less crystalline or an amorphous polymer is suitable while designing dosage forms intended for improved drug release or solubilization of active agents.

B. Thermal Properties:

In the amorphous region of the polymer, at lower temperature, the molecules of the polymer are in apparent frozen state, where the molecules can vibrate slightly but are not able to move significantly. This state is called as the glassy state. In this state, the polymer is brittle, hard and rigid analogous to glass. Hence the name glassy state. The glassy state shows hard, rigid, and brittle nature analogous to a crystalline solid with molecular disorder as a liquid. Now, when the polymer is heated, the polymer becomes soft and flexible similar to rubber. This state is called the rubbery state. The temperature at which the glassy state makes a transition to rubbery state is called the glass transition temperature (T_g). Thermal transitions in polymers can occur in different orders. In other words, the volume of a polymer can change with temperature as a first- or second-order transition. When a crystal melts, the polymer volume increases significantly as the solid turns to a liquid. The melting temperature (T_m) represents a first-order thermal transition in polymers. On the other hand, the volume of an amorphous polymer gradually changes over a wide temperature range or so-called glass transition temperature. This behavior represents a second-order thermal transition in polymers. From a drug delivery point, T_g is an important factor for solid dosage forms. For example, a chewable dosage form needs to be soft and flexible at mouth temperature of about 37°C. This means the polymer used as a chewable matrix should be softened at this temperature.

Polymers containing short chains or having lower molecular weight possess lower T_g values. The nature of polymer chain side group also affects the T_g. Bulky and polar side groups result in higher T_g. Groups such as phenyl, amide, sulfone, and carbonyl either inside the backbone or as a side group hanging on the backbone affect the overall polymer flexibility resulting in low T_g values. Similarly, linear polymer show low T_g values opposed to crosslinked polymers. Plasticizer molecules can increase the entropy and mobility of the polymer chains. This results in lowering of T_g values for plasticized polymers compared with their non-plasticized counterparts. Moreover, the molecular weight of the polymer also influences its glass transition temperature. Higher the molecular weight higher the T_g value. It is observed that T_g is increased up to the molecular weight of approximately 20 000, and after this limit, the T_g is not affected significantly.

C. Mechanical Properties: Polymeric materials have interesting mechanical properties which are often exploited in drug delivery science and technology. Few properties are discussed as follows.

(i) ***Strength:*** In simple words, the strength is the stress required to break the sample. There are several types of the strength, namely tensile (stretching of the polymer), compressional (compressing the polymer), flexural (bending of the polymer), torsional (twisting of the polymer), impact (hammering) and so on. The polymers follow the following order of increasing strength:

Linear polymers < Branched polymers < Cross-linked polymers < Network polymers

The strength of polymers increases with increase in molecular weight, cross-linking and crystallinity. With increasing molecular weight and hence the level of intermolecular forces, polymers display superior properties under an applied stress. As far as structure is concerned, a flexible polymer can perform better under stretching whereas a rigid polymer is better under compression. The rigid materials possess high Young's modulus (such as brittle polymers), and ductile polymers also possess similar elastic modulus, but with higher fracture toughness. However, elastomers have low values of Young's modulus and are rubbery in nature. The stress-strain behaviour of different types of materials are depicted in Fig 2.2.

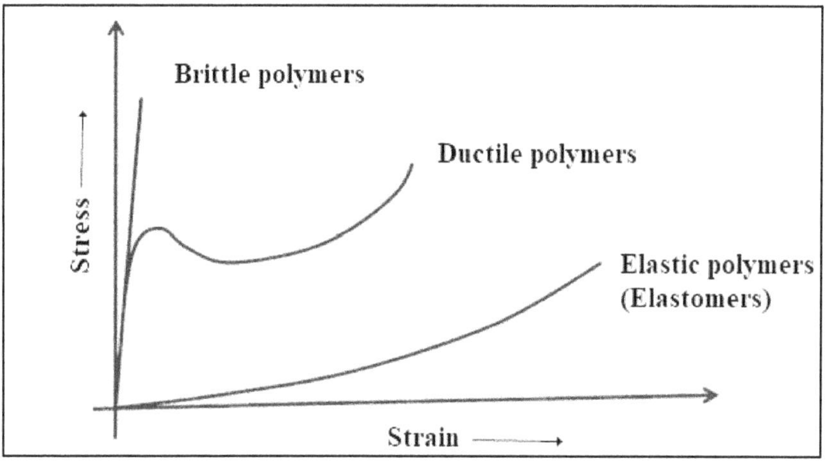

Fig.2.2 Stress-strain behaviour of different materials.

(ii) ***Viscoelastic Properties:*** There are two types of deformations: elastic and viscous. In the elastic deformation, the strain is generated at the moment the constant load (or stress) is applied, and this strain is maintained until the stress is not released. On removal of the stress, the material recovers its original dimensions completely, that is the deformation is reversible. However, in viscous deformation, the strain generated is not instantaneous and it is time dependent. The strain keeps on increasing with time on application of the constant load, that is, the recovery process is delayed. When the load is removed, the material does not return to its original dimensions completely, that is, this deformation is irreversible. Polymers show a combined behaviour of elastic and plastic deformation depending on the temperature and strain rate. At low temperature and high strain rate, elastic behaviour is observed, and at high temperature but low strain rate, the viscous behaviour is observed. The combined behaviour of viscosity and elasticity is observed at intermediate temperature and strain rate values. This behaviour is termed as viscoelasticity, and the polymer is termed as viscoelastic.

2.4 POLYMERS IN FORMULATIONS OF CDDS

Polymers are widely used in formulation of pharmaceutical dosage forms including controlled release drug delivery systems due to their versatile properties. The following section discusses the applications of polymers in controlled release drug delivery systems (CDDS).

(i) ***Oral Modified release/Sustained release systems:*** Sustained release and modified release dosage forms usually prolong the drug release time from the dosage forms in such a way that the systemic drug levels are within the therapeutic range for a prolonged period of time and thus

reduce the number of doses the patient must take to maintain a therapeutic effect. Polymers have been used in designing of sustained release products as release controlling/retarding materials. Both matrix type and reservoir type drug delivery devices (matrix tablets, microcapsules, microspheres, etc) are fabricated using hydrophilic and hydrophobic polymers with varying degrees of polymerization to retard the rate of release of drugs e.g., HPMC, MC, EC, PVP, PVA, tragacanth, acacia, starch, eudragits, etc. Special types of modified release products have been developed like gastroretentive systems, extended release systems, colon targeted systems, pulsatile delivery systems, targeted delivery systems, etc. using polymeric materials. The enteric coated tablets that prevent the drug release in stomach (thereby protect degradation of the drug in acidic environment) and delay the drug release preferably to intestine also use polymeric materials to achieve this enteric property e.g., hydroxypropyl methyl cellulose phthalate, cellulose acetate phthalate, shellac, etc. Many polymers exhibit mucoadhesive properties and hence are used in fabrication of mucoadhesive drug delivery systems. The examples of mucoadhesive polymers include polyacrylates, hyaluronan, chitosan, cellulose derivatives, etc.

(ii) ***Parenteral Controlled release formulations:*** PLA and PLGA are biodegradable polymers and have been used as surgical sutures and other biomedical applications since long. Earlier injectable sustained release formulations used these polymers for successful delivery of drug substances. Polymers for parenteral administration are injected or implanted as matrices in the form of microspheres, nanoparticles or reversible gels. For example, copolymers of polyethylene glycol (PEG) and PLGA have been found to possess thermoreversible properties. The copolymer formulations are soluble in aqueous systems and form a flowable solution under cold conditions. As the temperature is raised to approximately 37°C, the polymer solution undergoes rapid gelation to form a semisolid depot. A commercial example of very long-term sustained release via nondegradable polymer implants is the Norplant implant, designed for sustained delivery of levonorgestrel for up to five years.

(iii) ***Transdermal Delivery Systems:*** Transdermal drug delivery systems (as ointments, patches or films) uses the transdermal route to deliver the drug substances across the intact skin for systemic effects. A wide variety of polymeric materials has been used for development of transdermal drug delivery systems e.g., polyvinyl alcohol, ethyl cellulose, polyisobutylene, polyacrylate, polyamide, polyurea, ethylene vinyl acetate copolymer, etc. In the design of transdermal drug delivery systems, polymers are used to control the drug release, serve as release liner and backing membrane.

(iv) ***Ocular Implants:*** Nondegradable polymers are used as matrices for ocular implants. This application requires the polymer to be hydrophilic, to minimize local tissue irritation. Conventional ocular medicines (i.e., eye drops) have limitations such as rapid dilution, tear washout, poor patient compliance, and limited bioavailability. Ocular implants from hydrophilic polymer matrices that provide localized sustained release may overcome the above limitations. The first polymeric sustained release product to reach the market was *Ocusert®*, a pilocarpine sustained release ocular implant developed by Alza. *Ocusert®* has the drug reservoir as a thin disc of pilocarpine–alginate complex sandwiched between two transparent discs of microporous membrane fabricated from ethylene–vinyl acetate copolymer. The microporous membranes permit the tear fluid to penetrate into the drug reservoir compartment to dissolve pilocarpine from the complex. Pilocarpine molecules are then released at a constant rate upto a week for management of glaucoma.

(v) ***Stimuli Responsive Drug Delivery Systems:*** Polymeric materials such as hydrogels have been developed as stimuli-responsive materials, which can undergo abrupt volume change in response to small changes in environmental factors like temperature, pH, ionic strength, magnetic/ electric field, etc. This unique characteristic can be used for controlled drug delivery applications. These polymers are often called as "intelligent" or "smart" polymers. Examples of such polymers include poly(methylmethacrylate), poly-N-isoproply acrylamide, poly(acrylic acid), polyacrylamide, poly(N,N-dimethylacrylamide), etc.

2.5 CHAPTER AT A GLANCE

Term	Description
Polymer classification	Natural Polymers, Semi-synthetic Polymers, Synthetic Polymers, Linear Polymers, Branch chain polymers, Cross-linked Polymers, Homopolymer, Heteropolymer or co-polymer, Elastomers, Fibres, Thermoplastics, Thermosetting polymers, Biodegradable.
Polymer properties	**Physical Properties:** Degree of Polymerization and Molecular Weight, Polymer Crystallinity; Thermal Properties; Mechanical Properties: Strength, Visco elastic properties
Polymer applications	Oral modified release/sustained release formulations, Parenteral controlled release formulation, Transdermal delivery systems, Ocular implants, Stimuli-responsive drug delivery systems.

EXERCISES

Multiple choice Questions

1. An oligomer typically contains-
   (a) 2-3 monomer units
   (b) 30-100 monomer units
   (c) more than 200 monomer units.
   (d) no monomer units at all
2. Thermodynamically polymers cannot exist in gaseous state because-
   (a) polymers have high molecular weight
   (b) Polymers have viscoelastic properties
   (c) polymers have high melting point
   (d) None of the above
3. Which of the following is a synthetic polymer?
   (a) Carbopol (b) HPMC
   (c) Sodium carboxymethyl cellulose (d) Starch
4. Homopolymers are-
   (a) High molecular weight polymers
   (b) Plasticized polymers
   (c) Polymers with single type of monomer units
   (d) Polymers with 30-100 monomer units
5. Which of the following statement is correct?
   (a) Crystalline polymers are often transparent.
   (b) Mechanical strength of polymers decreases with increased crystallinity.
   (c) Polymers never exist in amorphous state.
   (d) Linear polymers are crystalline in nature.
6. Glass transition temperature in polymers is-
   (a) the temperature at which glassy state makes transition to rubbery state
   (b) the temperature at which rubbery state makes transition to glassy state
   (c) the temperature at which the polymer melts
   (d) the temperature at which the polymer solidifies
7. Suitable addition of plasticizers to polymers often-
   (a) Increases the glass transition temperature
   (b) Decreases the melting point
   (c) Decreases the glass transition temperature
   (d) Increases the melting point

8. Crosslinking of polymers-
   (a) Increases its glass transition temperature
   (b) Decreases its glass transition temperature
   (c) Increases its crystallinity
   (d) Decreases its melting point
9. The strength of polymer increases with-
   (a) Increased crystallinity, molecular weight and crosslinking
   (b) Increased crystallinity and decreased degree of polymerization
   (c) Decreased crystallinity and increased crosslinking
   (d) All of the above
10. Which of the following is a "smart" polymer-
   (a) Starch (b) HPMC (c) Carbopol (d) poly(N,N-dimethylacrylamide)

Short Answer Questions

1. Write a note on the physical properties of polymers.
2. Explain how polymers are used in ocular implants.
3. Comment on the mechanical properties of polymers.
4. What is glass transition temperature of polymers? Explain

Long Answer Questions

1. Classify polymers with suitable examples.
2. Give a detailed account of the various properties of polymers relevant to drug delivery.
3. Present a brief note on the applications of polymers in controlled release drug delivery systems.
4. Discuss the role and application of polymers in oral modified release systems and transdermal drug delivery.
5. Discuss the mechanical and thermal properties of polymers useful for drug delivery applications.

Answer Key MCQs

(1) – (b), (2) – (a), (3) – (a), (4) – (c), (5) – (d), (6) – (a), (7) –(c), (8) –(a), (9) –(a), (10) –(d)

BIBLIOGRAPHY

1. Rodriguez F. Principles of Polymer Systems, Taylor & Francis, Philadelphia, PA, 1996.

2. Uhrich KE, Cannizzaro SM, Langer RS, Shakesheff KM. Polymeric systems for controlled drug release. Chem Rev 1999, 99:3181-3198.

3. Florence AT and Attwood D. Physicochemical Principles of Pharmacy, 4th Ed., Pharmaceutical Press, London, 2006, Chapter 8, pp. 273–322.

Chapter 3

MICROENCAPSULATION

♦ LEARNING OBJECTIVES ♦

***After completing this lesson, the Reader should be able to understand*:**

- **Microencapsulation as a drug delivery platform**
- **The various advantages, disadvantages and pharmaceutical applications of microencapsulation**
- **The methods adopted to affect microencapsulation of drug substances**

3.1 INTRODUCTION

Microencapsulation may be defined as a process of application of a thin layer of polymeric coating to individual core materials (solid or liquid) of arbitrary particle size ranging from 1-5000 μm to produce small sized capsules with many useful properties. The resultant products of microencapsulation are often called as microcapsules, microspheres, micromatrices or microparticles. Although the terms are often used interchangeably, technological distinctions related to pharmaceutical sciences can be made as follows. Microcapsules are made up of one or more core substances (solid or liquid) that are surrounded by a distinct capsule wall, whereas micromatrices are polymeric matrices in which the encapsulated substances are homogeneously dispersed. Microparticles or microspheres are general terminologies that involve both. All these micron sized particulates are often clubbed under Multi-particulate systems in drug delivery technology.

In a relatively simple form, a microcapsule is a small sphere with a uniform wall around it. The material inside the microcapsule is referred to as the core, internal phase, or fill, whereas the wall is sometimes called a shell, coating, or membrane. A representative SEM image of microcapsule is presented in Fig. 3.1. The microencapsulation technology has been widely exploited in formulation of drug substances apart from other areas like food, cosmetics, agricultural and consumer products. These microparticulate systems are delivered via oral, parenteral, topical, transdermal, intranasal, intraocular and pulmonary routes.

3.2 ADVANTAGES AND APPLICATIONS OF MICROENCAPSULATION

The encapsulation techniques have been advanced to such a level that not only small molecular weight drugs but also macromolecules, such as proteins and genes, can be delivered via microparticle carriers. Although the technological advances have led to commercialization of several microparticulate products in recent years, many technical problems are to be overcome yet. The few recent applications of the technology are listed below.

(i) Bioadhesive drug delivery systems.
(ii) Controlled /sustained drug delivery.
(iii) Targeted drug delivery with improved cellular uptake.
(iv) Oral delivery of macromolecules, protein/peptides like insulin, heparin, etc.
(v) Delivery of genes, DNA, etc.
(vi) Delivery of vaccines.

The advantages of microencapsulation may be summarized as follows:

Advantages/Applications

(i) This method has the advantage of converting liquid drugs into a free-flowing powder form and hence improve their handling.
(ii) Sensitive drugs can be protected from adverse environmental factors and hence improving their stability. For example, vitamins and unsaturated fatty acids are degraded by oxygen. Many biological cells are sensitive to shear. Many drugs are prone to hydrolysis in presence of moisture. Some drugs and probiotics are destroyed during gastric transit. When incorporated in microcapsules, all these systems will be protected to some extent against the chemical, physicochemical and mechanical environmental conditions.
(iii) Vaporization of many volatile drugs and essential oils e.g. methyl salicylate and peppermint oil can be prevented by microencapsulation.

(iv) Incompatibility among the drugs can be prevented by microencapsulation and hence a single layered tablet can be manufactured containing two or more chemically incompatible drugs.

(v) Taste and odor masking can be achieved for drugs with bad taste and odor.

(vi) Particle size reduction improves the aqueous solubility of poorly soluble drugs and hence enhances bioavailability of drugs.

(vii) Sustained and controlled drug delivery can be achieved for better therapeutic outcomes.

(viii) Alteration in site of absorption can also be achieved by microencapsulation.

(ix) Many drugs have been microencapsulated to reduce toxicity and GI irritation including ferrous sulphate and KCl.

(x) Toxic chemicals such as insecticides may be microencapsulated to reduce the possibility of sensitization of plant operating personnel.

Disadvantages

(i) No single microencapsulation method is adaptable for all drug candidates (core materials).

(ii) In some instances, with certain methods of microencapsulation method, incomplete or discontinuous coating is observed leading to inefficient protection and instability of sensitive pharmaceutical substances.

(iii) Poor or inadequate reproducibility leading to quality issues.

(iv) Unstable release characteristics of the microencapsulated drugs.

(v) Economic constraints. The methods of microencapsulation are not cost-effective.

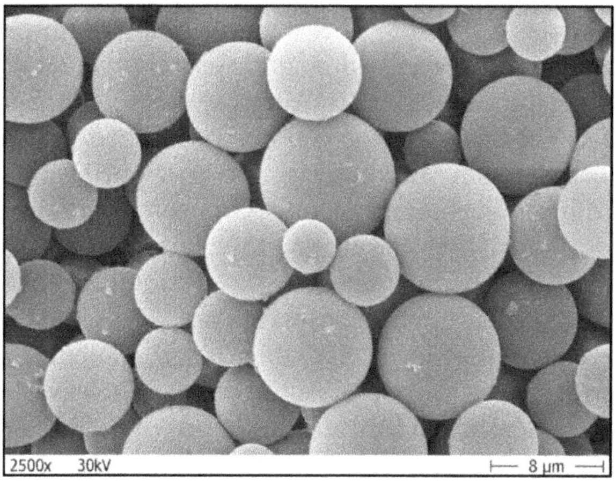

Fig.3.1 Representative SEM image of microcapsules.

The core and coating materials

Core materials can be either solid or liquid. The liquid core can be a solution or a dispersion of drug substances. The solid core may be composed of drug alone or with other excipients like stabilizers, release modulators, etc. The selection of appropriate coating material decides the physical and chemical properties of the resultant microcapsules/microspheres. While selecting a polymer the product requirements like protection, stabilization, release characteristics, etc are considered carefully. The polymer should be capable of forming a uniform film that is cohesive with the core material. It should be chemically compatible, non-reactive with the core material and provide the desired coating properties such as strength, flexibility, impermeability, optical properties and stability.

Generally hydrophilic polymers, hydrophobic polymers (or) a combination of both are used for the microencapsulation process. A number of coating materials have been used successfully; examples of these include gelatin, polyvinyl alcohol, ethyl cellulose, cellulose acetate phthalate, etc.

3.3 METHODS OF MICROENCAPSULATION

Diverse methods are adopted to fabricate microcapsules in pharmaceutical industries which include air suspension, coacervation, spray drying, solvent evaporation, pan coating, etc. The methods are discussed as follows.

(i) Air Suspension (Wurster method):

The method of air suspension has already been widely exploited in macroencapsulation process (e.g., tablet coating) and applicable for encapsulation of micron and sub micron sized particles also. This method uses fluid-bed coating processes to impart coating to the small sized core drug particles. In brief, the method involves dispersion of solid, particulate core materials (drugs) in a supporting air stream and spray coating of the air-suspended core particles with polymeric coating materials. The quality of the yield is often superior to other methods of microencapsulation. The coating film is applied more evenly and the coated film is more homogeneous. The coated particles are lifted on the air stream, which dries the coating as the particles are carried away from the nozzle. The particle drying rates are proportional to volume and temperature of the supporting air stream. The particles rise on the air stream, then settle down, and then begin another cycle. The cycles continue until the desired film thickness is achieved. The process is particularly well suited for uniform coating of particles with a polymeric membrane in a single operation. The coating materials can be applied in the form of aqueous solution, non-aqueous solution, emulsions, dispersions or hot-melts.

The efficient and effective encapsulation in air suspension method require a precise control over the key processing variables. The core material properties like density, surface area, melting point, solubility, friability, crystallinity, and flowability significantly affects the coating process. The coating material related factors like concentration of coating material (or, melting point of coating material), amount of coating materials and application rate.The quality of the supporting air for fluidization also influences the coating process. The volume of fluidizing air, the temperature of inlet and outlet, etc.

(ii) Coacervation-Phase separation:

The method of coacervation and phase separation was adopted by The National Cash Register Corporation. The manufacturing process involves three consecutive steps carried out under continuous agitation.

Step 1: *Formation of three immiscible chemical phases.*

Step 2: *Deposition of the coating materials over the core particles.*

Step 3: *Rigidization of the coating.*

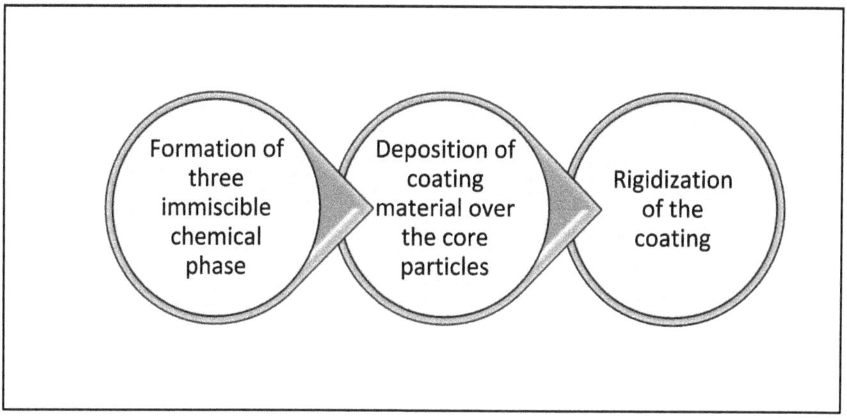

Fig.3.2 Steps in coacervation-phase separation.

In the first step, three immiscible chemical phases i.e. a liquid manufacturing vehicle phase, a core material phase, and a coating material phase are formed. For the formation of these three phases, the core materials are dispersed in a solution of coating materials. The solvent for the coating materials are the liquid manufacturing vehicle. Now, the coating polymer is in solubilized state in the liquid manufacturing vehicle. To induce phase separation of the polymer so as to form the coating material phase, the method of coacervation-phase separation is adopted which forms a phase of immiscible polymer in a liquid state. The phase separation can be achieved by many methods like changing the temperature of polymer solution, salt addition, non-solvent addition, incompatible polymer addition, etc.

In the second step, the liquid polymer coating materials get deposited over the core materials. This process requires careful physical mixing of the liquid coating materials and the core materials within the liquid manufacturing vehicle phase. The polymer coating gets deposited over the core materials upon adsorption of the polymer at the interface between the core material and the liquid vehicle phase. This accomplishes coating of the polymer over the core materials. However, the polymer coating, at this step, is still in wet stage.

In the third and the final step, rigidization of the coating is carried out by adopting any of the suitable methods like thermal, crosslinking, desolvation, etc. The objective of rigidization is to obtain self-sustaining microcapsules. The process is explained in the Fig 3.3.

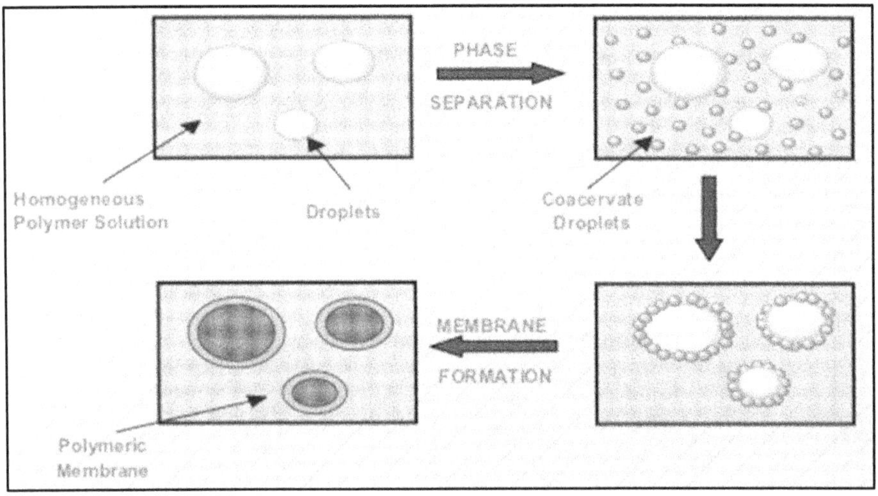

Fig.3.3 Coacervation and Phase-separation method.

The various methods to induce coacervation and phase-separation are discussed as follows.

(a) ***Temperature change:*** In order to understand the concept, the binary phase diagram for temperature-composition system comprising of a binary system of polymer and solvent may be referred at Fig 3.4.

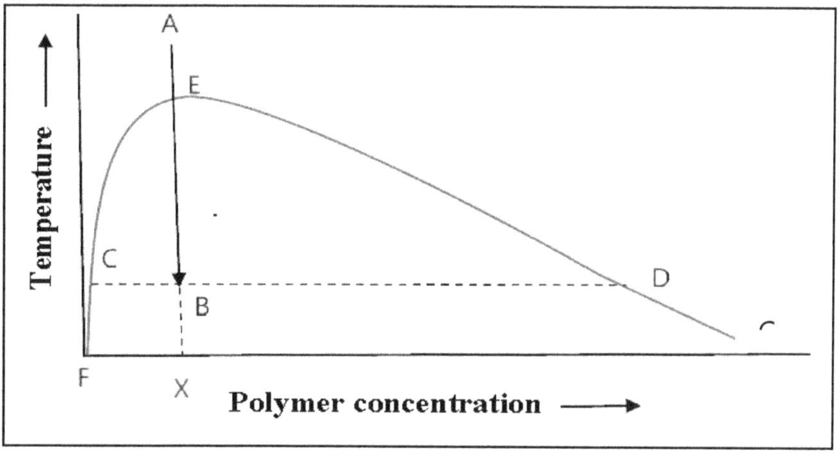

Fig.3.4 Phase diagram showing temperature induced coacervation.

A system having an overall composition, represented as point "X" on the abscissa, exists as a single phase, homogeneous solution at all points above the phase-boundary curve, FEG. As the temperature of the system is decreased from point "A" along the arrowed line AEB, the phase boundary is crossed at point "E", and the two-phase region is entered. Phase separation of the dissolved polymer occurs in the form of immiscible polymer liquid droplets. Under optimal polymer concentration, agitation and temperature, the liquid polymer droplets, then, coalesce around the dispersed core material particles and form the embryonic microcapsules. With decreasing the temperature, the liquid manufacturing vehicle phase becomes "polymer- poor" and the coating material phase becomes "polymer- rich". The loss of solvent by the polymer rich phase causes gelation of polymer, and hence rigidization or solidification of the polymer coating.

Microencapsulation of N-acetyl p-amino-phenol (water-soluble core) by highly substituted ethylcellulose polymer (EC; water-insoluble coating) exemplifies the concept of coacervation and phase separation by temperature change. The highly substituted EC is insoluble in cyclohexane (liquid manufacturing vehicle) at room temperature, but is soluble at elevated temperature. To affect the microencapsulation, EC is solubilized in cyclohexane at its boiling point to form a homogeneous solution of polymer (2% by weight). Then, the core materials, N-acetyl p-amino-phenol in finely divided crystalline state is dispersed in the above solution with constant agitation at a coating to core material (dry) ratio of 1:2. When the system is cooled under continuous stirring, phase separation and coacervation of EC occurs leading to formation of embryonic microcapsules. Further, reduction of temperature to room-temperature causes gelation and rigidization or solidification of the coating material over the microcapsules. Subsequently, the microcapsules are separated from cyclohexane by adopting any suitable separation technique i.e. filtration, decantation, centrifugation, etc.

(b) ***Incompatible polymer addition:*** In this method, the phase separation is induced by addition of an incompatible polymer (Y) into a system comprising of a polymeric solution (X) in a liquid manufacturing vehicle with dispersed core material particles. Essentially, the liquid manufacturing vehicle is chosen in such a manner that the polymer "X" and "Y" are soluble in it and the core materials are insoluble. The demixing of the polymer "X" occurs because of addition of soluble and incompatible polymer "Y" and subsequently affecting the microencapsulation of the dispersed core materials.

The microencapsulation of methylene blue hydrochloride (MB) with EC explains this method of coacervation and phase-separation. EC is dissolved in toluene (2% by weight) and then MB (insoluble in toluene) is dispersed in the polymer solution under continuous stirring (at core:coat ratio of 4:1). Phase separation of EC occurs upon slow addition of liquid polybutadiene at sufficient quantity, 25 times the content of EC. Polybutadiene is sufficiently soluble in toluene and incompatible with EC and hence causes demixing of EC affecting microencapsulation of the dispersed core particles (MB). Rigidization of the EC coating is done by addition of non-solvent for the coating polymer (EC) such as hexane. Subsequent washing cycles with hexane removes polybutadiene (it is soluble in hexane) and solidifies EC. Finally, the microcapsules are collected from the manufacturing vehicle (toluene) following a suitable separation method.

(c) ***Non-solvent addition:*** Addition of a non-solvent to the polymer solution causes the demixing of the polymer. This phenomenon is exploited for microencapsulation of methylscopolamine hydrobromide (MS). A 5% (w/v) solution of cellulose acetate butyrate (CAB) is prepared in methyl ethyl ketone and finely divided MS is dispersed in it under continuous stirring. The core to coat ratio (MS:CAB) is fixed at 2:1. The mixture is heated to about 55°C and then isopropyl ether (a non-solvent) is added slowly to affect the phase separation of CAB and subsequent microencapsulation of the suspended core materials, MS. The microcapsules are separated upon cooling the system to room temperature followed by washing with isopropyl ether and drying under vacuum.

(d) ***Salt addition:*** Addition of soluble inorganic salts to aqueous solutions of few polymers effect phase separation of the polymers and the concept is used for microencapsulation. Microencapsulation of oil-soluble vitamin exemplifies the method. Oil-soluble vitamin is dissolved in corn oil and emulsified to a desired droplet size in a 10% gelatin solution having an isoelectric point at about pH 8.9. The o/w emulsion is prepared by using

20 parts oil in 100 parts water, by weight. The process of emulsification is conducted at around 50°C, above the gelation temperature of gelatin. The temperature maintained at this point, slowly a 20% solution of sodium sulfate is added under stirring to affect the phase-separation. The ratio of volume of salt solution to emulsion is fixed at 4:10. The microencapsulated oil droplets loaded with the vitamin are collected and subjected to rigidization by transferring them to a 7% (w/v) solution of sodium sulfate maintained at 19°C. The microcapsules are dried by spray drying technique.

*(e) **Polymer-polymer interaction:*** Oppositely charged polyelectrolytes often interact to form complexes having reduced solubility leading to phase separation. Gelatin and gum Arabic are examples of such polyelectrolytes that interact. Gelatin possesses a net positive charge below its isoelectric point and gum arabic possesses a net negative charge. The microencapsulation of methyl salicylate (a water insoluble liquid) can be affected by this method. Aqueous solution of gum Arabic and gelation is prepared at the concentration of 2% each for the polymers. The homogeneous solutions are mixed in equal volumes and diluted to twice their volume with water and maintained at a temperature of 40-45°C and adjusted to pH 4.5. Under this optimal condition the oppositely charged polyelectrolytes interact and form an insoluble complex leading to phase-separation. Subsequently, the liquid core material is added at a core to coat ratio of 25:1. The liquid core material is emulsified with stirring to obtain the desired droplet size. Further, the system is gradually cooled to 25°C over a duration of one hour under continuous stirring. During this cooling period the phase separation occurs and subsequently the core material emulsion droplets are microencapsulated with gelatin-gum arabic complex. The microcapsules are rigidized by reducing the temperature further to 10°C.

(iii) Multi Orifice Centrifugal Process: It is a mechanical process for production of microcapsules utilizing centrifugal force to hurl a core material particle through an enveloping microencapsulation membrane subsequently affecting microencapsulation of the core. Liquids are encapsulated using a rotating extrusion head containing concentric nozzles. In this process, a jet of core liquid is surrounded by a sheath of wall solution or melt. As the jet moves through the air it breaks down into droplets of core, each coated with the wall solution. While the droplets are in flight, a molten wall may be hardened or the solvent may be evaporated from the wall solution. This process is excellent for forming particles of 400–2,000μm diameter. Since the drops are formed by the breakup of a liquid jet, the process is only suitable for liquid or slurry. A high production rate can be achieved, i.e., up to 22.5 kg of microcapsules can be produced per nozzle per hour per head. Process variables include; rotational speed of cylinder, flow rate of the core and coating material, the concentration and viscosity of the coating material, viscosity and surface tension of core material.

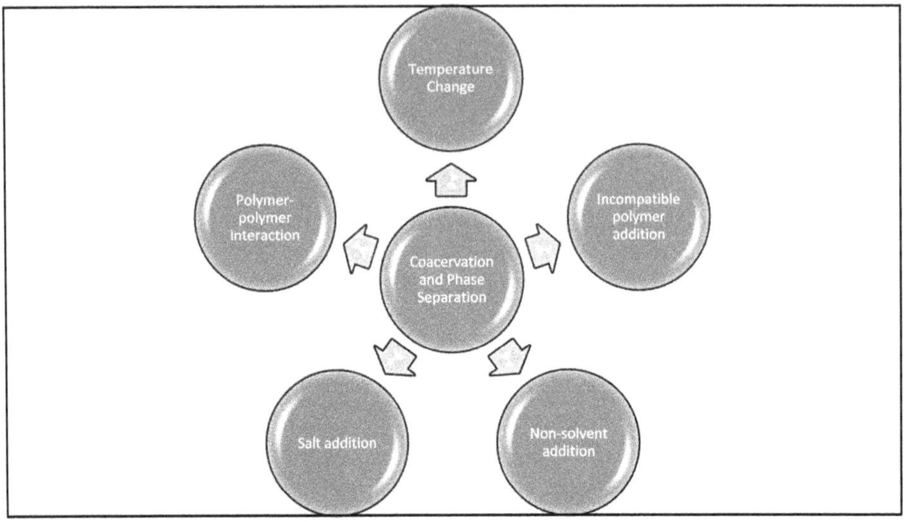

Fig.3.5 Coacervation and phase separation methods.

(iv) **Pan Coating:** Relatively large particles can be encapsulated by pan coating. Size of solid particles should be greater than 600 μm to achieve effective coating using this method. This method has been effectively used for preparation of controlled release beads. Drugs are coated onto the surface of various spherical substrates such as nonpareil sugar seeds, and subsequently coated with protective polymer coatings. The coating is applied as a coating solution or as an atomized spray using suitable nozzles to the solid cores in a coating pan. To remove the coating solvent, warm air is circulated in the pan or drying is carried out in ovens. Various designs of coating pans exist in pharmaceutical industries with many process variables.

(v) **Spray Drying/Spray Congealing:** The methods of spray drying and spray congealing are similar in many aspects. In both the methods, the core materials are dispersed in a liquified coating material and subsequently the core/coat mixture is sprayed or introduced to an environment where rapid solidification of the coating is affected. The difference between the two methods lies in the technique by which the solidification is accomplished. In case of spray drying, the rigidization is accomplished by rapid evaporation of the coating solvent. However, in case of spray congealing, coating solidification is affected by thermally congealing a molten coating material or by solidifying the dissolved coating material by introduction of non-solvents.

Spray drying method yields spherical microcapsules in the size range of 5-600 μm. Intriguingly, spray drying produces microcapsules with low bulk density due to the porous nature of the coated particles. This is an efficient method for encapsulation of solid and liquid cores. Many liquid flavouring agents has been microencapsulated using spray drying method yielding free flowing solid particulates. The spray congealing method also uses the same spray drying equipment with minor modification to facilitate use of molten coating materials.

(vi) **Solvent Evaporation:** The process is carried out in liquid manufacturing vehicle. The coating material is dissolved in a suitable volatile solvent which is essentially immiscible with the liquid manufacturing vehicle. The core material is either dissolved or dispersed in the coating material solution. The mixture is agitated in the liquid manufacturing vehicle to obtain the microcapsules. Heating the mixture evaporates the volatile solvent leaving behind the coating polymer alone over the cores. In case, the core material is dispersed in the polymer solution, the coat polymer shrinks over the core yielding a reservoir type microcapsule. In case, the core material is dissolved in the coating material solution, a matrix-type microcapsule or microsphere is formed. After complete removal of the volatile coating solvent, the microcapsules are separated from the liquid manufacturing vehicle after cooling to room temperature.

(vii) **Interfacial Polymerization:** This method involves polymerization of monomer units located at the interface between the core material and a continuous phase in which the core material is dissolved. The continuous phase or the core material supporting phase is often a liquid or gas.

(viii) **Supercritical Fluid Methods:** The supercritical fluid method is a relatively new method and often regarded as a green method for pharmaceutical processing, which can minimize the use of organic solvents and harsh manufacturing conditions taking advantage of two distinctive properties of supercritical fluids (i.e., high compressibility and liquid-like density). This method can be broadly divided into two parts: rapid expansion of supercritical solutions (RESS), which utilizes the supercritical fluid (e.g., carbon dioxide) as a solvent for the polymer, and supercritical antisolvent crystallization (SAS), using the fluid as an antisolvent that causes polymer precipitation. The details are beyond the scope of this book.

3.4 TIME LINE

1955	Barrett K. Green received a patent for the process of microencapsulation.
1959	The method of phase separation for microencapsulation was proposed.
1959	Interfacial polymerization for microencapsulation demonstrated by DuPont.

3.5 CHAPTER AT A GLANCE

Term	Description
Microencapsulation	A process of application of a thin layer of polymeric coating to individual core materials (solid or liquid) of arbitrary particle size ranging from 1-5000 μm to produce small sized capsules with many useful properties.
Core material	The material inside the microcapsule is referred to as the core material.
Coating material	The wall is called a shell, coating, or membrane and often is polymeric in nature.
Advantages/applications	(i) Conversion of liquid cores into a free-flowing powder form. (ii) Protection of sensitive drugs/substances from adverse environmental factors. (iii) Prevention of vaporization of many volatile drugs/cores. (iv) Incompatibility among the drugs can be prevented by microencapsulation in a single layered tablet. (v) Taste and odor masking of drug substances. (vi) Particle size reduction improves the aqueous solubility of poorly soluble drugs and hence enhances bioavailability of drugs. (vii) Sustained and controlled drug delivery including alteration in site of absorption. (ix) Products with reduced toxicity and GI irritation. (x) Safety of plant operating personnel.
Microencapsulation methods	Air suspension; Coacervation phase separation; Multi orifice centrifugal process; Pan coating; Spray drying/spray congealing; Solvent evaporation; Interfacial polymerization; Supercritical fluid method.

EXERCISES

Multiple choice Questions

1. Rigidization of microcapsules in air suspension method is accomplished by:
   (a) Repeated washing with non-solvent addition.
   (b) Thermal quenching.
   (c) Hot air blowers.
   (d) none of the above.
2. Which of the following is not a distinct phase in coacervation/phase separation process?
   (a) Core material phase
   (b) Coating material phase
   (c) Liquid manufacturing vehicle
   (d) Organic phase
3. Which of the following is a mechanical method for microencapsulation?
   (a) Air suspension
   (b) Coacervation
   (c) Multi orifice centrifugal method
   (d) Supercritical fluid method
4. Which of the following microencapsulation method utilizes polymer melts?
   (a) Spray drying (b) Spray congealing
   (c) Coacervation (d) Air suspension
5. Which of the following is a coating material in microencapsulation?
   (a) Ethyl cellulose (b) Ethyl alcohol
   (c) Sodium lauryl sulfate (d) Indomethacin
6. Air suspension method is also called as-
   (a) Nelson-Wagner method (b) Peppa's method
   (c) Coacervation method (d) Wurster method

7. Drug loading on nonpareil sugar seeds can be achieved with-
   (a) Coacervation (b) Pan Coating
   (c) Multi orifice centrifugal method (d) None of the above
8. Which microencapsulation method yields porous and low bulk density microcapsules?
   (a) Coacervation and phase separation method (b) Spray drying method
   (c) Pan coating method (d) Centrifugation method
9. In which of the following conditions matrix type microcapsules are formed in solvent evaporation method?
   (a) When the core material is in liquid state
   (b) When the core is dissolved in coating material solution
   (c) When the coating polymer is insoluble
   (d) When the core material is insoluble
10. Which of the following microencapsulation method is considered as a "green" method?
    (a) Pan coating method
    (b) Air suspension method
    (c) Super critical fluid method
    (d) Coacervation method

Short Answer Questions

1. What are the various advantages of microencapsulation?
2. Explain in brief about air suspension method for microencapsulation.
3. How is phase separation affected by non-solvent addition? Explain with an example.
4. Differentiate between spray drying and spray congealing for micro-encapsulation.
5. Explain in brief about solvent evaporation method for microencapsulation.

Long Answer Questions

1. Illustrate with suitable examples, the various methods of microencapsulation for pharmaceuticals.
2. Present a note on the various applications of microencapsulation in pharmaceutical sector.

3. What are the limitations of microencapsulation as a pharmaceutical process? Write a short note on coacervation and phase separation method for microencapsulation.
4. What are the advantages of microencapsulation. Add a note on multi-orifice centrifugal method for microencapsulation.
5. Enlist the various method of microencapsulation. Discuss in brief about air suspension method for microencapsulation.

Answer Key MCQs

(1) – (c), (2) – (d), (3) – (c), (4) – (b), (5) – (a), (6) – (d), (7) – (b), (8) – (b), (9) – (b), (10) – (c)

BIBLIOGRAPHY

1. Whateley TL. Microcapsules: preparation by interfacial polymerization and interfacial complexation and their application. In Microencapsulation: Methods and Industrial Applications; Benita, S., Ed.; Dekker: New York, U.S.A., 1996; 73, 349–375.
2. Santos IRD, Richard J, Pech B, Thies C, Benoit JP. Microencapsulation of protein particles within lipids using a novel supercritical fluid process. Int. J. Pharm. 2002, 242 (1–2), 69–78.

Chapter 4

MUCOSAL DRUG DELIVERY

♦ **LEARNING OBJECTIVES** ♦

After completing this lesson, the Reader should be able to understand:

- **Various mucosal drug delivery systems.**
- **Barriers to mucosal drug delivery.**
- **Principles of of mucoadhesion and bioadhesion.**
- **Factors affecting mucoadhesion and mucosal drug delivery.**
- **Advantages and disadvantages of mucosal drug delivery.**
- **Formulation of buccal dosage forms.**

4.1 INTRODUCTION

Bioavailability is considered as the key parameter for successful drug delivery by any route and parenteral invasive routes like subcutaneous, intramuscular and intravenous are considered as the standard with superior bioavailability. However, the invasive parenteral routes are associated with pain and discomfort to the patient and moreover, the drug products are often expensive due to strict manufacturing regulation of aseptic drugs and require trained personnel for drug administration. In this context, mucosal sites viz. oral (buccal), nasal, ocular, pulmonary mucosa, rectal and vaginal mucosa presents logically best alternates. Delivery of drugs to or via the mucosal surfaces, including the airways, the gastrointestinal (GI) tract and the genital tract, is called mucosal drug delivery. Anatomical make up of these sites with thin epithelium lining, trans-membrane network and rich blood supply makes an impressive route for huge variety of therapeutic molecules to get into blood stream. Systemic mucosal delivery of drugs via the nose and lungs, the oral (buccal) cavity and the genital tract circumvents the liver and thus avoid hepatic first-pass metabolism, which may be advantageously exploited.

Mucoadhesion and bioadhesion

Drug absorption is often limited by the residence time of the drug at the site of absorption. In ocular delivery, for example, a drug solution is cleared by the lacrimal fluid within a few minutes after application. Therefore, mucoadhesion is an important strategy in order to prolong the mucosal residence time of drug delivery systems. Both systemic and local delivery can be optimized with mucoadhesive dosage forms by retaining in intimate contact with the absorption site or the site of action, which results in high local drug concentrations and a high flux through the absorbing tissue. In drug delivery sciences, mucoadhesion is defined as the state in which a material and mucus or a mucous membrane are held together for prolonged period of time by interfacial forces. Mucoadhesives are synthetic or natural polymers which interact with the mucus layer covering the mucosal epithelial surface and mucin molecules constituting a major part of mucus. Bioadhesion is a broader term, which include mucoadhesion, and is defined as the ability of a material (synthetic or biological) to adhere to a biological tissue for an extended period of time.

Mucoadhesive drug delivery systems utilize the property of bioadhesion of certain water-soluble polymers which become adhesive on hydration and hence can be used for targeting a drug to a particular region of the body for extended periods of time. The mucosal layer lines a number of regions of the body including the gastrointestinal tract, the urogenital tract, the airways, the ear, nose, and eye. These represent potential sites for attachment of any bioadhesive system and, hence, the mucoadhesive drug delivery system may include the following:

(a) Buccal delivery system
(b) Sublingual delivery system
(c) Vaginal delivery system
(d) Rectal delivery system
(e) Nasal delivery system
(f) Ocular delivery system
(g) Gastrointestinal delivery system

To understand the mucosal drug delivery systems in a better way, one has to be acquainted with the anatomic features of mucosal layer and its physiologic aspects.

4.2 THE MUCOSAL LAYER AND BARRIERS TO DRUG DELIVERY

In several body cavities the single-layered (e.g., stomach, intestine, bronchi) or multi-layered (e.g., vagina and cornea) epithelia are moistured by the presence of a mucus gel layer. Single-layered epithelia contain goblet cells which secrete mucus onto the epithelial surface whereas multi-layered epithelia contain specialized glands such as salivary glands that secrete mucus onto the epithelial surface. The mucus gel consists of mucin glycoproteins, lipids, inorganic salts and up to 83% water. The mucin glycoproteins are the most important component for the structure, as their cysteine-rich subdomains can form intra- and/or intermolecular disulfide bonds. Because of the presence of sialic acid and sulfate, the mucus is negatively charged. The mucus layer is continuously released but also continuously eroded by enzymatic and mechanical challenges on the luminal surface. The thickness of this mucus layer differs widely between the various mucosal surfaces from less than 1 mm in the oral cavity to as much as 450 mm in the stomach.

The mucus has different functions which are more or less developed at the different body sites. First of all, it is a diffusion barrier for xenobiotics, especially for drugs. It also protects the mucosa in the stomach from the hydrochloric acid of the lumen. The mucus keeps the mucosal membrane moist and lubricated. Finally, Mucus has strong cohesive properties and firmly binds to the epithelial cell surface as a continuous gel layer.

Barriers to mucosal drug delivery:

The barriers to the mucosal drug delivery primarily include the mucus gel layer and, the mucosal tissue.

The thick mucus gel formed over the epithelial cell surface poses a significant barrier to drug permeation. The mesh space of mucus is a measure of the size of the pores between the entangled mucin fibers. In a recent study using human cervicovaginal mucus, a mean mesh space of 340 ± 70 nm was found with 80 % of the mesh spaces being larger than 200 nm. The mesh space of mucus greatly varies with its anatomical origin. Further, the rigidity of the mucus network is equally important for drug delivery. Rigidity of mucus network depends on the numbers and types of intermolecular interactions involved such as the electrostatic interactions. The hydrophilic nature and the presence of numerous negative charges allowing for drug interactions with the mucus components have also been shown to retard diffusion and thereby limit drug absorption.

Further, the mucosal tissue also plays an important role as barrier to drug delivery. The morphology of the epithelial absorption barrier varies according to the specific physiological site. Thus, the intestinal, nasal and lung epithelia are comprised of a monolayer of cells interconnected by tight and more loosely adherent junctions, whereas the epithelia in the oral cavity and the vagina are stratified and not tightly interconnected by junctions, but by an intercellular lipid matrix constituting a barrier for absorption. Thus, the epithelial absorption profile of drugs may vary with regard to the rate and the lag time depending on the specific mucosal epithelium targeted, as well as the physiochemical properties of the drug. Absorption across the epithelia may occur by passive transcellular or paracellular diffusion. Hydrophilic compounds, such as peptide drugs, prefer the paracellular route as the key route of absorbtion. Physical and chemical features of the drug determine if the compounds being administered obey transport via a transcellular or paracellular route. Only passive diffusion is involved in paracellular transport, whereas transcellular transport can take place by passive, facilitated or active transport processes. Only a small number of drugs can be transported via active transport systems. For instance, the intestinal absorption of di- and tri-peptides is by active transport by the carrier-mediated oligopeptide transporter. For uptake through the mucus pathways, both paracellular and transcellular are favored; nevertheless, in many cases both pathways are involved in the absorption process. Molecules exhibiting a radius greater than 15 Å show limited transport through the tight junctions, representing the restricted area for the paracellular route.

4.3 PRINCIPLES OF BIOADHESION/MUCOADHESION

For drug delivery purposes, the term bioadhesion implies attachment of a drug carrier system to a specified biological location. The biological surface can be epithelial tissue or the mucus coat on the surface of a tissue. If adhesive attachment is to a mucus coat, the phenomenon is referred to as mucoadhesion. In biological systems, bioadhesion can be classified into 3 types:

- **Type 1:** adhesion between two biological phases, for example, platelet aggregation and wound healing.

- **Type 2:** adhesion of a biological phase to an artificial substrate, for example, cell adhesion to culture dishes and biofilm formation on prosthetic devices and inserts.
- **Type 3:** adhesion of an artificial material to a biological substrate, for example, adhesion of synthetic hydrogels to soft tissues and adhesion of sealants to dental enamel.

A series of phenomena happens during bioadhesion process. The first stage involves an intimate contact between a bioadhesive and a membrane. In the second stage, after contact is established, penetration of the bioadhesive into the crevice of the tissue surface or interpenetration of the chains of the bioadhesive with those of the mucus takes place. One of the most important factors for bioadhesion is tissue surface roughness. Adhesive joints may fail at relatively low applied stresses if cracks, air bubbles, voids, inclusions, or other surface defects are present. Viscosity and wetting power are the most important factors for satisfactory bioadhesion. On a molecular level, mucoadhesion can be explained on the basis of molecular interactions. The interaction between two molecules is composed of attraction and repulsion. Attractive interactions arise from van der Waals forces, electrostatic attraction, and hydrogen bonding. Repulsive interactions occur because of electrostatic and steric repulsion. For mucoadhesion to occur, the attractive interaction should be larger than nonspecific repulsion. To explain the fundamental mechanisms of bioadhesion, several theories has been proposed as follows:

(i) ***Electronic theory:*** According to the electronic or the electrostatic theory, electron transfer occurs upon contact of an adhesive polymer with a mucus glycoprotein network because of differences in their electronic structures. This results in the formation of an electrical double layer at the interface. Adhesion occurs due to attractive forces across the double layer.

(ii) ***Adsorption theory:*** According to the adsorption theory, after an initial contact between two surfaces, the material adheres because of surface forces acting between the atoms in the two surfaces. The surface adherence results due to secondary chemical bonds originating from electrostatic forces, van der Waals forces, and hydrogen and hydrophobic bonds.

(iii) ***Wetting theory:*** It is applied to liquid or low-viscosity bio-adhesives systems. It explains adhesion as an embedding process,

where by adhesive agents penetrate into surface irregularities of the substrate and ultimately harden, producing many adhesive anchors. Free movement of the adhesive on the surface of the substrate means that it must overcome any surface tension effects present at the interface. The wetting theory calculates the contact angle and the thermodynamic work of adhesion. The work of adhesion (expressed in terms of surface and interfacial tension, Y) is defined as the energy per square centimeter released when an interface is formed.

The work of adhesion is given by the equation-

$$W_a = Y_A + Y_B - Y_{AB}$$

where A and B refer to the biological membrane and the bioadhesive formulation respectively. The work of cohesion is given by:

$$W_c = 2Y_A \text{ or } Y_B$$

For a bioadhesive material B spreading on a biological substrate A, the spreading coefficient is given by:

$$S_{B/A} = Y_A - (Y_B + Y_{AB})$$

$S_{B/A}$ should have a positive value for a bioadhesive material to adhere to a biological membrane.

(iv) ***Diffusion theory:*** According to diffusion theory, the polymer chains and the mucus mix to a sufficient depth to create a semipermanent adhesive bond. The existence of concentration gradients will drive the polymer chains of the bioadhesive into the mucus network and the glycoprotein mucin chains into the bioadhesive matrix until an equilibrium penetration depth is achieved. The exact depth needed for good bioadhesive bonds is unclear, but is estimated to be in the range of 0.2–0.5 µm. The exact depth to which the polymer chains penetrate the mucus depends on the diffusion coefficient and the time of contact. The mean diffusional depth of the bioadhesive polymer segments, "s", may be represented by the following equation-

$$s = (2tD)^{1/2}$$

where "D" is the diffusion coefficient and "t" is the contact time.

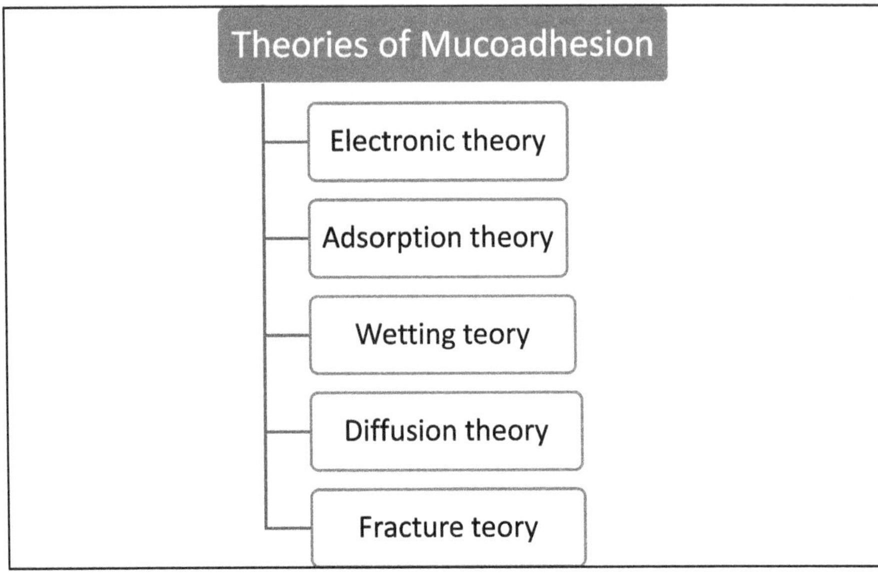

Fig.4.1 Summary of theories of mucoadhesion.

(v) ***Fracture theory:*** Fracture theory attempts to relate the difficulty of separation of two surfaces after adhesion. Fracture strength (G) equivalent to adhesive strength is given by the following equation-

$$G = (E\varepsilon/L)^{1/2}$$

where, "E" is the Young's modulus of elasticity, "ε" is the fracture energy, and L is the critical crack length when two surfaces are separated.

4.4 FACTORS INFLUENCING MUCOADHESION

Many factors or variables have potential to influence the quality of mucoadhesion and subsequently affect the mucosal drug delivery. The key factors include polymer related factors, environment related factors and physiological factors which are discussed as follows.

(i) ***Polymer related factors:*** The molecular weight, concentration, flexibility of polymer chain and spatial conformation of the polymer affects bioadhesion. The interpenetration of polymer molecules is favorable for low molecular weight polymers, whereas entanglements are favored for high molecular weight polymers. The optimum molecular weight for the maximum bioadhesion depends on the type of polymer. Their nature dictates the degree of swelling in water, which in turn determines interpenetration of polymer molecules within the mucus.

Some studies revealed that the bioadhesive force increases with the molecular weight of the bioadhesive polymer up to 100,000 Da, and that beyond this level there is not much effect. However, the adhesive strength of polyethylene oxide increases even up to molecular weights of 4,000,000 Da.

The concentration of polymers is also important for adequate bioadhesion. For solid dosage forms such as tablets, the higher the polymer concentration, the stronger the bioadhesion. Flexiblity of the polymer chain is important for interpenetration and entanglement. As water-soluble polymers become crosslinked, the mobility of the individual polymer chain decreases. As the cross-linking density increases, the effective length of the chain which can penetrate into the mucus layer decreases even further and mucoadhesive strength is reduced.

Spatial conformation of the polymer molecule also affects the bioadhesion. The helical conformation of polymers (e.g. dextran) may shield many active groups which are responsible for adhesion, unlike PEG polymers, which have a linear conformation.

(ii) ***Environment related factors:*** The pH affects the charge of the polymer and the charge of the mucosal surface because of the different dissociation of the functional groups of the polymeric and amino acid backbone, respectively. The degree of hydration of a polymer is dependent on its chemical structure and the pH.

To initially induce bioadhesion, the solid bioadhesive is placed in contact with the biological substrate and definite pressure is applied. The quantity of applied pressure and duration affects the bioadhesive strength. Higher pressure applied initially for contact, which can increase the depth of interpenetration, and longer initial contact time between the delivery system and the mucus, increase the mucoadhesive strength.

(iii) ***Physiological factors:*** The natural mucin turnover limits the residence time of the mucoadhesives on the mucus layer. The mucin turnover rate varies at different mucosal surfaces (anatomic differences) and in different subjects. The mucus turnover in humans has been estimated to be in the range of 12–24 h and is dependent on many other physiologic factors and presence of food.

Furthermore, diseases like gastric ulcers, common cold, bacterial or fungal infections or inflammation can change the mucosal physico-chemical properties.

4.5 TRANSMUCOSAL/BUCCAL PERMEABILITY OF DRUGS

The transmucosal permeability of drugs depend on three major factors i.e. mucosal membrane factor, physicochemical properties of the drug and other environmental factor.

(i) ***Mucosal membrane factor:*** The superficial layer of the oral mucosa is composed of a layer of stratified epithelial tissue. The epithelial cell membranes are essentially lipophilic, but the spaces between the cells are basically hydrophilic. Thus, the oral epithelium may be thought of as an area composed of lipophilic and hydrophilic regions. As a result, there are essentially two routes for drug transport across the oral mucosa: the paracellular route and the transcellular route. Although drugs are able to use both routes simultaneously, one route will be preferred over the other due to the inherent properties of the drug/permeant.

The paracellular route refers to passage of a drug through the space surrounding the individual epithelial cells. As noted above, the area between the epithelial cells is essentially hydrophilic in nature, although there may be lipophilic components secreted into this space. Because this area is hydrophilic, this is the preferred transport route for drugs that are hydrophilic in nature and have a molecular weight of less than approximately 500 Da. In contrast, the paracellular route is a transport barrier for drugs that are lipophilic in nature primarily because the solubility of a lipophilic compound in a hydrophilic environment is low.

The transcellular route refers to passage of a drug through the cells of the epithelial layer. The epithelial cell membranes are lipophilic, and so transport through the transcellular pathway is favored for lipophilic compounds. It should be noted that the intracellular space, e.g., the cytoplasm, is hydrophilic. However, the main resistance to drug transport by the transcellular route is the cellular membrane, and so transport across the intracellular space (cytoplasm) is relatively rapid and does not constitute a significant transport barrier. Transcellular transport is rapid for lipophilic compounds for a variety of reasons. For example, the relative surface area for the transcellular route is significantly larger than that for the paracellular route. In addition, the pathlength for a drug to cross the oral mucosa by transcellular transport is much shorter than for paracellular transport.

Transcellular absorption of drugs is mediated by passive diffusion. This is particularly true for low molecular weight lipophilic drugs. In essence, passive diffusion involves the transport of a drug from an area of high concentration to an area of low concentration. In the context of drug delivery by the oral mucosa, the area of high concentration is the oral cavity, whereas the area of low concentration is the blood supply. The low concentration gradient of the blood supply is maintained by normal blood flow, which continually carries absorbed drug away from the oral mucosa and results in the maintenance of "sink conditions."

Passive diffusion follows Fick's laws of diffusion, which state that the absorption rate is proportional to the drug concentration and the surface area available for drug absorption. However, there are other important considerations that affect the rate of diffusion, such as the ionization state of the drug molecule. In particular, the ionization state of a drug is important for drug diffusion through the transcellular route, because non-ionized drugs exhibit greater lipid solubility as compared to the ionized form. For this reason, the rate of passive diffusion through the transcellular route is related to the amount of drug that exists in the non-ionized form. Drug ionization state is, of course, related to the pKa of the individual drug, as well as the pH of the local environment as described by the Henderson–Hasselbalch equation.

(ii) ***Physicochemical properties of drugs:*** Permeation of a compound across the buccal mucosa is mainly dependent on molecular size, lipophilicity, and ionization. Small molecules (< 100 Da) are rapidly transported through the buccal mucosa. As the molecular size increases, permeability typically diminishes for hydrophilic substances. For unionized molecules, as the lipophilicity rises, permeability typically increases. For many ionizable drugs, maximum permeation occurs at a pH where the drug compound remains primarily unionized. Thus, assuming a saliva pH of approximately 7.2, as an example, either weakly basic drug compounds that have pKa values less than or equal to 7.2, or weakly acidic drugs that have pKa values greater than or equal to 7.2 would ensure that a large percentage (≥ 50 %) of the ionizable drug molecule existed in the unionized form.

(iii) ***Environmental factors:*** Environmental factors such as mucus, saliva, salivary glands, and movement of the oral tissues may also decrease the rate and extent of drug absorption across buccal mucosa.

Mucus is the intercellular ground matrix consisting of mucins and inorganic salts, which surrounds epithelial cells. It serves as a lubricant, thus facilitating movement of cells relative to one another. At buccal pH, mucous molecules join together to form a gelatinous layer over the epithelial cells with a thickness varying from about 40 to 300 μm. It plays a major role in the bioadhesion of drug delivery system.

The secretion from major and minor salivary glands is known as saliva. It is primarily composed of water (99 %), with a pH around 6.5–7.5. This pH plays an important role in the passive diffusion of unionized drugs. The normal resting (unstimulated) flow rate of saliva is approximately 100–500 μl/min, with a total volume of saliva in the oral cavity being approximately 1 ml. An increase in salivary secretion (due to mechanical pressure, chemicals in the diet, anticipation of a meal, etc.) makes it difficult for a delivery system to be retained for a significant amount of time at the absorption site. Similarly, any retentive system placed adjacent to the salivary gland may result in rapid dissolution/erosion of the delivery system.

Swallowing, talking, and eating may lead to dislodgement of the device in the oral cavity. Movement of the tissues is less when individuals are sleeping, but swallowing does occur during sleep. Typically, when the volume of saliva in the oral cavity reaches about 1.1 ml, an involuntary swallowing reflex is triggered, and the saliva is subsequently swallowed. The movement of the tongue may also influence the delivery of drugs from a mucoadhesive retentive system, owing to compression of the dosage form against the hard palate by the tongue, induction of suction pressure, and a general sweeping action of the tongue across the dosage form and tissues.

4.6 ADVANTAGES AND DISADVANTAGES

The advantages related to the use of mucoadhesive drug delivery systems include the following-

1. Increased dosage form residence time at the site of absorption or action.
2. Overall improved drug bioavailability.
3. Controlled and sustained drug delivery.
4. Reduced administration frequency and improved patient compliance.
5. Possibility of targeting particular body sites and tissues.
6. Avoids first-pass hepatic metabolism via the transmucosal nonoral routes.
7. Nasal mucosal offers large surface area of the nose and the thin, porous, highly vascularized nasal epithelium which ensures high absorption and rapid transport of the absorbed substances directly into the systemic blood circulation avoiding drug metabolism in the liver. If drugs are absorbed in the olfactory region they will be absorbed directly into the central nervous system bypassing the tight blood -brain barrier. Furthermore, the enzymatic activity of the epithelium is lower than the one of the GI tract and therefore higher bioavailability of active pharmaceutical ingredients (API) such as peptides and proteins can be achieved.

8. The buccal mucosa has a rich blood supply that flows directly into the jugular vein and thereby is sparing the drug from first-pass metabolism of the liver and degradation in the GI tract by enzymes.
9. Vaginal mucosa also avoids the hepatic first-pass metabolism and GI side-effects offering a good permeability to a wide range of compounds including peptides and proteins standing as an alternative to the parenteral route for drugs such as bromocriptine, oxytocin, calcitonin, human growth hormone and steroids used for replacement therapy or contraception.
10. The major problem of conventional ocular drug delivery is the small area for penetration, the presence of corneal epithelium as an absorption barrier, and the short contact time. Goblet cells on the conjunctival surface secrete mucin which is spread over the surface of the eye by blinking. Mucoadhesive polymers, as drug carrier systems, can interact with the mucus and prolong the residence time of the medication and thus increase their bioavailability.
11. Drugs and their conventional delivery systems show a high variation in the gastrointestinal residence time due to state-of-feeding and intestinal motility. Mucoadhesive delivery systems make an intimate contact with the mucosa increases the residence time and therefore higher local drug concentrations and improve absorption.

The disadvantages associated with mucoadhesive systems are described as follows:

1. A large variation exists in the mucosal membrane permeability depending on the anatomical site. E.g., buccal mucosal permeability is significantly lesser than intestinal mucosal permeability.
2. A large variation exists in the effective surface areas for absorption for different mucosal membranes. E.g., intestinal mucosa has the largest effective surface area for drug absorption.
3. Continuous secretion of saliva can affect the efficiency of oral mucosal drug delivery.
4. Lacrimal secretions affect the efficiency of ocular mucosal drug delivery.
5. Similar secretion of body fluids in other mucosal surfaces of intestine, nose, vagina, rectum, etc affect the respective mucosal drug delivery systems. Nasal and ophthalmic routes have another drawback of mucociliary drainage that would clear the dosage form from the site
6. Involuntary swallowing during oral mucosal drug delivery negatively affect the efficiency and sometimes, even may cause a choking hazard.
7. Poor patient acceptability due to bad taste during oral mucosal drug delivery. Eating and drinking is also prohibited which adds to the inconvenience.

8. Non-intestinal mucosal drug delivery (vaginal, rectal, buccal, etc.) may cause a significant inconvenience and tissue irritation to the patients.
9. Occurrence of local ulcerous effects due to prolonged contact of the drug with the mucus membrane.
10. Lack of a good model for in vitro screening to identify drugs suitable for mucosal administration.

4.7 FORMULATION OF BUCCAL DRUG DELIVERY SYSTEMS

Buccal drug delivery can have two different therapeutic aims i.e. either local therapy of the oral mucosa (e.g., antimycotics, antiviral agents, local anesthetics, corticosteroids etc.) or systemic therapy (e.g., propranolol, proteins, peptides, oligonucleotides, etc). However, the candidate drug molecules should have the desired properties for buccal drug delivery (see Table 4.1).

Table 4.1 Ideal drug candidate properties for buccal delivery.

Drug candidate properties	Ideal limits
Aqueous solubility	> 1 mg/ml
Lipophilicity	10 < oil:water partition coefficient < 1000
Molecular weight	< 500 Da
Melting point	< 200°C
pH of saturated aqueous solution	5–9
Required dose deliverable	< 25 mg/day

With a better understanding of the mechanism(s) of bioadhesion, several bioadhesive dosage forms have been reported. Because of the presence of a smooth and relatively immobile surface for placement of a bioadhesive dosage form, the buccal region appears to be more suitable for sustained delivery of therapeutic agents using a bioadhesive system. Since there is a limit to the size of the bioadhesive dosage form, only a limited amount of drug can be used in these systems. In general, any drug with a daily requirement of 25 mg or less is suitable for buccal delivery. Drugs with short biological half-lives; requiring a sustained effect; and exhibiting poor permeability, sensitivity to enzymatic degradation, and poor solubility may be successfully delivered via a bioadhesive oral delivery system. Relevant bioadhesive dosage forms in the buccal cavity include adhesive tablets, adhesive gels, adhesive patches, and adhesive ointments. The mucoadhesive buccal films/patches and tablets are usually fabricated in different geometry (see Fig.4.2). The directions of drug release are marked as arrows in the figure.

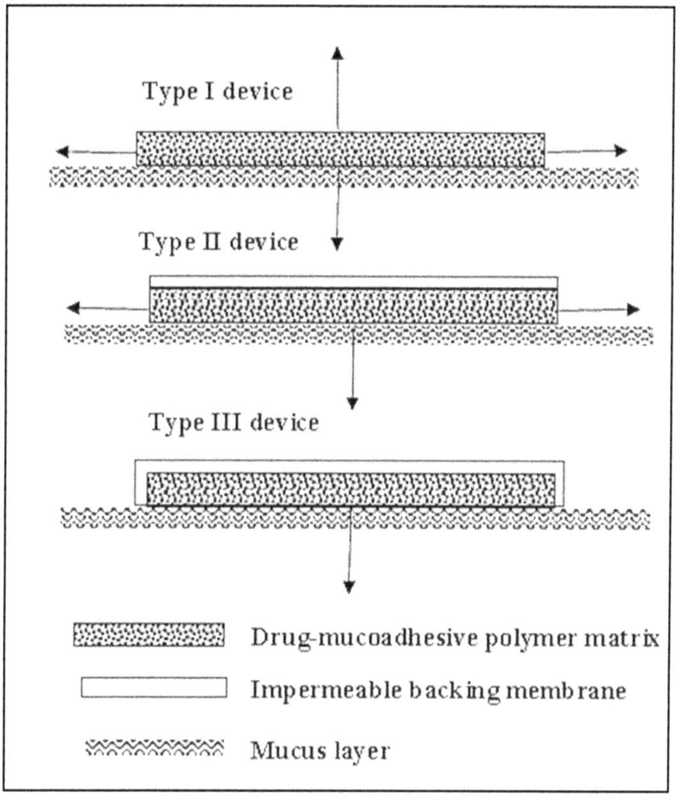

Fig.4.2 Types of buccal drug delivery devices.

Type I device- This is a single-layer device, from which drug can be released multi-directionally.

Type II device- It has an impermeable backing layer on top of the drug-loaded bioadhesive layer, and drug loss into oral cavity can be greatly decreased.

Type III device- This is a unidirectional release device, from which drug loss will be avoided and drug can penetrate only via the buccal mucosa.

The general formulation of buccal dosage forms includes various components like permeation enhancers, solubility enhancers, enzyme inhibitors and mucoadhesive agents.

(i) ***Permeation enhancers:*** Buccal penetration enhancers are capable of decreasing penetration barrier of the buccal mucosa by increasing cell membrane fluidity, extracting the structural intercellular and/or intracellular lipids, altering cellular proteins, or altering mucus structure and rheology. The buccal mucosa is multilayered without tight junctions, and effective penetration enhancers for transdermal and/or intestinal drug delivery may not have similar effects on buccal drug delivery.

Currently, the most commonly investigated penetration enhancers include bile salts, fatty acids, and sodium lauryl sulfate. Bile salts act by extraction of membrane protein or lipids, membrane fluidization, and reverse micellization in the membrane. They also have inhibitory effects on mucosal membrane peptidases. It is generally considered that buccal mucosal damage caused by bile salts would be reversible.

Fatty acids like oleic acid and cod liver oil extract has been reported as buccal permeation enhancers. Sodium lauryl sulfate has been reported to increase the buccal delivery of several drugs when included in various dosage forms. However, sodium lauryl sulfate was reported to cause marked irritation to the buccal epithelium.

(ii) ***Solubility enhancers:*** Despite the increased bioavailability of many drugs by avoiding first pass effect, poor solubility of drug in saliva may affect drug release from the device for subsequent uptake by buccal mucosa. Solubilization of a poorly water-soluble drug by complexing with cyclodextrin and delivering via the buccal mucosa is advantageous in increasing drug absorption and bioavailability. Solubility of imidazole antimycotics (e.g., miconazole, econazole, and clotrimazole) were found to improve upon formulation with hydroxypropyl-beta-cyclodextrin as inclusion complex. Apart from complexation, other routine strategies for enhancement of solubility can also be adopted for buccal drug delivery.

(iii) ***Enzyme inhibitors:*** The buccal mucosa has relatively low enzymatic activity, and lower incidences of drug inactivation compared to other mucosal sites. However, enzymes in saliva and buccal mucosa can still degrade drugs, particularly peptide/protein drugs. Several proteolytic enzymes were found in buccal epithelium. Co-administration of enzyme inhibitors is an useful strategy for improved absorption of protein/peptide drug. Enzyme inhibitors such as aprotinin, bestatin, puromycin, and bile salts stabilize protein drugs by affecting activity of proteolytic enzymes, altering the conformation of the peptide drug or forming micelles, and/or rendering the drug less accessible to enzymatic degradation. Particularly, as peptide/protein drugs are transported through the paracellular route, the cytosolic peptidases may be inaccessible for the drugs during their permeation. Aminopeptidases appeared to represent a major metabolic barrier to the buccal delivery of peptide drugs, and the absence of endopeptidase and carboxypeptidase is advantageous for the buccal delivery of peptide drugs.

(iv) ***Mucoadhesives:*** Mucoadhesives are used in the formulation of buccal drug delivery systems to improve its residence time and quality of contact with the mucosal tissue. Compared to other mucosal surfaces, the buccal regions seem to be more suitable for a bioadhesive system because of a smooth, relatively immobile surface and accessibility. The functional groups available on the surface of polymer conformation favoring bioadhesion include hydroxyls, carboxyls, amines, and amides. The bioadhesive polymer must have a critical molecular weight and an adequate length to allow chain interpenetration. Anionic polymers are usually preferred due to negatively charged mucin at physiological pH. Polymers with bioadhesive properties include biopolymers (e.g., chitosan and sodium alginate) and synthetic polymers (e.g., cellulose derivatives, polyacrylic polymers, polyvinylpyrrolidone, and polyvinyl alcohol). The above-mentioned nonspecific bioadhesives can be considered as first-generation bioadhesives. The duration of bioadhesion is largely determined by the fast turnover of mucus layer. Factors such as saliva secretion, food intake, local pH, and compositions of delivery systems also strongly affect bioadhesion. Lectins are proteins/glycoproteins that possess high specific affinity for carbohydrates. Recently, lectin-based second-generation bioadhesives have attracted considerable interest for oral drug delivery. The specific bioadhesion is also termed "cytoadhesion" and is a highly specific interaction between adhesives and cell surfaces. It was observed that lectin binding on human buccal cells occurred within 20 s and appeared not to be detached by saliva flushing. It seems possible to enhance drug delivery by anchoring the delivery device to the buccal epithelial cell with lectin-based specific bioadhesives.

4.8 DOSAGE FORMS IN BUCCAL DRUG DELIVERY

Brief outline of various dosage forms for buccal delivery is discussed as follows.

Buccal Tablets: Buccal tablets are usually small, flat, and oval shaped with a diameter of approximately 5–8 mm. Unlike conventional buccal tablets, buccal mucoadhesive tablets allow for drinking and speaking without major discomfort. They soften, adhere to the mucosa, and are retained in position until dissolution and/or release is complete. These tablets can be applied to different sites in the oral cavity, including the palate, the mucosa lining the cheek, as well as between the lip and the gums. Successive tablets can be applied to alternate sides of the mouth. However, the major drawback of buccal bioadhesive tablets is their lack of physical flexibility, leading to poor patient compliance for long-term and repeated use.

Bioadhesive tablets are usually prepared by direct compression, but wet granulation techniques can also be used. Tablets intended for buccal administration by insertion into the buccal pouch may dissolve or erode slowly; therefore, they are formulated and compressed with sufficient pressure only to give a hard tablet. In order to achieve unidirectional release, every face of the tablet, except the one that is in contact with the buccal mucosa, can be coated with water impermeable materials, such as ethyl cellulose, hydrogenated castor oil, etc., using either compression or spray coating. Multilayered tablets may be prepared by sequentially adding and compressing the ingredients layer by layer. If necessary, the drug may be formulated in certain physical states, such as microspheres, prior to direct compression in order to achieve some desirable properties, e.g. enhanced activity and prolonged drug release.

Buccal patches: Buccal patches may range from simple erodible and non-erodible adhesive disks attached to laminated systems in the size range of 1-16 cm^2. These can be designed to provide either unidirectional or bidirectional release of the drug. Patches are laminates consisting of an impermeable backing layer, a drug-containing reservoir layer from which the drug is released in a controlled manner, and a bioadhesive surface for mucosal attachment. Buccal patch systems are similar to those used in transdermal drug delivery.

Solvent casting and direct milling methods are commonly employed for preparation of buccal adhesive patches. In the solvent casting method, the intermediate sheet from which patches are punched is prepared by casting the solution of the drug and polymer(s) onto a backing layer sheet, and subsequently allowing the solvent(s) to evaporate. In the direct milling method, formulation constituents are homogeneously mixed and compressed to the desired thickness, and patches of predetermined size and shape are then cut or punched out. An impermeable backing layer may also be applied to control the direction of drug release, prevent drug loss, and minimize deformation and disintegration of the device during the application period.

Buccal films: Buccal films are relatively recently developed dosage form for buccal administration. Buccal films may be preferred over adhesive tablets in terms of flexibility and comfort. In addition, they can circumvent the relatively short residence time of oral gels on the mucosa, which are easily washed away and removed by saliva. Moreover, in the case of local delivery for oral diseases, the films also help protect the wound surface, thus helping to reduce pain and treat the disease more effectively.

An ideal film should be flexible, elastic, and soft, yet adequately strong to withstand breakage due to stress from mouth movements. It must also possess good bioadhesive strength in order to be retained in the mouth for the desired duration of action. Swelling of film, if it occurs, should not be too extensive in order to prevent discomfort.

Buccal films are usually manufactured by a solvent casting method. The drug and polymer(s) are first dissolved in a casting solvent or solvent mixture.

The solution is then cast into films, dried, and finally laminated with a backing layer or a release liner. The backing layer helps retard the diffusion of saliva into the drug layer, thus enhancing the adhesion time and reducing drug loss into the oral cavity. The solvent casting method is simple, but suffers from some disadvantages, including long processing time, high cost, and environmental concerns due to the solvents used. Recently, hot melt extrusion method is adopted to overcome the drawbacks.

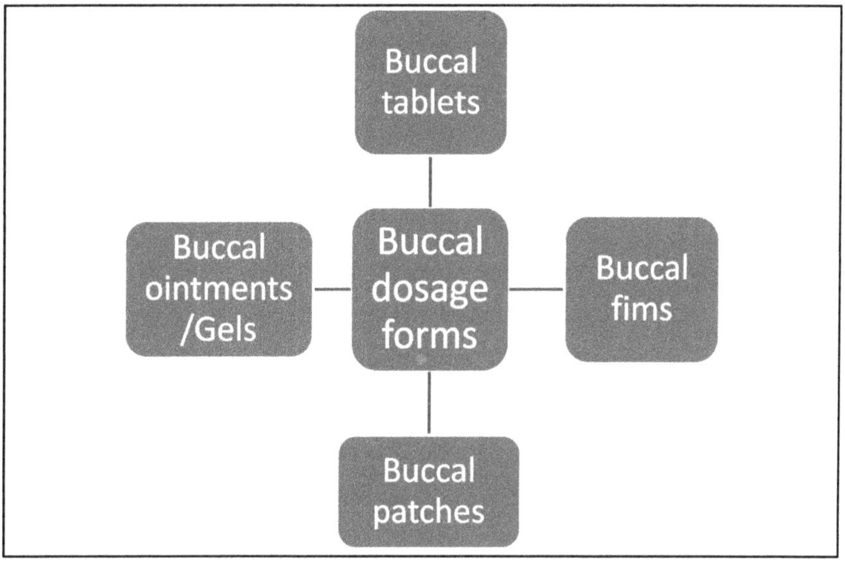

Fig.4.3 Summary of buccal dosage forms.

Buccal ointments and gels: In 1982, an ointment-type oral mucosal dosage form of prednisolone for the treatment of aphthae was developed containing carbopol-934 and white petrolatum as the base. Semisolid dosage forms, such as gels and ointments, have the advantage of excellent spreadability over the oral mucosa. However, drug dosing from semisolid dosage forms may not be as accurate as from tablets, patches, or films. Poor retention of the gels at the site of application has been overcome by using bioadhesive formulations. Certain bioadhesive polymers, e.g. poloxamer 407, sodium carboxy methylcellulose, carbopol, hyaluronic acid, xanthan gum, etc, undergo a phase change from a liquid to a semisolid. This change enhances the viscosity, which results in sustained and controlled release of drugs. Hydrogels are also very promising semisolid vehicle for buccal drug delivery.

4.9 CHAPTER AT A GLANCE

Term	Description
Mucoadhesion	It is defined as the state in which a material and mucus or a mucous membrane are held together for prolonged period of time by interfacial forces.
Bioadhesion	It is a broader term, which include mucoadhesion, and is defined as the ability of a material (synthetic or biological) to adhere to a biological tissue for an extended period of time.
Mucoadhesives	These are synthetic, semisynthetic or natural polymers which interact with the mucus layer covering the mucosal epithelial surface and mucin molecules constituting a major part of mucus.
Mucoadhesive drug delivery systems	These include Buccal delivery system, Sublingual delivery system, Vaginal delivery system, Rectal delivery system, Nasal delivery system, Ocular delivery system and Gastrointestinal delivery system.
Types of bioadhesion	Type 1- adhesion between two biological phases, for example, platelet aggregation and wound healing. Type 2- adhesion of a biological phase to an artificial substrate, for example, cell adhesion to culture dishes and biofilm formation on prosthetic devices and inserts. Type 3- adhesion of an artificial material to a biological substrate, for example, adhesion of synthetic hydrogels to soft tissues and adhesion of sealants to dental enamel.
Theories of bioadhesion	Electronic theory, adsorption theory, wetting theory, diffusion theory.
Factors affecting mucoadhesion	Polymer related, environment related, physiological factors.

Table *contd...*

Term	Description
Factors affecting mucosal permeation	Mucosal membrane related, physicochemical properties of drug, environmental factors.
Formulation of buccal drug delivery systems	Permeation enhancers, solubility enhancers, enzyme inhibitors, mucoadhesives
Buccal dosage forms	Tablets, patches, films, Ointments and gels.

EXERCISES

Multiple choice Questions

1. Mucus is negatively charged due to the presence of-
   (a) Sialic acid and sulfate (b) Chloride ion.
   (c) Hydrochloric acid (d) none of the above.
2. Absorption of protein drugs follows which of the following route for mucosal absorption?
   (a) Transcellular (b) Paracellular route
   (c) Both paracellular and transcellular (d) None of the above
3. Platelet aggregation during wound healing is exemplified by-
   (a) Type I bioadhesion
   (b) Type II bioadhesion
   (c) Type III bioadhesion
   (d) None of the above
4. Transcellular absorption is preferred by-
   (a) Hydrophilic compounds
   (b) Lipophilic compounds
   (c) BCS I drugs
   (d) All of the above

5. Which of the following is a buccal permeation enhancer
   (a) HPMC (b) Sodium CMC
   (c) Bile salt (d) Eudragit
6. Which of the following is a method for preparation of buccal films?
   (a) Solvent casting (b) Media milling
   (c) Emulsification (d) Top dowm
7. Which of the following is a common ingredient for buccal gels?
   (a) SiO_2 (b) carbopol-934
   (c) graphene (d) Crosspovidone
8. The ideal dose of drug in buccal delivery platform should be less than-
   (a) 2g (b) 1g
   (c) 500 mg (d) 25 mg
9. Which of the following best explains electronic theory of mucoadhesion?
   (a) Transfer of electrons occurs between the polymer and mucus glycoprotein.
   (b) Transfer of electron occurs between the adhesive polymer and saliva.
   (c) Transfer of electron between the electronic chip and the buccal patch.
   (d) All of the above
10. Which of the following is an example of highly effective cytoadhesive?
   (a) Lectin (b) Starch
   (c) colloidal silica (d) PLGA

Short Answer Questions

1. Write a short note on bioadhesion.
2. Explain the barriers to mucosal drug delivery.
3. Explain the wetting theory for bioadhesion.
4. Explain how polymers affect mucoadhesion.
5. Explain how the physicochemical properties of permeant drugs affect the transmucosal permeability.

Long Answer Questions

1. Define mucoadhesion. Discuss about the various advantages and disadvantages of mucosal drug delivery.
2. Detail the theories of bioadhesion useful to understand mucoadhesive drug delivery systems.
3. Discuss the various factors affecting transmucosal permeability of drugs.
4. Present a generalized note on formulation of buccal drug delivery systems.
5. Write a note on various dosage forms for buccal drug delivery.

Answer Key MCQs

(1) – (a), (2) – (b), (3) – (a), (4) – (b), (5) – (c), (6) – (a), (7) – (b), (8) – (d), (9) – (a), (10) – (a),

BIBLIOGRAPHY

1. Hombach J, Bernkop-Schnürch A. Mucoadhesive Drug Delivery Systems. In: Schäfer-Korting M. (eds) Drug Delivery. Handbook of Experimental Pharmacology, 2010. vol 197. Springer, Berlin, Heidelberg.
2. Ahuja A, Khar RK, Ali J. Mucoadhesive drug delivery systems. Drug Dev Ind Pharm. 1997, 23:489–515.

Chapter 5

IMPLANTABLE DRUG DELIVERY SYSTEMS

♦ LEARNING OBJECTIVES ♦

***After completing this lesson, the Reader should be able to understand*:**

- **Various advantages and disadvantages of implantable drug delivery systems.**
- **Classification and types of implants.**
- **Principles and concepts associated with various types of implants.**
- **Design approaches and drug release process from implantable systems.**

5.1 INTRODUCTION

The oral route remains the most popular and convenient method of drug delivery, with many techno-therapeutic advantages. However, along with other common routes such as transdermal, or intravenous (IV) injection, it is also associated with a number of limitations. Many drugs are not suitable for delivery via the oral route. This may be as a result of: drug degradation in the gastrointestinal tract (GIT); first pass metabolism; or compliance issues. In addition, many newly discovered drugs compounds do not possess the ideal physicochemical properties (e.g. solubility) for oral delivery. Intravenous delivery may overcome some of the issues associated with oral delivery such as: first pass metabolism; degradation in the GIT; or poor solubility and bioavailability. However, this route is not free from limitations. A healthcare professional will be required for administration, and there may be sterility or specific storage issues. It is also an invasive delivery technique which may be unsuitable for those patients who suffer from needle phobia. The transdermal route offers advantages such as: avoidance of first pass metabolism; avoidance of gastro-intestinal degradation; and non-invasiveness. However, it also has a number of issues which prevent it becoming the ideal drug delivery route. Very few drug compounds possess the specific properties such as: low molecular weight; a Log P value between 1 and 3; good solubility; and high partition coefficient, that are required to pass through the stratum corneum barrier, without help from additional methods such as the use of iontophoresis or microneedles. Hence, there is a need for a novel drug delivery platform. A promising alternative delivery method is the use of implantable devices to deliver drug compounds.

Implantable drug delivery systems (IDDSs) are designed to store and deliver small and precise doses of therapeutic agents into the blood stream or to the specific tissue sites, subsequently replacing the need of daily administration of drugs required for the long-term continuous treatment of many disease conditions.

Implants can be used as delivery systems for either systemic or local therapeutic effects. For systemic therapeutic effects, implants are typically administered SC, intramuscularly, or intravenously, whereby the incorporated drug is delivered from the implant and absorbed into the blood circulation. Implants for local effects are placed into specific body sites, where the drug acts locally, with relatively negligible absorption into the systemic circulation. The IDDSs, fabricated of either degradable or nondegradable polymers, are able to modulate, through a wide range of parameters, the rate of released drug(s) for a period of hours, weeks, or months. Such implants have been utilized clinically for decades providing long-term delivery of contraceptives, hormones, and other therapeutic agents.

Implant morphology is typically cylindrical, with monolithic devices at the millimeter or centimeter scale being most commonly employed. Implantation is typically done in subcutaneous or intramuscular tissue, with the aid of special implantation devices, needles, or the use of micro-surgery. Subcutaneous tissue or intramuscular tissue are ideal locations for implantation of drug-depot devices, due to high fat content that facilitates slow drug absorption, minimal innervation, good hemoperfusion, and a lower possibility of localized inflammation (low reactivity to the insertion of foreign materials). In addition to subcutaneous implantation, various other body regions have also successfully served as implantation sites, particularly for delivery to localized tissue such as intravaginal, intravascular, intraocular, intrathecal, intracranial, and peritoneal. Perhaps the most common clinical application to date targets cardiac or carotid arteries as sites for drug-eluting stents (DES), delivering therapy to intravascular locations. The other main applications of such devices have been in the treatment of solid tumors with potent anticancer agents, and delivery of antibiotics for treatment of periodontal disease. The various advantages and disadvantages of these IDDSs are summarized as follows.

Advantages:

1. Improved control of drug levels at the specific site of action. This is due to the elimination of "peaks and troughs" resulting from periodic dosing and uneven dosing intervals. A well designed IDDSs releases drug at constant rate over long period of time. This then leads to fewer side effects from too high or too low a dose. In addition, less total drug is required to elicit the same therapeutic effect.
2. Drugs are delivered as near as possible to their target sites of action and undesirable effects on other sites in the body are minimised.
3. Some protection of drugs that are rapidly metabolised or have short in vivo half-lives is afforded by IDDSs.
4. For drugs that cannot be administered by other routes and where compliance is likely to be a major problem.
5. In cases of extreme allergies or side effects to drugs already administered, immediate removal of implants is possible in contrast to injectable drug delivery systems and in many cases less uncomfortable and traumatic as compared to "stomach pumps (if a stomach pump is indeed possible) with oral drug delivery systems.
6. If the only therapeutically active form of a drug can be administered via the I.V. route, e.g. insulin, an IDDSs may be more suitable and less painful to patients over a long period of time.

Disadvantages:

1. Toxicity or lack of biocompatibility of the materials used for the implant.
2. Harmful by products from IDDSs may form, specifically for biodegradable forms.
3. Most IDDSs require minor surgery to implant and to remove from the administered site if it is not a biodegradable system.
4. Pain and discomfort may be caused by the presence of the implant.
5. IDDSs can be more expensive than non IDDSs due to the cost of the polymer, pump, or manufacturing procedure.
6. Leaks and variable, imprecise drug release may occur in IDDSs.

5.2 CLASSIFICATION OF IDDSs

Implants can be broadly subdivided into passive and active systems. Passive systems can be further classified into nondegradable and degradable implants, that typically have no moving parts or mechanisms. Active systems employ some energy-dependent method for providing a positive driving force to modulate drug release. These energy sources may be as diverse as osmotic pressure gradients or electromechanical drives.

(i) **Passive implants:** Passive implants tend to be relatively simple, homogenous and singular devices, typically comprising the simple packaging of drugs in a biocompatible material or matrix. The biocompatible materials used for the design are usually polymeric in nature. By definition, they do not contain any moving parts, and depend on a passive, diffusion-mediated phenomenon to modulate drug release. Delivery kinetics are partially tunable by the choice of drug, its concentration, overall implant morphology, matrix material and surface properties. The passive implants are further classified as follows.

(a) ***Non-biodegradable implantable drug delivery systems:*** Non-biodegradable implants are commonly prepared using polymers such as silicones, poly(urethanes), poly(acrylates) or copolymers such as poly (ethyelene vinyl acetate) etc. This type of device can be monolithic or reservoir type implant. Monolithic type implants are made from a polymer matrix in which the drug is homogeneously dispersed. On the other hand, reservoir-type implants contain a compact drug core covered by a permeable non-biodegradable membrane. The membrane thickness and the permeability of the drug through the membrane will govern the release kinetics. Non-biodegradable implantable drug delivery systems have been extensively used for contraceptive delivery. These devices are structurally resilient and robust over their lifetime.

One of the earliest and widely deployed, nondegradable reservoir implants is Norplant® developed in 1980 for delivery of levonorgestrel. When implanted subcutaneously, typically on the inside upper arm of female users, it is capable of offering contraceptive protection for up to 5 years.

However, the main drawback of non-biodegradable implants is that after depleting their drug load, they need to be removed. The materials used to prepare these devices show good long-term biocompatibility, but sometimes they can cause infections, tissue damage or cosmetic disfigurement. Accordingly, once all the drug has been released, they are normally extracted to prevent any adverse effects.

(b) ***Biodegradable implantable drug delivery systems:*** These devices are made using polymers or block copolymers that can be broken down into smaller fragments that will be subsequently excreted or absorbed by the body. Normally they are made using polymers such as poly(caprolactone) (PCL), poly (lactic acid) (PLA) or poly (lactic-co-glycolic acid) (PLGA). These materials have been extensively studied and their degradation kinetics can be easily tuned to adjust the drug release rate. The main advantage of this type of implant is that they do not need to be extracted after implantation, as they will be degraded by the body of the patient.

They can be manufactured using the same designs described in the previous section: monolithic implants and reservoir-type implants. One drawback of this particular type of device is that they are more complex to develop than the non-biodegradable ones. The range of potential materials that can be used is reduced, and the regulatory requirements are stricter as the material will be left behind in the body. Finally, the degradation of the polymeric matrix is the main driving force for drug release. However, this can be highly variable in each patient.

There are various commercial biodegradable implants available in the drug market. Selected examples include the Gliadel® wafer for the treatment of brain tumors, Zoladex® for treatment of advanced prostate cancer and advanced breast cancer, and Profact® or Suprefact® Depot for treatment of hormone-responsive cancers, such as prostate cancer or breast cancer and in assisted reproduction.

Some disadvantages of biodegradable IDDSs are: their higher complexity, development cost, regulatory requirements, and the lack of availability of polymers with the exact physical properties needed, including mechanical strength and tunable degradation kinetics. In general, the development of biodegradable systems is a more complicated task than formulating nondegradable systems. When fabricating new biodegradable systems, variables to be taken into consideration include the in vivo degradation kinetics of the polymer, which must ideally remain constant to maintain sustained release of the drug. Unfortunately, these can be highly variable, depending upon patient age and disease state.

(ii) Active or dynamic implants: Dynamic implant systems are based on a positive driving force to enable and control drug release. As a result, these are typically able to modulate drug doses and delivery rates much more precisely than passive systems. However, this comes at a higher cost, both in terms of complexity and device price.

(a) Osmotic pumps: Two solutions of different solute concentrations separated by a semipermeable membrane will establish osmotic pressure across the membrane such that there will be a net flow of water (the solvent) through the membrane from the low-concentration solution to the high concentration solution. An equilibrium state will be reached when the difference in pressure between the two solutions is equal to the osmotic pressure.

The main components of an osmotic micropump include the pharmaceutical drug (solute), an osmotic agent, a semipermeable membrane, a solvent (usually water), and a delivery orifice. Osmotic agents, also known as osmogens, are used to increase the osmotic pressure, which is directly proportional to the drug delivery rate.

Osmotic micropumps can be classified into three types based on the compartmental separation of the pharmaceutical drug, the osmotic agent, and the solvent, which is normally water derived from surrounding aqueous body tissue fluids. In its simplest form, an osmotic pump consists of a single compartment in which the drug is separated from the solvent that flows through a semipermeable membrane to dissolve the drug (See Fig 5.1). The drug acts as the osmotic agent and its solubility determines the drug release rate, which is kept relatively constant as long as the drug solution remains in saturation.

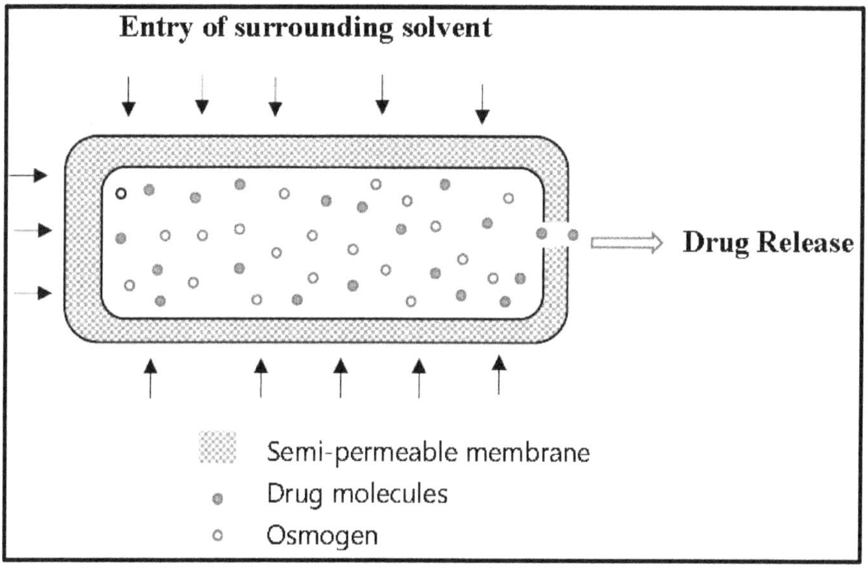

Fig.5.1 Schematic diagram of an one-compartment osmotic pump.

In a two-compartment osmotic micropump, an osmotic agent is dissolved by water derived from surrounding aqueous body tissue fluids to create the osmotic pressure. The micropump consists of two compartments or reservoirs, a drug reservoir and an osmotic agent reservoir both separated by a moveable barrier or partition. When the osmotic agent dissolves, the resultant pressure of the saturated osmotic agent pushes against the barrier, displacing the drug solution toward the orifice of the micropump.

An alternative implementation is to have a flexible membrane wall for the osmotic agent reservoir that can expand or swell under pressure, thus exerting pressure on the drug solution to flow through the orifice of the micropump (see Fig 5.2).

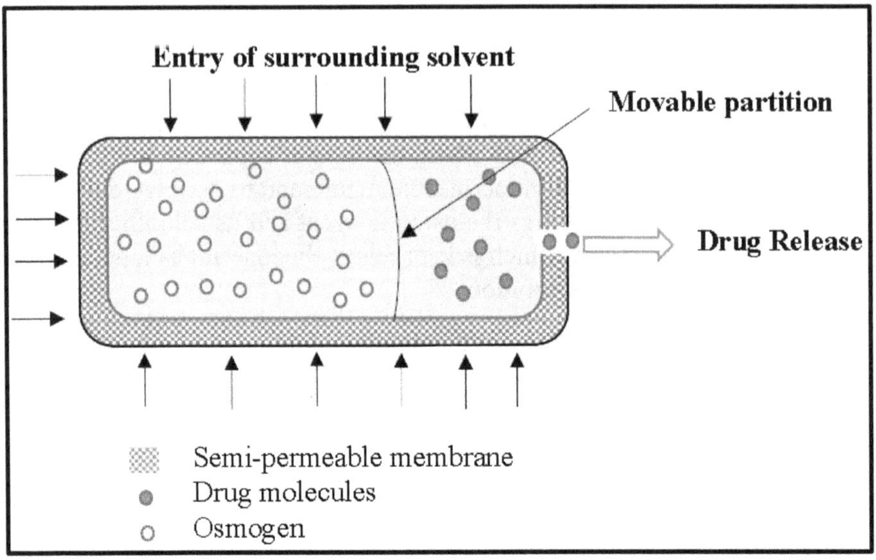

Fig.5.2 Schematic diagram of a two-compartment osmotic pump.

Micropumps can also be implemented having three or more compartments. Three-compartment micropumps are an extension of two compartments in which the extra compartment holds the solvent rather than relying on aqueous body tissue fluids to act as the solvent.

The fundamental equation for all osmotically driven pumps is given by:

$$dm/dt = KA(\Delta\pi)C/h$$

where, dm/dt is drug release rate through the outlet orifice of the osmotic pump, K is the permeability of the semipermeable membrane, $\Delta\pi$ is the osmotic pressure gradient, A is the surface area of the semipermeable membrane, h is the thickness of the membrane, and C is the drug concentration of the dispensed solution.

(b) ***Propellant infusion pumps:*** Though the osmotic pumps offer a higher level of control and zero-order release, compared to biodegradable passive IDDSs, the volume of drug that can be delivered is a major limitation. To overcome this drawback, an alternative design utilizes propellant gas instead of an osmotic agent to generate a constant positive pressure for zero-order drug release.

The use of a compressed gas allows for a larger volume of drug to be stored and released. A good example of this technology is the Infusaid® (Infusaid Corp., Sharon MA), which is a fully implantable fixed-rate pump. In this design, the drug formulation (e.g. insulin) chamber is separated from fluorocarbon propellant chamber by a metal bellows encased in disk-shaped titanium housing. At body temperature, the vapour pressure exerted by the propellant gas forces fluid from the drug chamber through a filter and a flow regulator, and provides a constant rate of drug ejection at a given temperature. The delivery rate is adjusted by changing the drug concentration in the pump reservoir. The overall package is approximately 9 cm in diameter by 3 cm in height and has been utilized for insulin delivery, anticoagulant therapy, and cancer chemotherapy.

(c) ***Electro-mechanical implants:*** These are mostly metallic implants. While osmotic and propellant-driven constant pressure pumps work well for small volumes of medication, this may be a severe limitation for certain chronic diseases requiring daily infusion of medication, precluding their use over long time spans. In such cases, it may be necessary to consider larger implants, wherein the storage capacity of the pump may be replenished from time to time, while the pumping mechanisms stay implanted. By necessity, this implies the use of electrically powered mechanical pumps, typically with moving parts and advanced control systems.

The Synchromed pump, developed by Medtronic Inc., is an example of a peristaltic pump implant, featuring external micro-electronic control of the delivery rate. It has been employed for pain management using intrathecal delivery of opioids, treatment of severe spasticity using baclofen, and for other indications. The pump consists of an outer titanium shell that houses the pump mechanism and controller, a reservoir holding the drug solution, and a battery. It can be conveniently refilled with a needle and syringe via a silicone rubber septum on the system. The implant dimensions are 8.8 cm in diameter and 2.5 cm thickness. The system is typically implanted in the abdominal cavity; delivery of baclofen is enabled by a silicone catheter tunnelled to the intrathecal space.

Electromechanical infusion technology has been rapidly growing and offers some unique solutions for biomedical applications, particularly to address unmet medical needs related to precision dosing. Micro electromechanical systems (MEMS) technology enables the manufacture of small devices using microfabrication techniques, similar to that used to fabricate silicon-based computer chips. MEMS technology has been used to construct micro-reservoirs, micropumps, nano-porous membranes, nanoparticles, valves, sensors, micro-catheters, and other structures using biocompatible materials appropriate for drug administration. Numerous drug delivery implants based on micro- or nano-fabrication technologies are being developed.

The wireless Micro CHIPS DDS contraceptive implant is an active system in that it contains micro reservoirs of 30 μg of the hormone levonorgestrel released daily over a 16 year period and the process can be deactivated and reactivated at any time using a short-range wireless remote control unit to minimize accidental interference from external sources. The Micro CHIPS implant with parathyroid hormone reservoir is also used for the treatment of osteoporosis.

(d) ***Injectable in situ forming implants:*** Injectable in situ forming implants are liquid formulations comprised of biodegradable polymers mixed with bioactive therapeutic agents which can be injected into a target tissue. Once in place, the solution forms a solid or semisolid depot from which drugs can be released in a controlled manner. This liquid to solid phase transition takes place in response to a stimulus such as temperature, pH, enzymatic activity, or solvent miscibility. In contrast to preformed implant systems which often require local anaesthesia and minimally invasive surgical placement, *in situ* systems are more convenient. The mechanism of transition from liquid to solid include (i) thermoplastic pastes, (ii) thermally induced gelling systems, (iii) in situ cross-linked systems, (iv) in situ solidifying organogels, and (iv) in situ precipitating or phase inverting implants.

Thermoplastic pastes (or thermopastes) are polymers that can be injected in the molten form and solidify as they cool down to body temperature. These polymers typically have a low melting temperature, ranging from 25 to 65°C. Common thermopastes include PLA, PGA, PCL, and poly (trimethylene carbonate), etc.

Thermally induced gelling systems are liquid at room temperature, and form a gel at temperatures above the lower critical solution temperature (LCST). Lower critical phase separation is governed by the balance between hydrophobic and hydrophilic moieties on the polymer chain and is driven by the negative entropy of mixing. The Gibbs free energy change for the mixing of two phases is negative below the LCST and positive above. When temperature increases to the LCST, the hydrogen bonding between polymer and water becomes energetically unfavourable compared to polymer–polymer and water–water interactions. Then an abrupt transition occurs as the hydrated hydrophilic molecule quickly dehydrates and changes to a more hydrophobic structure. A number of polymer modifications can be used to alter the temperature at which this transition occurs. Examples of this system include poly (N-isopropyl acrylamide) (poly(NIPAAM)), PEO–PPO–PEO copolymers (Pluronics®), and PEG–PLA as well as PEG–PLGA–PEG copolymers.

A number of *in situ* forming implant systems have been used in clinical applications e.g. Eligard® (Tolmar Pharmaceuticals, Inc.), Atridox® (Zila Inc, Fort Collins, CO), Zoladex® (AstraZeneca, UK), etc. Eligard is a formulation of leuprolide acetate in the polymer solution Atrigel® (Atrix Laboratories, Fort Collins, CO), which consists of PLGA (PLA:PGA=75:25) dissolved in N-methyl-2-pyrrolidone. Leuprolide acetate can be released for a period of up to 6 months from this system, and suppresses plasma testosterone levels which inhibits prostatic tumor growth.

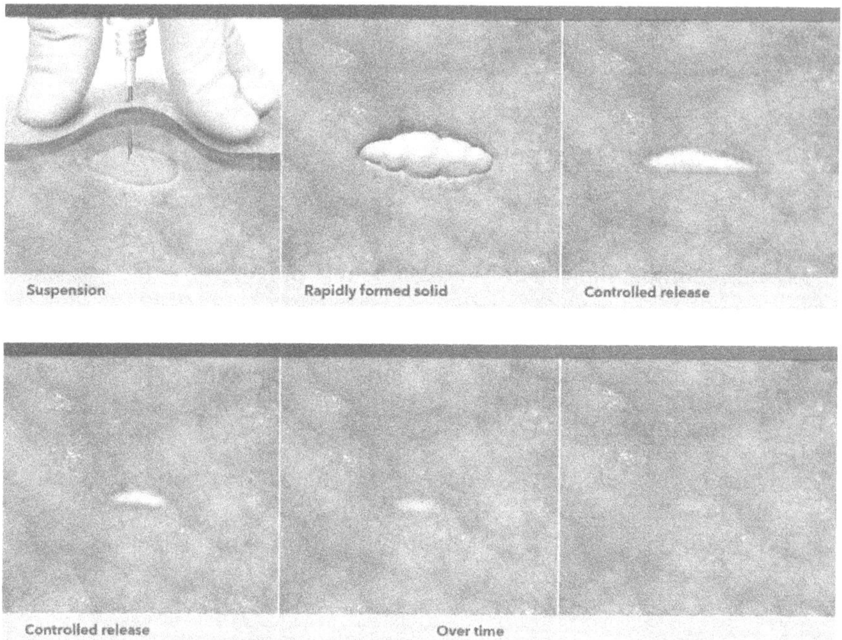

Fig.5.3 The in situ implant Eligard® with permission from Tolmar Pharmaceuticals, Inc.

5.3. CHAPTER AT A GLANCE

Term	Description
Implantable drug delivery systems	These are drug delivery systems to store and deliver small and precise doses of therapeutic agents into the blood stream or to the specific tissue sites, subsequently replacing the need of daily administration of drugs required for the long-term continuous treatment of many disease conditions.
Types of implants	Passive systems (Biodegradable systems, Non-biodegradable systems), Active or dynamic systems (Osmotic pumps, propellant infusion pumps, Electro-mechanical implants, Injectable in situ forming implants)
Osmotic pump types	One compartment, two compartments and three compartments

EXERCISES

Multiple choice Questions

1. Silicones are example of:
   (a) Biocompatible and non-biodegradable polymer.
   (b) Non-biocompatible and biodegradable polymer.
   (c) Non-biocompatible and non-biodegradale polymer.
   (d) Biocompatible and biodegradable polymer.
2. Which of the following is a non-biodegradable reservoir type passive implant?
   (a) Eligard (b) Norplant
   (c) Synchromed (d) Infusaid
3. Which of the following is a major drawback of non-biodegradable passive implants?
   (a) Drug release is not controlled
   (b) Tissue incompatibility
   (c) Need to remove the implant after depletion of drug load
   (d) None of the above
4. Which of the following is a biodegradable passive implant-
   (a) Eligard (b) Infusaid
   (c) Norplant (d) Zoladex
5. Which of the following is an example of thermoplastic pastes-
   (a) PLA (b) HPMC
   (c) EC (c) Carbopol

Short Answer Questions

1. What are the advantages of implantable drug delivery systems?
2. Write a short note on non-biodegradable passive implants.
3. Write a short notes on osmotic pumps as implantable device.
4. What are the limitations of implants as drug delivery systems?

Long Answer Questions

1. Discuss in brief about the passive implantable drug delivery systems.
2. Discuss in brief about dynamic implantable therapeutic devices.
3. What are the advantages of implantable drug delivery systems? Add a note on osmotic pumps.
4. What are the limitations of implantable systems? Add a note on injectable in situ forming implants.
5. Compare and contrast between biodegradable and non-biodegradable implants. What are the various applications of implantable systems?

Answer Key MCQs

(1) – (a), (2) – (b), (3) – (c), (4) – (d), (5) – (a)

BIBLIOGRAPHY

1. Fu Y, Kao WJ. Drug release kinetics and transport mechanisms of nondegradable and degradable polymeric delivery systems. Expert Opin. Drug Deliv. 2010, 7, 429 - 444.
2. Stewart SA, Domínguez-Robles J, Donnelly RF, and Larrañeta E. Implantable Polymeric Drug Delivery Devices: Classification, Manufacture, Materials, and Clinical Applications. Polymers (Basel). 2018, 10(12): 1379.
3. Danckwerts M and Fassihi A. Implantable Controlled Release Drug Delivery Systems: A Review, Drug Dev Ind Pharm. 1991, 17(11): 1465-502.

Chapter 6

TRANSDERMAL DRUG DELIVERY SYSTEMS

♦ LEARNING OBJECTIVES ♦

After completing this lesson, the Reader should be able to understand:

- **The concept and design of Transdermal drug delivery system**
- **Factors affecting permeation of drugs across the skin**
- **Formulation approaches of TDDS**
- **TDDS designs**

6.1 INTRODUCTION

The development of drug delivery systems aims at enhancing drug absorption and efficacy by redesigning the delivery processes rather than the drug molecules or the chemical entities. *When the aim is to deliver drugs through skin in predetermined and controlled fashion, the result is transdermal drug delivery.* Transdermal delivery systems provide the following advantages over conventional therapy.

- Gastrointestinal absorption problems are avoided.
- First-pass effect is avoided, thus minimizing drug input.
- Drugs with narrow therapeutic range can be delivered.
- Better control of blood levels for potent drugs is possible.
- Patient compliance can be increased.
- Drugs with short half-lives are utilized.

- This approach is useful when oral administration is to be avoided or is contraindicated.
- Can be utilized for non-invasive vaccination purpose.
- The pharmacokinetic profiles of drugs are more uniform with fewer peaks, thus minimizing the risk of toxic side effects.
- A large surface area of skin and ease of access allows many placement options on the skin for transdermal absorption.
- Reduction in reduction of dosing frequencies and is also suitable for patients who are unconscious or vomiting.
- Therapy can be quickly terminated by simple removal of the system from the skin surface.

However, transdermal drug delivery is not useful when required to deliver large doses of drug(s), when the drug or the formulation is skin sensitizing or irritating, when the drug is extensively metabolized in skin, or when molecular size is large enough to prevent the molecules from diffusing through the skin.

I. PERCUTANEOUS ABSORPTION

Percutaneous absorption is the penetration of substances into various layers of skin and permeation across the skin into the systemic circulation. It is a step wise process involving:

i. *Penetration*: The entry of a substance into a particular layer of the skin;

ii. Partitioning from the stratum corneum into the aqueous viable epidermis;

iii. Diffusion through the viable epidermis and into the upper dermis;

iv. *Permeation*: The penetration of molecules from one layer into another, which is different both functionally and structurally from the first layer;

v. *Absorption*: The uptake of a substance into the systemic circulation.

A molecule may use two diffusional routes to penetrate normal intact skin, the appendageal route and the transepidermal route (Figure 6-1).

(i) Appendageal route: Appendageal route comprises transport via sweat glands and hair follicles with their associated sebaceous glands. These routes circumvent penetration through the stratum corneum and are therefore known as "shunt" routes. This route is considered to be of minor importance because of its relatively small area, approximately 0.1 % of the total skin area.

(ii) Transepidermal route: It involves the passage of molecules through the stratum corneum, an architecturally diverse, multi-layered and multicellular barrier. For drugs, which mainly cross-intact horny layer, two potential micro routes of entry exist, the transcellular (intracellular) and paracellular (intercellular) pathways.

a) ***Transcellular***: Transcellular pathway means transport of molecules across epithelial cellular membrane. These include passive transport of small molecules, active transport of ionic and polar compounds and endocytosis and transcytosis of macromolecules.

b) ***Paracellular***: Paracellular pathway means transport of molecules around or between the cells. Tight junctions or similar situations exist between the cells.

The principal pathway taken by a permeant (drug) is governed primarily by the partition coefficient. Hydrophilic drugs partition preferentially into the intracellular domains, whereas lipophilic drugs traverse the stratum corneum via the intercellular route. Most drugs permeate the stratum corneum by both routes. However, the tortuous intercellular pathway is widely considered to provide the principal route and major barrier to the permeation of most drugs. The effective transdermal drug delivery can be formulated by considering the factors as drug, skin and the vehicles that can be broadly classified as biological and physicochemical factors.

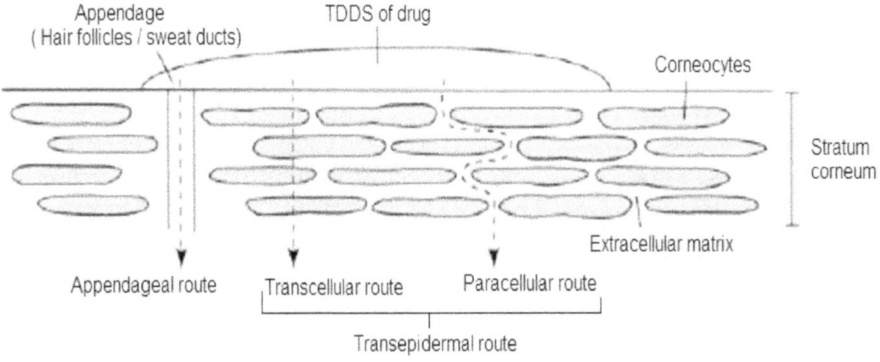

Fig.6.1 Diffusional routes for penetration of molecules across intact skin.

A. Biological factors

i) ***Skin condition***: Acids and alkalis, many solvents like chloroform, methanol damage the skin cells and promotes penetration. Diseased state of patient alters the skin conditions. The intact skin is better barrier but the above mentioned conditions affect penetration.

ii) ***Skin age***: The young skin is more permeable than older. Children are more sensitive for skin absorption of toxins. Thus, skin age is one of the factors affecting penetration of drug in TDDS.

iii) ***Blood supply***: Changes in peripheral circulation can affect transdermal absorption.

iv) ***Regional skin site***: Thickness of skin, nature of stratum corneum and density of appendages vary site to site. These factors affect significantly penetration.

v) ***Skin metabolism***: Skin metabolizes steroids, hormones, chemical carcinogens and some drugs. So skin metabolism determines efficacy of drug permeated through the skin.

vi) ***Species differences***: The skin thickness, density of appendages and keratinization of skin vary species to species, so affects the penetration.

B. Physicochemical factors

i) ***Skin hydration***: When in contact with water, the permeability of skin increases significantly. Thus humectants are added to the TDDS formulation.

ii) ***Temperature and pH***: The permeation of drug increase many folds with temperature. Weak acids and weak bases dissociate depending on the pH of skin and pKa or pKb values and the proportion of unionized drug determines the drug concentration in skin. Thus, temperature and pH are important factors affecting drug penetration.

iii) ***Diffusion coefficient***: Penetration of drug depends on diffusion coefficient of drug. At a given temperature the diffusion coefficient of drug depends on properties of drug, diffusion medium and interaction between them.

iv) ***Drug concentration***: The flux is proportional to the concentration gradient across the barrier and concentration gradient will be higher if the concentration of drug will be more across the barrier.

v) ***Partition coefficient***: The optimal partition coefficient is required for good action. Drugs with high K partition themselves in the lipid portion of skin. The drugs with low partition coefficient will not permeate readily.

vi) ***Molecular size and shape***: Drug absorption is inversely related to molecular weight; small molecules penetrate faster than large ones.

Approaches for Permeation Enhancement

Technologies used to modify the barrier properties of the stratum corneum can be divided into passive/chemical or active/physical methodologies (Figure 6.2). Passive methods include the influencing of drug and vehicle interactions and optimization of formulation, in order to modify the stratum corneum structure. Passive methods are relatively easy to incorporate into transdermal patches such as chemical enhancers and emulsions. However, the main drawback of passive methods may be a lag time in drug release incurred with obvious negative influence on rapid onset drugs, such as insulin.

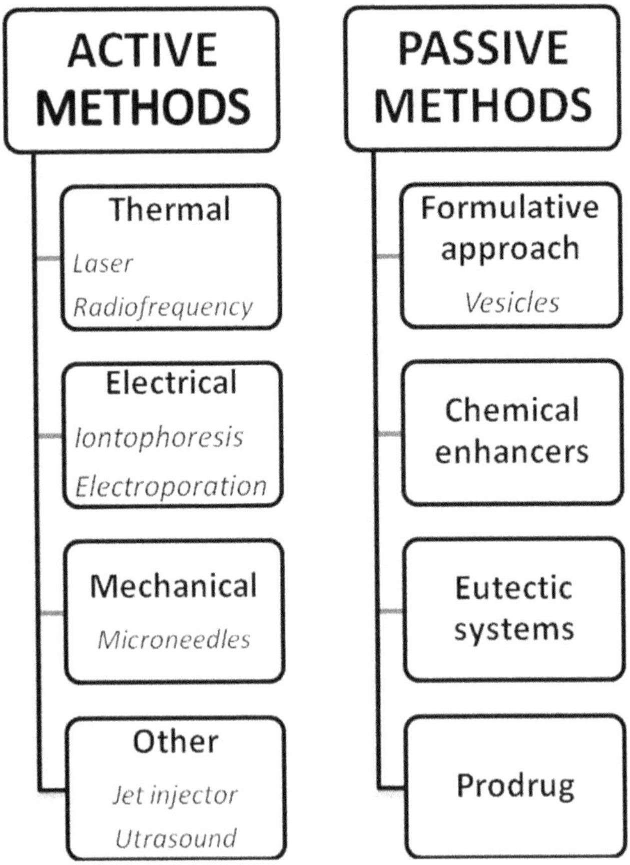

Fig.6.2 Methods employed to modify permeation of drugs.

One of the most widely used passive approaches is the use of chemical penetration enhancers which facilitate drug permeation across the skin by increasing drug partitioning into the barrier domain of the stratum corneum, without long-term damage to the skin. Penetration enhancers have several mechanisms of action such as: increasing the fluidity of the stratum corneum lipid bilayers, interaction with intercellular proteins, disruption or extraction of intercellular lipids, increase of the drug's thermodynamic activity and increase in stratum corneum hydration. Several types of penetration enhancers are known and they can be divided into several groups based on their chemical structure, rather than their mechanism of action. Most of these have mixed modes of action so it is difficult to classify them according to this characteristic. Examples of commonly investigated penetration enhancers are alcohols, sulphoxides, azone, pyrrolidones, essential oil, terpenes and terpenoids, fatty acids, water and urea.

The penetration enhancers follow three main mechanisms (i) causing disruptions in the highly organized structure of stratum corneum, (ii) interaction with proteins present intercellularly, and (ii) improved drug partitioning in the stratum corneum with help of co-enhancer. The enhancers act by manipulating any of the three pathways. There are two ways to achieve this, by bringing about a conformational change in the skin proteins or by swelling of the solvent. The fatty acid enhancers for example make the stratum corneum more lipophilic. The purpose of the enhancers is to make the drug more easily soluble in the stratum corneum and thus make them diffuse into the skin surface. However, the major limitation for penetration enhancers is that their efficacy is often closely correlated with the occurrence of skin irritation.

II. FACTORS IN TRANSDERMAL MEDICATION

The design, development, and success of transdermal delivery systems can be traced to four factors, which are interrelated. These are (a) drug formulation, (b) biopharmaceutics of the drug, (c) characteristics of skin, and (d) adhesion of the system to skin. Figure 6-3 describes these interrelationships graphically. Each of these factors in turn is then influenced by several other subfactors, which are briefly outlined in Table 6-1.

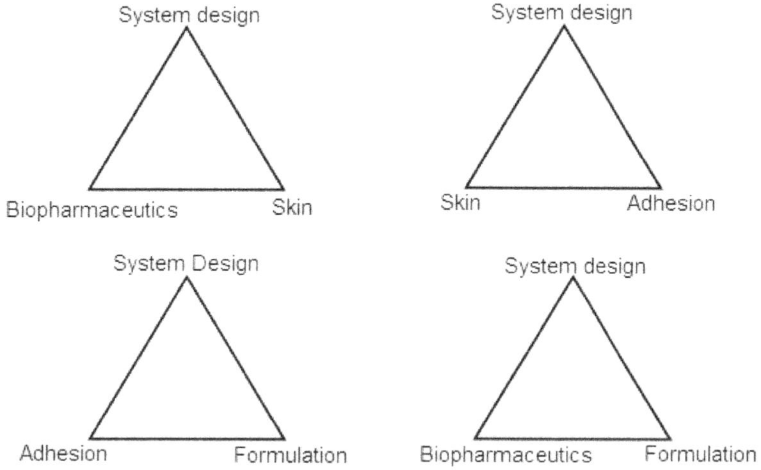

Fig.6.3 Factors and interrelationships in transdermal delivery system design.

Table 6.1 Subfactors affecting the factors in transdermal medication.

The *formulation* characteristics that determine the efficacy of the device are:	The design of the delivery device depends on the following *skin* parameters:	The adhesion parameters that determine the device design are the skin and adhesive formulation. Latter is affected by:	The biopharmaceutical parameters affecting the design of delivery devices are:
Boundary layers Thickness Temperature Geometry of system Vehicles Porosity of membranes Tortuosity	Species (Caucasian/ Black) Condition of skin (healthy/diseased, pretreated, secretion, hair density, etc.) Site-to-site permeability	Size and shape Cohesiveness Curing Arrangement of other layers Flexible/non-flexible and breathable/non-breathable backing material Type and characteristics of the polymer	Half-life of the drug Pharmacological blood levels Therapeutic window Amount of drug required to penetrate the skin Hydration state of skin

III. DRUG CANDIDATE FOR TDDS

The transdermal route of administration cannot be employed for all drugs. The drug selection is based on its physicochemical properties, pharmacokinetic parameters and biological factors. Physiochemical factors such as solubility, crystallinity, molecular weight, polarity, melting point and partition coefficient must be considered. The pharmacokinetic information of the drug is a critical factor in deciding its suitability for delivery by the transdermal route as it is suitable only for low dose drugs. The resulting plasma concentration of active agent depends on the clearance. Another important factor is the half-life, which provides information on the disposition of a drug and determines whether a transdermal delivery can be developed or not. The biological factors like skin irritation, site of application of the patch are important considerations. For example scopolamine patch for motion sickness is applied backside of the ear and Transderm-Nitro is applied on the chest. The occlusive or allergic response is significant for the drugs presented to the skin as it determines the acceptability of the device. Table 6-2 summarizes the desirable properties of a drug candidate for TDDS and the factors to be considered for the TDDS dose calculation.

Table 6.2 A summary of desirable properties of a drug candidate for TDDS and the factors to be considered for the TDDS dose calculation.

Physicochemical	Pharmacokinetic	Biological
Solubility Crystallinity Polarity Molecular weight: < 400 daltons Melting point: Log P (octanol-water) between 1-4	**Dose:** low (< 20 mg/day) Half-life: Less than 10 hours Volume of distribution Total body clearance Therapeutic index: Low Bioavailability: Low oral bioavailability	Skin toxicity: Non irritating and non-sensitizing Site of application Allergic reactions Skin metabolism Skin permeability: >0.5 × 10^{-3} cm/h

IV. TYPE OF TRANSDERMAL DEVICES

Primarily, there are five categories of transdermal drug delivery devices (Figure 6.4). Precisely, there are two concepts in the design of transdermal delivery systems namely, the reservoir type and the matrix type. The others are extensions of these two concepts. These concepts are discussed in the preceding text.

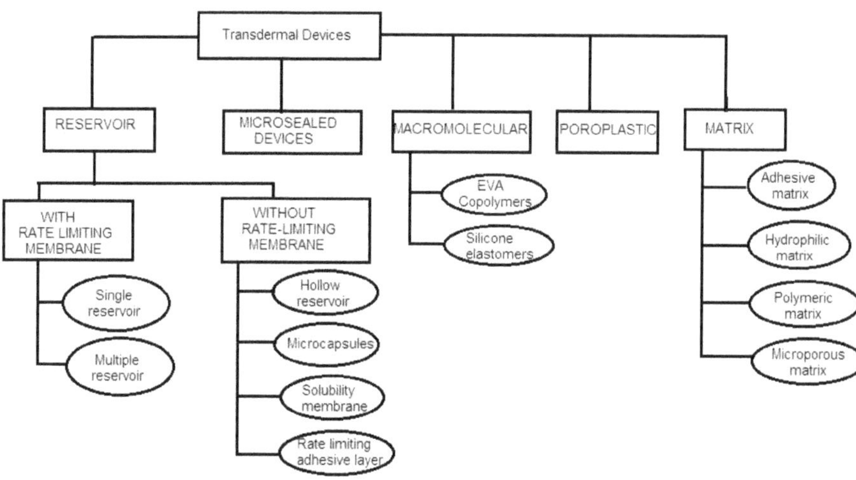

Fig.6.4 Classification of transdermal drug delivery systems.

I. RESERVOIR TYPE DEVICES

A. Reservoir type devices with rate-limiting membrane

(i) ***Single reservoir rate limiting membrane devices***: In the reservoir type of devices the drug is stored in a reservoir from which it diffuses across a rate-limiting membrane to the site of absorption. Figure 6-5 depicts a typical reservoir type of device with rate-controlling membrane.

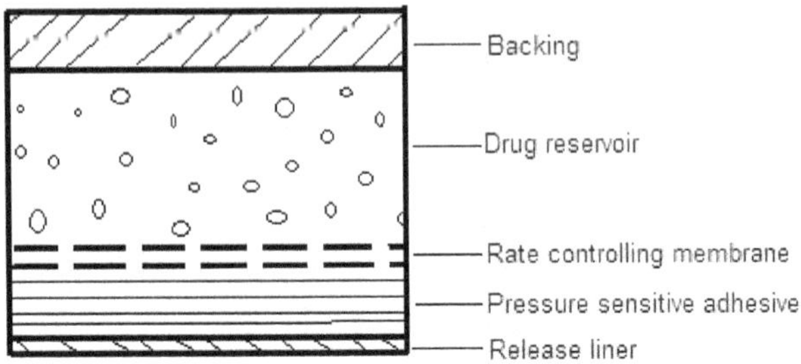

Fig.6.5 Diagram for single reservoir type TDDS with rate controlling membrane.

In the system the adhesive polymers are dissolved in a vehicle and drug is added while another solution of the drug is prepared separately. The drug layer and the adhesive layer are then coated as a thin continuous film onto a moving web passing through drying ovens. Once the layers have dried, the drug layer, the adhesive layer, the rate-controlling membrane, and the backing layer, along with the release liner, are laminated together. Then individual units are punched out.

This type of system is useful when the stratum corneum is not the principal rate-limiting barrier for the diffusion of drug(s) and rate control from the device is desirable. The advantage it offers is the near-constant release rate of drug from device. However, rupturing of the rate-limiting membrane may result in a quicker than desired release of drug from the device. The examples of reservoir type of transdermal device are Catapress-TTS (Boehringer-Ingelheim), Transderm-Scop (Ciba Pharmaceuticals), Tramsderm-Nitro (Ciba Pharmaceuticals), and Estraderm (Ciba Pharmaceuticals) systems. Transderm-Scop (scopolamine) and Catapress-TTS (clonidine) patches are known as multilaminates. The design of all the four devices is basically similar. They all contain backing membrane, reservoir of drug, rate-limiting membrane, adhesive, and a peel-off release liner. However, there are several processing differences. In the Transderm-Nitro and Estraderm systems the drug reservoir is filled as liquid (Estraderm) or ointment (Transderm-Nitro) between the impermeable backing and the rate-limiting membrane. The design details of Transderm-Scop (Figure 6-6a), Transderm-Nitro (b), Catapress-TTS (c) and Estraderm (d) are summarized in Table 6-3.

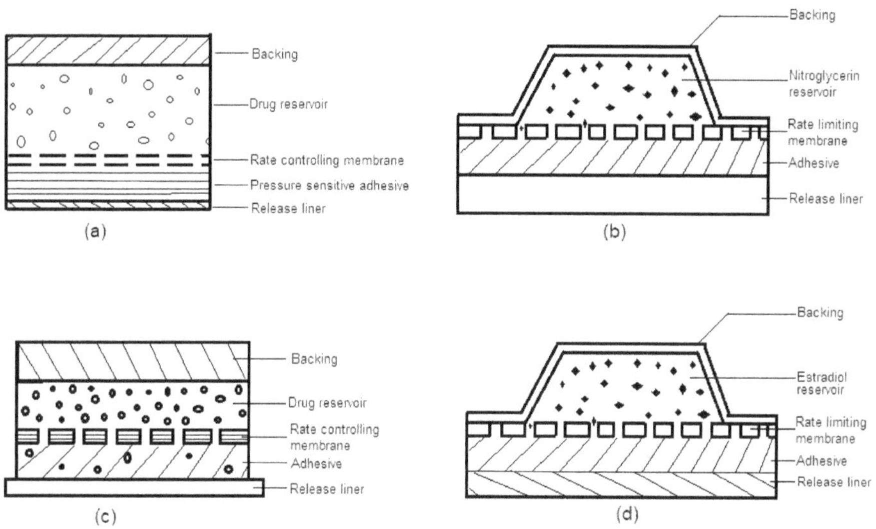

Fig.6.6 Diagrammatic representation of (a) Transderm-Scop, (b) Transderm-Nitro, (c) Catapress-TTS, and (d) Estraderm.

Table 6.3 Component details of various commercialized TDDS.

Component	Transderm-Scop	Transderm-Nitro	Catapress-TTS	Estraderm
Backing	Polyethylene terephthalate, metallized polypropylene, metallized PVC, or metallized polyethylene	Metallized plastic	Pigmented polyester film	Aluminized polyethylene terephthalate
Reservoir	Scopolamine in mineral oil (10-100 cp), polyisobutylene)	Nitroglycerin on lactose in colloidal SiO_2 and silicone medical fluid	clonidine in mineral oil, poly-isobutylene, and colloidal SiO_2;	Estradiol in ethanol and hydroxy-propylcellulose
Microporous membrane	Polypropylene or PVC or cellulose acetate nitrate or polyacrylonitrile of 0.1 to 0.85 porosity and 1 to 10 tortuosity and 0.01 to 0.001 cm thickness	Ethylene vinyl acetate (EVAc) copolymer	Microporous polypropylene membrane	EVA copolymer

Table *contd....*

Component	Transderm-Scop	Transderm-Nitro	Catapress-TTS	Estraderm
Adhesive	Polyisobutylene (high molecular weight, low molecular weight) and mineral oil	Pressure-sensitive silicone adhesive	Pressure-sensitive silicone adhesive	High molecular weight and low molecular weight polyiso-butylene in light mineral oil
Release liner	siliconized PVC / poly-propylene /polyethylene terephthalate	Siliconized polyethylene terephthalate	Siliconized polyethylene terephthalate	Siliconized polyethylene terephthalate

Another type of reservoir system with rate-limiting membrane was designed and patented by the Hercon Division for the transdermal delivery of drugs. The USFDA approved system consists of three polymer layers as depicted in Figure 6-7.

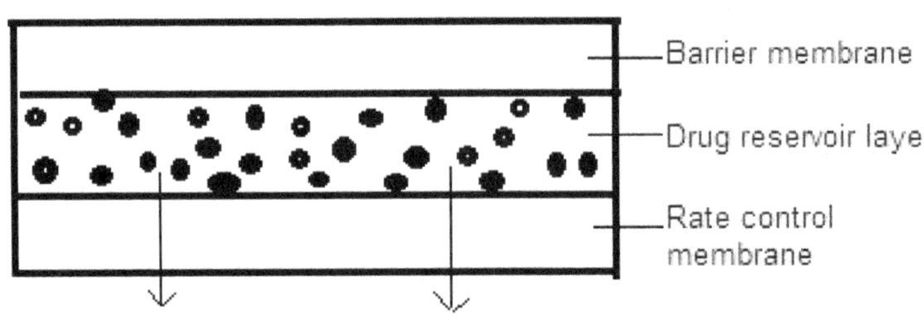

Fig.6.7 Hercon nitroglycerin TDDS.

The central layer is the drug reservoir. One of the outer sides of the reservoir is the impermeable (barrier membrane); while the other layer is the rate-controlling layer, which contacts the skin. A peripheral adhesive ring (not shown) on the barrier layer secures the system on the skin. The advantages of this system include its flexibility, the possibility of varying rate control by varying the polymers in the reservoir and the control layers, and the accommodation of both the solids and liquid reservoir.

(ii) ***Multi-reservoir rate limiting membrane devices*:** A characteristic feature of these systems is that an enhancer is stored in a compartment, separate from the drug reservoir. The system represented in Figure 6-8a has an impermeable backing, followed by the reservoir of a vehicle or an enhancer, a rate-limiting membrane, and a drug reservoir in the adhesive. The reservoir may also contain stabilizer, diluents, and other inert materials such as a gelling agent. The rate-limiting membrane is meant to control the permeation rate of the vehicle/enhancer and should preferably be impermeable to the drug. The drug is dispersed in any pressure-sensitive adhesive. In one structural modification of this system, the drug reservoir is accommodated between the rate-limiting membrane and the adhesive layer as a separate compartment (Figure 6-8b). Multi-reservoir type devices are useful where intimate contact between the vehicle/enhancer and the drug is not desired.

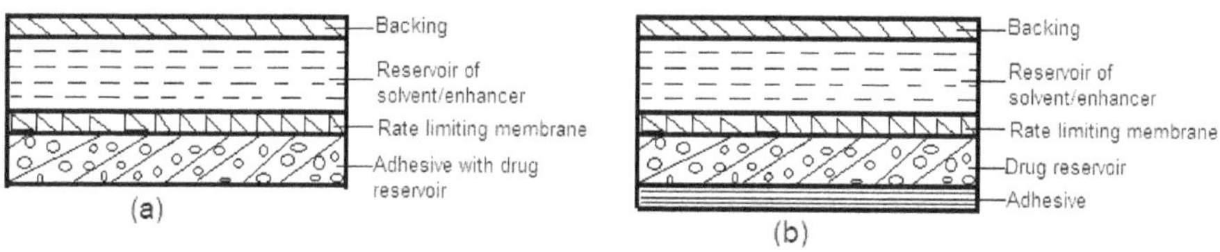

Fig.6.8 Scheme for (a) multireservoir and (b) modified multireservoir type TDDS.

Another modification of such systems is depicted in Figure 6.9a where both the enhancer and the drug are dispersed in an adhesive polymer or a polymeric matrix followed by an adhesive overlay. The enhancer or vehicle is microencapsulated inside a diffusion-controlling membrane (made of microporous material), and these microcapsules together with the drug are dispersed in an adhesive polymeric matrix that adheres well to the skin. The release rate of enhancer from the microcapsules governs the release rate of drug from the formulation. A similar type of system containing a peripheral ring of adhesive (Figure 6-9b) can be fabricated when the drug and the enhancer have lower than desired permeation rates through the adhesive layer.

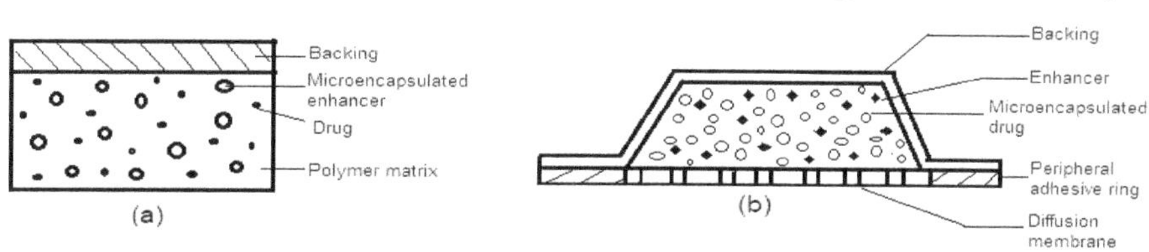

Fig.6.9 Scheme for TDDS containing (a) microencapsulated enhancer, and (b) microencapsulated enhancer and peripheral adhesive ring.

B. Reservoir type devices without rate limiting membrane

(i) ***Devices with rate limiting adhesive layer*:** In the previously described reservoir systems with rate-limiting membranes, the drug reservoir was sandwiched between an impermeable backing and a microporous rate-controlling membrane. The adhesive diffusion control reservoir types of device differ in that a dispersion of drug in the adhesive polymer (reservoir) is spread as a thin layer on the impermeable backing. Layers of rate-limiting adhesive polymers without any drug are then spread on top of the reservoir layer.

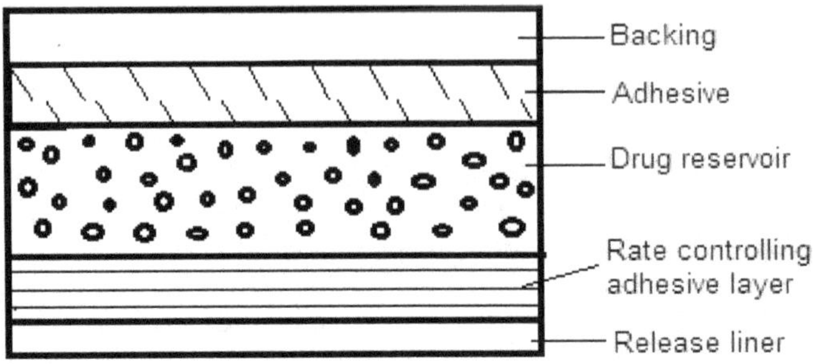

Fig.6.10 Diagrammatic representation of adhesive diffusion control type TDDS.

This concept has been utilized by Pharma-Schwartz (Monheim, Germany) for the development of transdermal nitroglycerin delivery system, Deponit (Figure 6-10).

(ii) ***Microencapsulated drug reservoir type devices*:** When the drug is dispersed as microcapsules all throughout the contact adhesive, the rate-controlling step in the delivery is the diffusion of the drug through the walls of the microcapsules. The permeation rate of drug across the microcapsule is a function of the porosity, thickness, and diffusion coefficients of the membrane and also of the solubility of the drug in the membrane. The most important component in such a system is the microencapsulation agent. Several hydrophilic or hydrophobic polymers are available for this purpose. Hydrophilic polyether gels, cross-linked polyvinyl alcohols/partially hydrolyzed acetate, acrylates, and methacrylates are some examples of hydrophilic polymers, while hydrophobic polymers may be exemplified by silicones, soft nylon, and plasticized or unplasticized polyvinyl. The microencapsules are then dispersed into pressure-sensitive adhesives and a thin layer of the dispersion is cast on the backing material, as indicated in Figure 6-11. The thickness of the adhesive layer varies with the amount of drug required for loading.

(iii) ***Reservoir devices with solubility membranes*:** The drug is dispersed in a polymer matrix as reservoir which is sandwiched between an impermeable backing and a solubility membrane (Figure 6-11). The non-reservoir side of the solubility membrane is coated with a pressure-sensitive adhesive. The system is characterized by two rate-controlling steps: (a) the polymeric matrix material which is capable of dissolving the drug and thus controls the rate of the passage of drug to the solubility membrane, and dissolution of the drug in the solubility membrane.

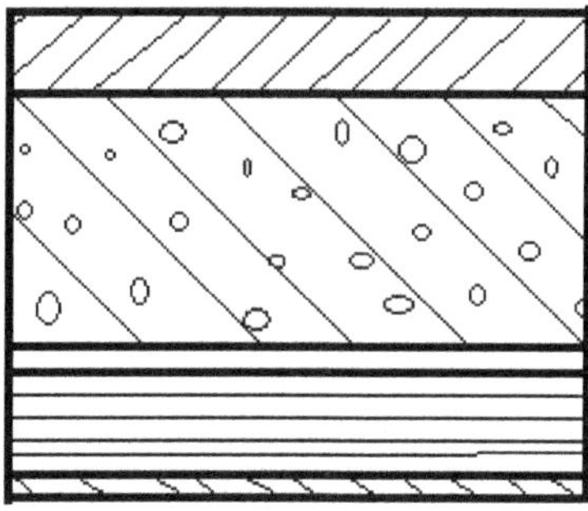

Fig.6.11 Representation of TDDS with solubility membranes.

This solubility membrane may be formed of any of the microencapsulation agents described previously. The solubility profile of the drug is different the two rate-controlling steps, and thus precise delivery of the drug to the adhesive can be attained by varying the ratio or the com-position of the polymeric matrix and the solubility membrane.

(iv) ***Hollow reservoir devices*:** Figure 6.12 illustrates a reservoir type of transdermal delivery system, in which the reservoir is in the form of a hollow cylinder having an impermeable backing and a rate-limiting membrane that controls the release of drug into the adhesive layer. The reservoir may be prepared by one of the following procedures: (a) by moulding into a hollow container with the drug entrapped, or (b) by forming an envelope of polymeric materials that is permeable to passage of drug with the drug encased. The microencapsulating agents described earlier are suitable for the preparation of the reservoir.

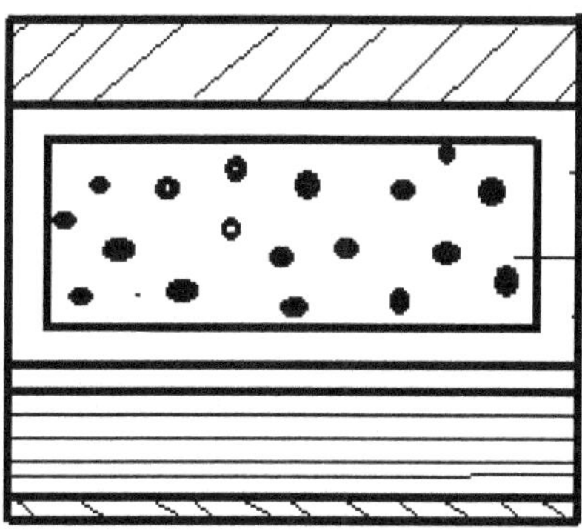

Fig.6.12 Diagram for hollow cylindrical reservoir type TDDS.

The delivery rate of the drug is governed by the thickness and diffusivity of the lower reservoir wall /membrane. The reservoir of a TDDS may contain some pharmaceutical excipients (saline, sterile water, dextrose, lactose, mineral oil, light vegetable oils, triglycerides of lower fatty acids, glycols, polyvinyl pyrrolidone, Klucel, etc.) in addition to the drug.

B. MATRIX TYPE DEVICES

The drug in a matrix-type system is uniformly dispersed throughout a hydrophilic or lipophilic polymer matrix, which is then cured into a polymeric disk of predetermined thickness and surface area. The matrix is then glued to aluminium foil, which is sealed to drug-impermeable backing through an absorbent pad. Mostly such systems do not have an adhesive overlay but instead possess a peripheral adhesive ring. Figure 6-13 illustrates a typical matrix type of transdermal delivery device. Several structural modifications are possible as discussed later in this section.

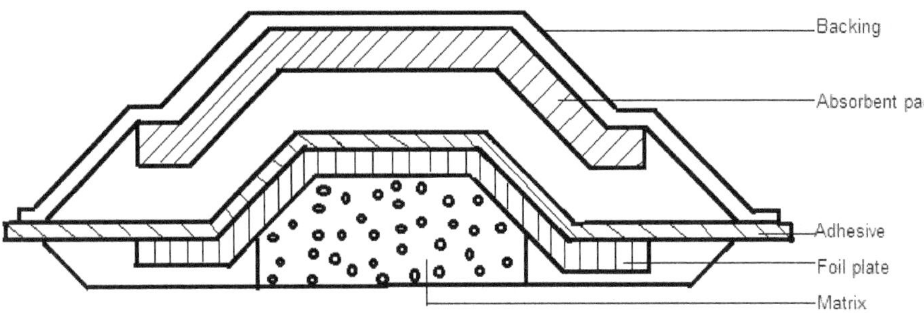

Fig.6.13 A typical matrix type TDDS.

The polymeric matrix is saturated with a dispersion or solution of drug in a solvent. The solvent molecules are organized by the polymer network such that the dispersed and/or dissolved drug is held in the microspaces of the network. Such an orientation and organization of drug and solvent molecules inside the polymeric network is affected to a great degree by the ionization of the polymer cross-linking and configuration of the polymer. The matrix should have the following characteristics:

- There should be zero chemical interaction of the matrix polymers with the drug.
- The matrix should not impart excessive resistance to the diffusion of the entrapped drug.
- It should be stable and be able to hold the drug in stable condition.
- It should be non-irritating to skin and also should adhere well to the skin to provide an appropriate bridging between the skin and the drug.
- Structural integrity should be maintained at high temperatures and humidities.

Commonly employed agents for matrix formulation are ethylene vinyl acetate copolymers, polyesters, microporous polypropylenes, polyvinyl chloride, polyvinyl pyrrolidone and polysaccharides.

(i) ***Polymeric matrix type transdermal devices*:** The polymeric matrix type of transdermal delivery devices is exemplified by Nitro-Dur (Key Pharmaceuticals, Miami, Florida), as shown in Figure 6-14.

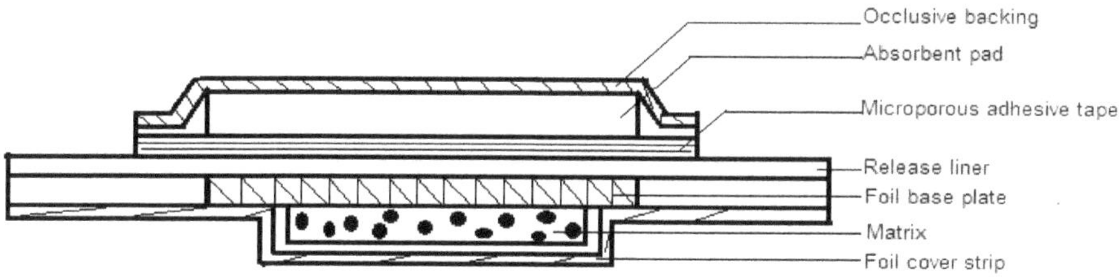

Fig.6.14 The scheme for Nitro-Dur matrix device.

(ii) The critical components in the design of Nitro-Dur containing nitroglycerin (GTN) fall into four categories: (a) aluminium foil package, (h) absorbent pad, (c) adhesion components, and (d) polymer-GTN matrix. Because of the complicated design of the system (Figure 6-13), selection of proper components is critical. The aluminium foil package is made up of an aluminium foil release liner (cover strip) and an aluminium foil base plate. The GTN matrix is completely surrounded by these two components during its shelf life. At the time of application, the aluminium foil cover strip is peeled off, exposing the matrix. The aluminium foil base plate and the cover strip serve to eliminate the possibility that GTN and other potentially volatile components will evaporate. The foil base plate stays behind the matrix for the duration of the application and thus serves as a barrier for GTN and other liquid components of the matrix. The microporous adhesive tape allows for the permeation of excessive moisture and maintenance of good adhesion during wear. The pressure-sensitive adhesive is behind the release liner at the periphery of the matrix to provide adhesion of the unit to the skin. The peripheral adhesive does not interfere with the diffusivity of the drug. The polymeric matrix of Nitro-Dur consists of PVA and PVP forming the lattice structure, while the GTN and other liquid components occupy the interstices. The release of GTN from the matrix is dependent on the extent of polymer cross-linking. The release from matrix-type devices shows a square root of time dependence:

(iii) $$\left[\frac{dM}{dt} = \frac{LC_m\ D_m}{2t}\right]^{1/2}$$ .....Eq. 6-1

Where, L is the loading dose in the matrix, C_m is the concentration of the drug in the matrix, and D_m the diffusion coefficient of the drug in the polymer.

(iv) ***Microporous matrix type device*:** The device (Figure 6-15) consists of a backing material and a drug-containing microporous matrix, which rests on a pressure-sensitive adhesive layer. The drug passes through the rate-controlling microporous material. The matrix is impregnated with a diffusive medium in which the drug can dissolve and which also determines the drug release rate. The drug permeation is also governed by the pressure-induced viscous flow of drug molecules through the pores of the microporous matrix. By varying composition, pore size, effective thickness of the microporous rate-controlling material, viscosity of formulation, and impregnating solvent, the delivery rate can be controlled and varied.

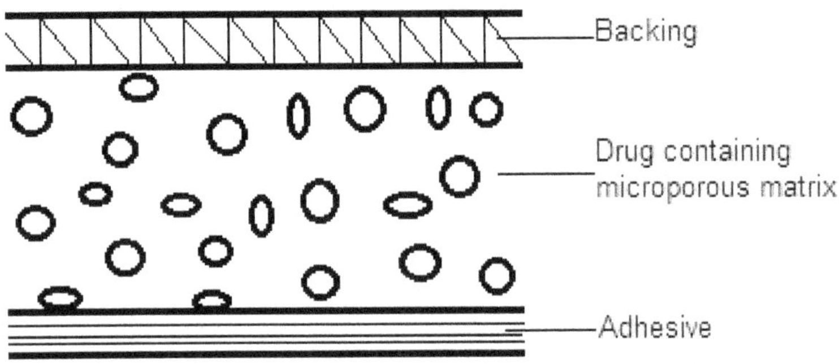

Fig.6.15 Microporous matrix type TDDS.

The microporous materials may be isotropic (uniform structure throughout the matrix), or anisotropic (heterogeneous structure). The materials usually employed for this purpose include polyamides, polyvinyl chloride, polysulfones, acrylonitriles, polycarbonates, polyvinylidene fluoride, acrylic resins, polyurethanes, polyvinyl acetate and cellulose esters. The drug is usually added to the matrix material in a liquid form and is uniformly distributed.

(v) ***Hydrophilic Matrix Devices (Lec-Tec Matrix)*:** The device consists of a semi-solid state polymeric matrix acting as a reservoir as well as a hydrophilic bridge to the skin, which facilitates drug permeation into and through the skin by wetting the skin. The hydrophilic matrix consists of polysaccharides or synthetic hydrophilic polymers. The matrix also contains hydrogen-bonding liquids such as water, glycerol, propylene glycol, and polyethylene glycol. The formulation may also include an aqueous emulsion of adhesive to improve the tack of the patch. The system is self-adhering and can be removed and reapplied. The transdermal delivery rate from such a system is a function of the matrix formulation, the hydrophilic bridges formed between the system and the skin, and the drug concentration within the aqueous phase of the skin.

(vi) ***Adhesive matrix devices*:** This system is characterized by an adhesive matrix, which also acts as a reservoir of drug and is exemplified by Nitro-Dur II (Key Pharmaceuticals) as shown in Figure 6-16.

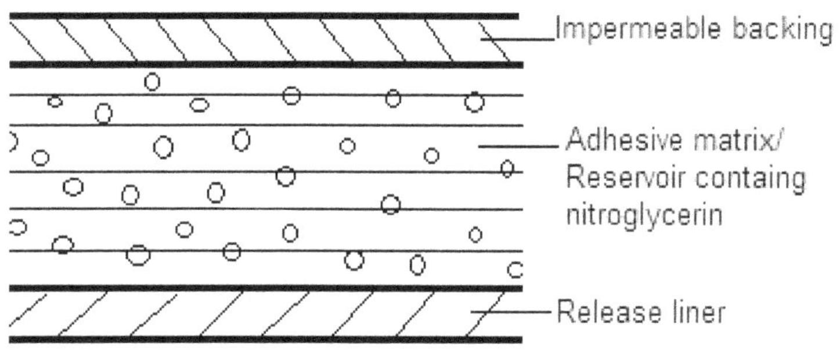

Fig.6.16 Diagrammatic representation of the Nitro Dur II.

The nitroglycerin is dispersed in an acrylic adhesive. This acts as an adhesive matrix, which is coated onto a Saranex type of backing material with a clear polypropylene type of release liner.

C. MICROSEALED DELIVERY DEVICES

The microsealed transdermal device is the result of the hybridization of the reservoir and matrix types of system and is represented by Nitro Disc (G. D. Searle Pharmaceuticals, Chicago). In this system (Figure 6-17) an aqueous suspension of drug is prepared in a water-soluble polymer.

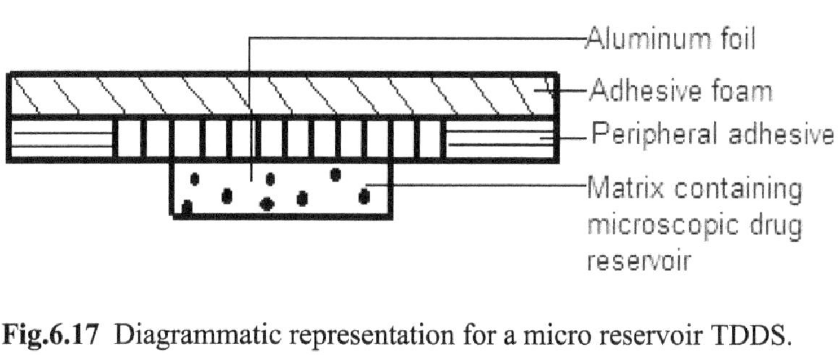

Fig.6.17 Diagrammatic representation for a micro reservoir TDDS.

The suspension is then dispersed into a lipid-soluble polymer with high-speed-shear force, to form microscopic spherical reservoirs with the drug entrapped. Immediately, the system is cross-linked by the addition of polymeric cross-linking agents, and a matrix is formed. This matrix is then attached to an aluminum foil plate at the back, to prevent evaporation of the GTN. The aluminium foil plate is then attached to an adhesive polyurethane (flexible) foam pad which forms the backing. This system has a peripheral adhesive ring.

D. POROPLASTIC OR MOLECULON TYPE DEVICES

The Poroplastic devices developed at Moleculon (Cambridge, Massachusetts) utilize Poroplastic films. The poroplastic films consist of ultramicroporous cellulose triacetate membranes which are non-sensitizing to the skin and are fairly stable at biological pH. The film is made utilizing the concept of the water coagulation of cellulose triacetate solution in organic acids at low temperatures. The coagulation is performed under controlled conditions and the extent of water content may be varied to a great degree. The percent weight of water in a poroplastic film is used to give an identification number for different grades of poroplastic films. The water may be exchanged subsequently for another vehicle by a diffusional exchange process, and hence a poroplastic membrane is also known as "solid composed mostly of liquid." The liquid in the film is held by capillary action; therefore poroplastics are also compared to molecular sponges but with a much smaller pore size. Some of the vehicles for a poroplastic film include polyethylene glycols (low molecular weight), propylene glycol, water, alcohols, aliphatic esters, mineral oils, silicone fluids, and glycerol. The poroplastics are available in different molecular weight cut off ranges, which are directly related to the percentage of water present in the film. The greater the amount of water in the film, the greater is the pore diameter. For example, for films with 70% water the apparent pore diameter is 0.0014 pm, for 85% water the pore diameter is 0.0025 pro, and for 92% water content the pore diameter is 0.006 μm. The cellulose triacetate film is chemically inert and functions primarily to hold the vehicle and the drug. Thus the permeation rate is basically governed by the formulation and the vehicle characteristics. The design features of the three types of poroplastic transdermal device are summarized in Table 6-4 and shown in Figure 6-18.

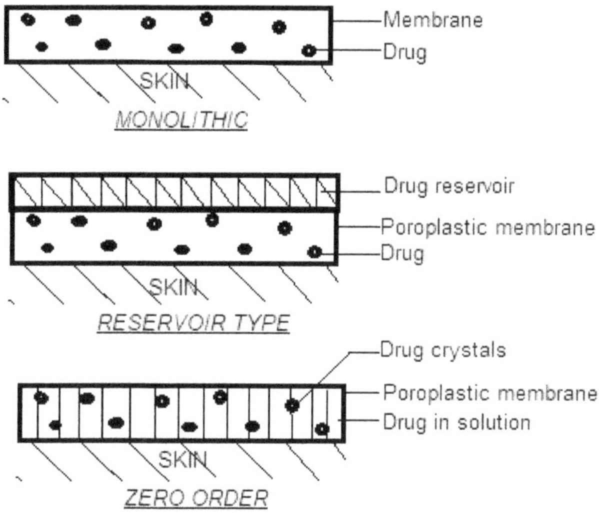

Fig.6.18 Various types of poroplastic TDDS.

Table 6.4 Design features of poroplastic patches.

Simple monolithic	Zero order	Reservoir
1. Drug solution in membrane.	1. Drug crystals are present in membrane.	1. Concentrated solution of drug behind the poroplastic film acts as a distinct reservoir.
2. Drug content depletes with time and ermeability decreases.	2. As drug permeates, more crystals dissolve to maintain saturated solution.	2. As drug permeates out of the film, more drug enters the film from the reservoir

E. TRANSDERMAL DELIVERY OF MACROMOLECULES

Typical requirements for transdermal delivery of drugs include low molecular weight (≤ 500-1000, preferably ≤ 500), low melting characteristics (150 - 200°F), aqueous solutions neither too acidic nor too basic (between 5 and 9 pH units, preferably in the pH range of 6.0- 8.0), and preferably unit oil /water partition coefficient. The macromolecules do not possess these characteristics and hence are not ideal candidates for transdermal delivery. However, attempts have been made to characterize diffusional properties of some low molecular weight peptides. Advances have been made lately in the fabrication of systems for the rate-controlled delivery of macromolecules (hormones, enzymes, interferon, bioactive peptides, etc.). The devices under consideration may be divided into two categories: (a) devices based on ethylene vinyl acetate copolymers (EVAc) and (b) devices based on silicone elastomers. Both systems utilize one common concept: that is, because of the large molecular size of drug, the matrix must have channels to facilitate the release of macromolecules. These devices are used as implants, but since the release is diffusion controlled and the technology are modified to suit transdermal delivery.

(i) ***EVAc copolvmer type macromolecule delivery devices***: The general procedure for designing EVAc copolymer-type macromolecule delivery systems essentially follows the flowchart shown in Figure 6-19a.

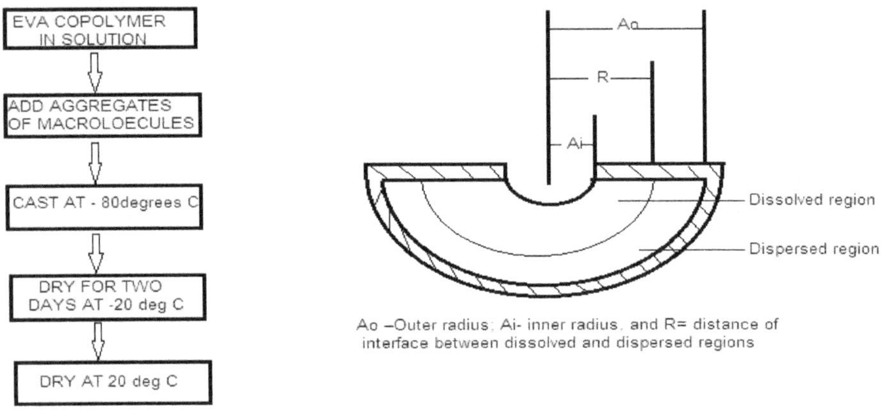

Fig.6.19 (a) Fabrication process for casting macromolecular delivery system containing EVAc copolymers, (b) Diagram of hemispherical TDDS.

This procedure creates channels which facilitate the release of the drug. The diffusion-controlled EVAc matrix type of device for the delivery of macromolecules may be hemi-sphere shaped (Figure 6-19b) or of the magnetically modulated release type. Magnetically modulated devices modulate the release rate, whenever needed, by the application of magnetic field. The basic principle of construction is similar to that described in Figure 6-19a.

(ii) ***Silicone elastomer-type macromolecutar delivery devices***: This type of device is made by using different medical-grade silicone elastomers in certain ratios. The macromolecular powder is added to the mixture very slowly, with constant mixing, and then a calculated amount of polymerizing agent is also added. The mixture is kept under vacuum and then extruded into a Tygon or Silastic tubing and allowed to cure overnight at room temperature. When the cross-linking is complete, the tubing is cut into small pieces of preset dimensions. One end of the tubing is coated with impermeable Silastic coating, while the other end is left open to allow the drug release.

V. PRESSURE-SENSITIVE ADHESIVES

Pressure-sensitive adhesives are very similar to contact adhesives, the major difference being the requirement of pressure to affect the bond. Pressure-sensitive materials usually consist of a rubbery elastomer and a modifying tackifier. Usually, these systems are highly thixotropic and have good "quick tack." The pressure sensitive adhesives used in transdermal delivery devices may be classified into three categories: butyl rubbers and polyisobutylenes, acrylics, and silicones.

VI. TACKIFIERS

The adhesive properties of pressure-sensitive adhesives depend primarily on the viscoelastic properties of the adhesive mass. In such adhesive formulations, the elastomer adds the elastic component while a tackifier provides the viscous properties. The principal properties of adhesives are tack, resistance to peel and resistance to shear, and these are controlled by the characteristics of the elastomer-tackifier mixture. A good adhesive has a proper balance of these properties. The tackifiers used in sensitive adhesives are divided into two types: rosin types and hydrocarbon resins. The rosin group consists of rosin, modified rosins, their esters, and so on. The hydrocarbon resin group consists of polyterpenes, synthetic hydrocarbons, phenolic resins, and similar compounds.

VII. RELEASE COATINGS

Release liners are an integral component of transdermal delivery devices. They provide protection from undesirable contact of the product with other surfaces. Several factors contribute toward the properties of the release coatings used in the release liners. The release coating should not be wetted by the adhesive; that is, contact between the release liner and the adhesive should be poor. A smooth but tough plastic film may be used as a release liner without any release coating. Better anchorage of adhesive to backing may also be imparted by prime coatings to provide better release of the release liner. One of the most important considerations is that the surface of release liner be non-porous so as to prevent the soft-adhesive flow into the pores which would otherwise result in the need for increased unwinding force. The release coating should meet the following requirements:

1. The coating should provide an adequate release. The release level should be low enough to permit an easy unwind. The release should be slow at low peel angle and fast at 900 peel.
2. The release should be reproducible, also meaning that the release should not depend on the amount of release agent.
3. The release agent should be firmly anchored to the surface of the release liner or the release backing and should not be susceptible to being transferred to the adhesive.

The release coating is normally applied as a dilute solution or as dispersion over the release backing (2-3 g/m^2). The most recent development in silicone release technology consists of the solvent less silicone coatings, which are applied at 100% solids level. These were designed specifically for pressure-sensitive release and consist of a vinyl functional polymethyl hydrogen siloxane cross-linker and a noble metal catalyst. They can give thin films (0.03- 0.04 mm thick).

VIII. CONCLUSION AND FUTURE PROSPECTS

Transdermal patches represent an outcome of growth in skin science and technology, clinical observation and evidence-based studies. Since the inception, the passive transdermal drug delivery systems have evolved phenomenally evidenced by a range of commercial TDDS. Currently, the focus is on active transdermal delivery systems that are based on minimal or non-invasive approaches such as iontophoresis, microneedles, electroporation and sonophoresis. However, the development of active TDDS patches has been hampered by commercial and technical issues. The transdermal delivery systems, particularly patches, are increasingly being used in the pediatric population. A specific example is the methylphenidate patch for the treatment of attention deficit hyperactivity disorder. However, while transdermal delivery can be regarded as a convenient non-invasive method of drug delivery for term infants and older children requiring smaller doses than adults, formulation challenges remain for premature neonates with an immature skin barrier.

6.2 TIMELINE

1940s	First quantitative systemic delivery (Zondek's system)
1950s	Individualized delivery system: nitroglycerin ointment
1960s	Topical delivery device (Wurster & Kramer's system). Passive non-invasive patches.
1970s-1980s	First patch system – the reservoir – introduced for scopolamine, nitroglycerin, clonidine and oestradiol.
1979	The first transdermal patch approved for systemic delivery of scopolamine for treatment of motion sickness.
1980s-1990s	Next generation patches – matrix and drug-in-adhesive (e.g. fentanyl and nicotine patches).
2000s	Cutaneous solutions (e.g. Patchless Patch®, Evamist®). Active patches (e.g. iontophoresis, Zecuity®). Minimally invasive patches (e.g. microneedles, Nanopatch®).
Currently	Transdermal delivery is currently restricted to approximately 17 drug molecules that are approved by the US FDA.

6.3 CHAPTER AT A GLANCE

Term	Description
Transdermal	Transdermal is a route of administration wherein active ingredients are delivered across the skin for systemic distribution.
TDDS	Is topically administered dosage form in the form of patches which deliver drugs for systemic effects at a predetermined and controlled rate.
Percutaneous absorption	Percutaneous absorption is the penetration of substances into various layers of skin and permeation across the skin into the systemic circulation
Reservoir delivery system	In a reservoir system the drug is either molecular dissolved or dispersed in a reservoir that is surrounded by a rate limiting inert membrane.
Matrix delivery system	In a matrix or monolithic delivery system the drug is either molecular dissolved or dispersed inside a matrix
Rate controlling membrane	The property of the membrane which affect the desired degree of rate control of the drug delivery device in which the membrane is used
Pressure sensitive adhesive	(PSA, self-adhesive, self-stick adhesive) is a type of non reactive adhesive which forms a bond when pressure is applied to bond the adhesive with the adherend. No solvent, water, or heat is needed to activate the adhesive.
Backing layer	A backing is a layer of something such as cloth that is put onto the back of something in order to strengthen or protect it.
Tacky	Not dry sticky to touch
Tack	It can be described as a measure of viscous flow under conditions of fast strain rates and low stress magnitudes, while shear adhesion (creep) is a measure of viscous now at low strain rates and medium stress levels.
Peel adhesion	Peel adhesion is a measure of resist to flow at intermediate strain rates and medium to high stress levels and is also a measure of the cohesive strength of the adhesive.

EXERCISES

Multiple choice Questions

1. Which of the following biopharmaceutical factors does not affect the design of TDDS?
   (a) Half life of drug (b) Plasma blood levels
   (c) Distribution volume (d) Therapeutic window
2. Catapress TTS is the TDDS for
   (a) Clonidine (b) Scopolamine
   (c) Nitroglycerin (d) Estrogen
3. In matrix type TDDS the drug is uniformly dispersed throughout
   (a) A lipophilic polymer matrix
   (b) a hydrophilic polymer matrix
   (c) Lipophilic or hydrophilic polymer matrix
   (d) None of the above
4. Which of the following is not a typical requirement for the drug to be designed as TDDS?
   (a) Molecular weight <500
   (b) Low melting characteristics
   (c) Low absorption
   (d) Unit oil/water coefficient
5. Which of the following are not pressure sensitive adhesives?
   (a) Butyl rubber (b) polyisobutylenes
   (c) hydrocarbon resins (d) Silicones
6. A tackifier in the pressure sensitive adhesive provides
   (a) Viscous properties
   (b) Reduction in glass transition temperature
   (c) Softness
   (d) Flexibility
7. Poroplastic type TDDS are made of
   (a) Cellulose phthalate (b) Cellulose triacetate
   (c) Saranex (d) Polyacrylamides

8. Which of the following is not a type of reservoir type TDDS?
   (a) Microcapsules type
   (b) Solubility membrane type
   (c) Rate limiting adhesive layer type
   (d) Microsealed drug delivery device
9. System design of a TDDS is affected by
   (a) Skin (b) Adhesion
   (c) Formulation (d) All of the above
10. TDDS for macromolecules can be fabricated using
   (a) EVAc
   (b) Isobutylenes
   (c) Polyesters
   (d) Methyl based silicones

Short Answer Questions

1. With the help of neat diagram explain the design of matrix based TDDS.
2. What do you understand by poroplastic TDDS patches? Highlight the design features.
3. Write a short note on release liners.
4. What are the desirable features of an ideal drug candidate for TDDS?
5. Enumerate the advantages of TDDS over conventional therapy.
6. Explain the drug permeation routes

Long Answer Questions

1. Classify reservoir type TDDS. Describe the reservoir systems without rate limiting membrane with neat diagrams.
2. Describe various types of matrix type TDDS.
3. Describe the factors affecting permeation of drugs across the skin..
4. Write notes on (i) Microsealed delivery devices, and (ii) TDDS for macromolecules.
5. What do you understand by percutaneous absorption? How can it be enhanced?
6. Explain the factors and subfactors affecting transdermal delivery of drugs.

Answer Key MCQs

(1) – (c), (2) – (a), (3) – (c), (4) – (c), (5) – (c), (6) – (a), (7) – (b), (8) – (d), (9) – (d), (10) – (a).

BIBLIOGRAPHY

1. Othman A, Khan HMS, Sarfaraz M, Arafat M, Ijaz S, Hameed A, Transdermal patches: Design and current approaches to painless drug delivery, Acta Pharmaceutica, 2019, 69(2) 197-215.
2. Peterson TA, Transdermal Drug Formulation and Process Development, Formulation, Fill & Finish 2003 18-21.
3. Uchechi O, Ogbonna JDN, Attama AA, Nanoparticles for Dermal and Transdermal Drug Delivery, 2014 Available from: https://www.intechopen.com/books/application-of-nanotechnology-in-drug-delivery/nanoparticles-for-dermal-and-transdermal-drug-delivery, DOI: 10.5772/58672.
4. Roohnikan M, Laszlo E, Babity S, Brambill D, A Snapshot of Transdermal and Topical Drug Delivery Research in Canada Pharmaceutics 2019, 11, 256; doi:10.3390/pharmaceutics11060256.
5. Transdermal Permeation of Drugs in Various Animal Species Hiroaki Todo, Pharmaceutics 2017, 9, 33; doi:10.3390/pharmaceutics9030033.
6. Leite-Silva VR, de Almeida MM, Fradin A, Grice JE, Roberts MS, Delivery of drugs applied topically to the skin Expert Rev. Dermatol.2012, 7(4), 383–397,

Chapter

7

GASTRORETENTIVE DRUG DELIVERY SYSTEMS

♦ LEARNING OBJECTIVES ♦

After completing this lesson, the Reader should be able to understand:

- **Concept and Design of GRDDS**
- **Formulation approaches of GRDDS**
- **Types of GRDDS**
- **Applications of GRDDS**

7.1 INTRODUCTION

Oral drug delivery systems are ideal if they are single dose systems that deliver the drug directly to the target site and maintain the desired drug concentration with a long duration of action in order to provide better patient compliance. The physicochemical properties of most of the weakly basic drugs, such as high solubility at an acidic pH but poor solubility at an alkaline pH, result in poor absorption of the drug from the intestine. Gastroretentive drug delivery systems (GRDDS) sustain drug release, reduce drug bio burden and wastage, improve the solubility of drug(s) that are less soluble in intestinal pH and enhance bioavailability. Prolonged gastric retention in the stomach could be advantageous for treatment of gastric pathologies such as gastroesophagal reflux. The controlled and prolonged drug release of GRDDS also helps to minimize mucosal irritation caused by many drugs.

GRDDS have certain disadvantages, including incompatibility with drugs that cause irritation and/or lesions to the gastric mucosa. The absorption of the drug from the GRDDS is dependent on gastroretention that in turn may be affected by the presence of food in the stomach, variations in the stomach emptying time, constantly changing environment of the gastrointestinal tract, and the physical attributes of the drug delivery system (e.g. density and size). Gastric emptying of floating dosage forms in bedridden patients may occur at random and is highly dependent on the diameter and size of the formulation.

Therefore, it is advisable that patients should not be administered floating dosage forms just prior to bedtime.

Stomach

The stomach is divided into three main parts: fundus, body and antrum (pylorus). The proximal portion referred to as fundus and the body functions as storage for undigested food. The antrum is the primary site for mixing motions and acts as gastric emptying pump by propeller actions.

Gastric emptying happens in both, the fasting and fed states. However, the motility pattern is different in are varied upon pattern of motility. In this phenomenon, series of electric events take place in cycles via stomach and intestine every 2 to 3 hours. There occurs a phenomenon of interdigestive myloelectric cycle or migrating myloelectric cycle (MMC), which is divided in four phases as shown in Figure 7.1. Gastroretention strongly depends on a complicated and unpredictable gastric emptying with MMC motility of the stomach. In the case of the fed state, the gastric emptying time is slowed as the onset of the MMC is interrupted. For example, the feeding state results in a lag time (i.e. 30 min - 4 h) prior to the onset of gastric emptying.

Phase I Basal phase	Phase II Preburst phase	Phase III Burst phase	Phase IV
• Lasts from 30 to 60 min with rare contractions and is characterized by lack of secretory, electrical, and contractile activity.	• Lasts for 20 to 40 min with intermittent contractions, during which contractile motions increase in frequency and size.	• Lasts for 10 to 20 min with intense and regular contractions for short period, termed housekeeper waves that sweep off undigested food.	• Lasts for 0 to 5 minutes and is the transition period between Phases III and I.

Fig.7.1 Phases of migrating myloelectric cycle.

Factors impacting GRDDS efficacy

The factors impacting the gastric residence time of GRDDS can be divided into two categories namely those related to human aspect, and (ii) mechanism. For the human aspect the following parameters are of importance:

7.1 Food

Food affects the motility of the stomach and hence plays a major role in gastric retention behaviour. The gastric residence time is short in fasting state because of higher motility than in the fed state. In the fed state, the retention time is extended and hence the drug delivery is sustained. The nature of the food, i.e., volume, viscosity and caloric content are significant factors; therefore a high fat meal strongly increases the gastric residence time (GRT). Independent from the composition of the food itself, the frequency of the intake will significantly increase the GRT because of lower MCC overall activity.

7.2 The Pylorus Limitation

During the digestion the pylorus size is reduced to about 2 - 3 mm, in comparison to 12.8 ± 7.0 mm in inert phase. The gastric peristaltic effect exerts forces sufficient enough to disintegrate dosage forms of sufficient size with a hardness ≤ 1.89 Newton. Therefore, all particles which have a diameter inferior to 5 mm can pass through the pylorus to duodenum.

7.3 Gender, Posture and Age

Generally stomach emptying is slower in women compared to men, regardless of weight, height, body surface area and even when the hormonal changes due to the menstrual cycle are normalized. Elderly people generally show extended GRT independent from posture or gender.

7.4 Size and Shape of Monolithic Dosage Form

Bigger the dosage form, greater the gastroretentive time. Floating dosage forms are less concerned by this basic concept. Different shapes have been proposed (Figure 1), ring-shaped and tetrahedron-shaped devices are reported to have better gastroretentive time compared with other shapes.

7.5 Monolithic Versus Multiple Unit System

Monolithic dosage (single unit e.g. floating tablet) form may demonstrate "all or nothing" effect. This means that either the dosage form may exhibit gastroretentional properties and eventually exit the stomach; or it may be emptied from the stomach due to peristaltic movement (gastric emptying) thus terminating the gastroretentive action. Multiple units exhibit a better predictable release and specificity of gastroretentive dosage form, they avoid the possible.

Drug candidates suitable for GRDDS

a) Drugs which have site-specific absorption in the stomach, or upper part of intestine.

b) Drugs those are unstable in the lower part of gastrointestinal tract.

c) Drugs required to exert local therapeutic action in stomach e.g. metronidazole, amoxicillin.

d) Drugs poorly soluble or insoluble in intestinal fluids e.g. verapamil, ofloxacin, captopril.

e) Drugs with variable bioavailability e.g. acyclovir, rivastigmine.

Box 1

Drugs that would be benefit from increased residence in stomach		
Acyclovir	Biposophonates	Captopril
Furosemide	Metformin	Gabapentin
Levodopa	Baclofen	Ciprofloxacin
Metronidazole	Verapamil	Rivastgmine

Furthermore, as the total gastrointestinal transit time of the dosage form is increased by prolonging the gastric residence time, these systems can also be used as extended release devices with a reduced frequency of administration and, thus, improved patient compliance. In contrast, a prolonged residence time in the stomach is not desirable for drugs that:

- Cause gastric lesions (e.g., NSAIDs).
- Are unstable in the acidic pH of the stomach.
- Undergo a significant first-pass effect (e.g., nifedipine).

Gastroretentive Formulations

In the past few decades, a plethora of gastroretentive drug delivery systems have been developed that include: high density systems that sink and are retained in the lower portion of the stomach, low density systems that exhibit buoyancy in gastric fluid, mucoadhesive systems that exhibit bioadhesion to stomach mucosa and adhere to the gastric wall, extendible/unfoldable/swellable systems that limit emptying of the dosage forms through the pyloric sphincter, magnetic systems, superporous hydrogel systems, raft forming systems and biodegradable hydrogel systems (Fig 7.2). Most gastroretentive drug delivery systems are single-unit dosage forms, which have in common the risk of losing their effect too early due to their all-or-none emptying from the stomach. To overcome this restriction, multiple-unit floating or bioadhesive systems have been proposed. These distribute uniformly within the gastric content and gradually empty from the stomach, possibly resulting in longer-lasting effects and reduced intersubject variabilities.

The process of gastrointestinal transit in humans and its implications for drug delivery are well understood (Box 2). Dosage forms administered to a fed stomach will have delayed emptying. A multi particulate system (microspheres / pellets) can mix with food and as a consequence, will usually empty with the food over an extended period of time. If the administered particles are large, they will not be able to pass through the constricted pylorus with the digested food, and will have to wait until the stomach is empty and in fasted state. Exactly when the particles will empty also depends on their number and their relative positions in stomach. Hence a dosage form larger than 15 mm and administered with food is expected to achieve gastroretention. Such a dosage form will therefore have an opportunity to empty after the food has left the stomach when fasted state occurs.

Box 2

Gastrointestinal transit of pharmaceutical dosage forms

Many factors that control the gastrointestinal transit of pharmaceutical dosage forms are summarized below:

- Gastric emptying is governed by feeding status.
- Objects less than 10 mm in size can empty from the fed stomach.
- Objects larger than 20 mm in size will be retained in the fed stomach.
- The transit time in small intestine is ≈ 3h.
- A dosage form can reach colon in 4-5 h.
- Transit in colon is lengthy (≈ 20 hours)

1. High density system GRDDS

These are high density systems close to 2.5 g/cm^3 that achieve significant retention in the lower part of stomach. Commonly used excipients of these systems include barium sulfate, zinc oxide, iron powder, and titanium dioxide. Gastric contents have a density close to water (1.004 g/cm^3). When the patient is upright small high-density pellets sink to the bottom of the stomach (Fig. 7.3) where they get entrapped in the folds of the antrum and withstand the peristaltic waves of the stomach wall. Thus increasing the gastrointestinal tract time from 5.8 to 25 h.

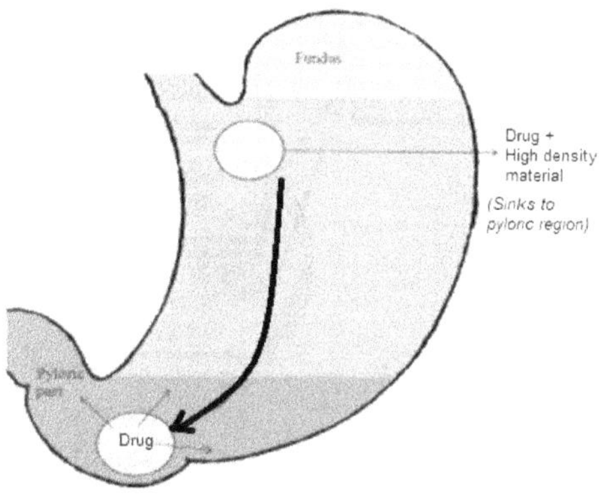

Fig.7.2 GRDDS based on high density.

Even though this system has the potential to improve the GRT, it is difficult to design high-density pellets containing high-dose drugs. Although encouraging results were reported in ruminants these systems seem to be less effective in human beings; therefore, no such system is available commercially.

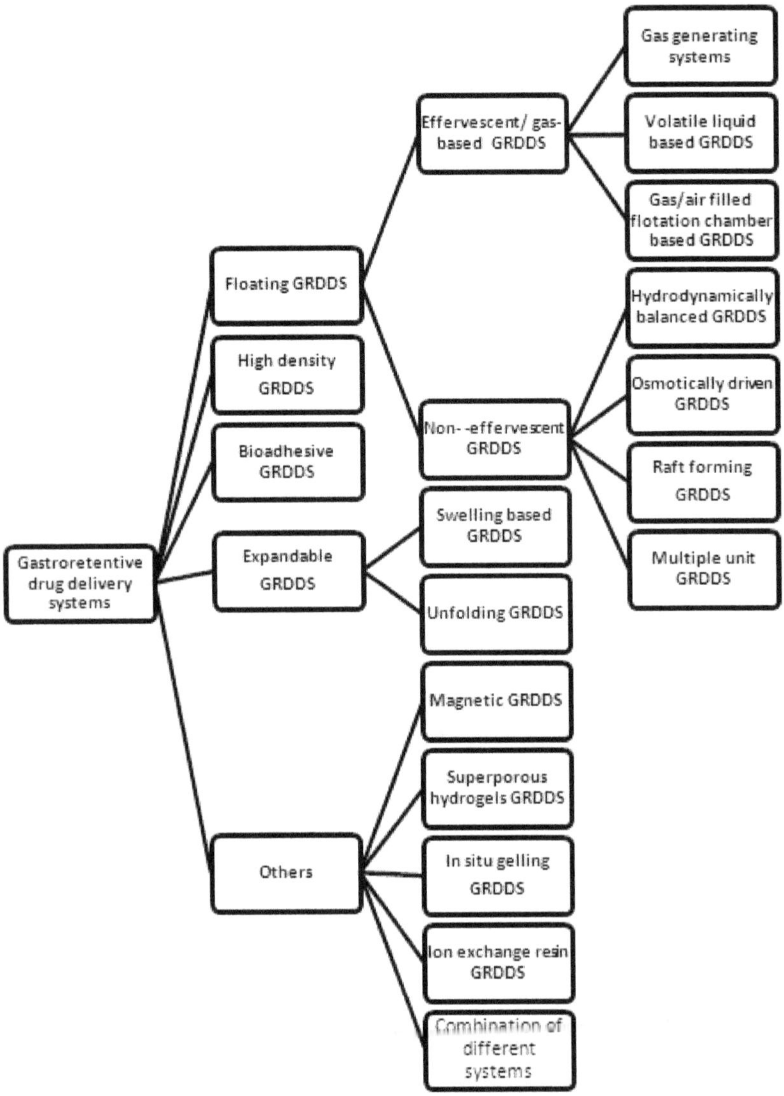

Fig.7.3 Diagrammatic classification of GRDDS.

2. Floating GRDDS or low density system

Among the various GRDDS approaches, floating drug delivery systems by virtue of their low density remain buoyant above the gastric content for the prolonged period of time and thus provide a continuous local release of the drug in the stomach. Even though, floating drug delivery systems are predominantly used as they do not adversely affect the motility of the GIT, the major setback for these systems is that they are effective only when the fluid level in the stomach is sufficiently high. However, when the stomach is emptied by the movement of fluid and food to the small intestine and the tablet localizes to the pylorus, the buoyancy of the dosage form may be hindered.

Floating characteristics of a gastric retentive dosage form is assessed by onset of floating, floating duration but also floating strength.

The floating strength has not been quantified extensively. However, it represents an important characteristic as the dosage form has to float in vivo even in the presence of food. As higher floating strength increases the probability of the oral dosage form to remain afloat, this attribute plays a major role in reducing food effects on gastric retention. Several approaches of non-effervescent and effervescent formulation technologies have been developed in order to customize gastric residence time of the formulations. The floating systems can be classified according to their effervescence behavior as **effervescent** and **non-effervescent GRDDS.**

(i) ***Effervescent/Gaseous systems*:** Floating of dosage forms can be achieved by the inclusion of a gas generating agent in an inert matrix or by use of inert gas/volatile liquid. Floatability can be achieved by generation of gas bubbles. CO_2 can be generated *in situ* by incorporation of carbonates or bicarbonates, which react with acid either the natural gastric acid or co-formulated as citric or tartaric acid. The optimal stoichiometric ratio of citric acid and sodium bicarbonate for gas generation is reported to be 0.76:1. The approach has been used for single (Fig. 7.4) and multiple unit systems.

Gas-generating systems inevitably have a lag time before floating on the stomach contents, during which the dosage form may undergo premature evacuation through the pyloric sphincter. Low-density systems (<1 g/cm^3) with immediate buoyancy have therefore been developed. They are made of low-density materials, entrapping oil or air. An alternative is to incorporate a matrix with entrapped liquid, which forms a gas at body temperature.

The floating GRDDS based on volatile solvent comprises of a chamber which contains liquid (e.g. ether) that converts into gaseous state at body temperature thus causing the chamber to inflate in stomach. The inflatable chamber loaded with drug reservoir (drug impregnated with polymeric matrix) is encapsulated in a gelatin capsule as shown in Figure 7.5. On ingestion gelatin dissolves releasing the drug compartment and inflatable chamber. The latter automatically inflates and retains the drug reservoir chamber in the stomach for continuous drug release.

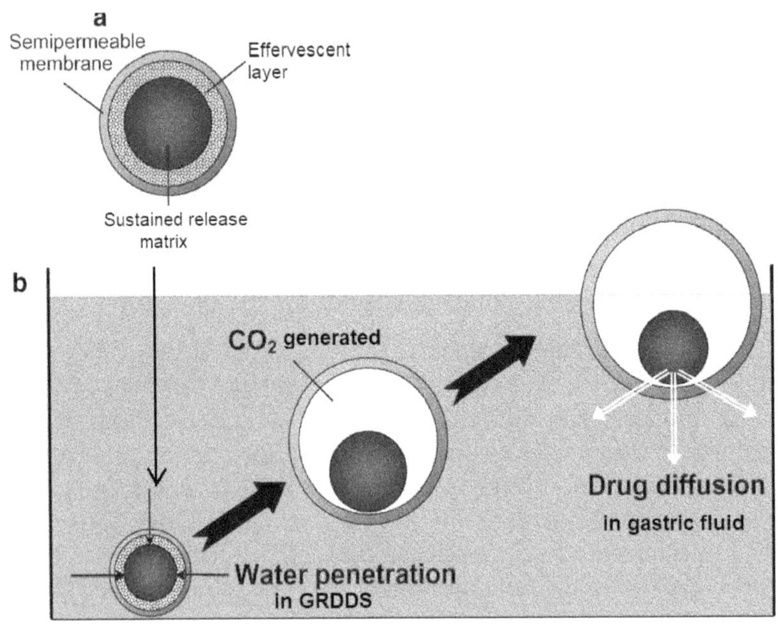

Fig.7.4 Single unit gas generating low density GRDDS.

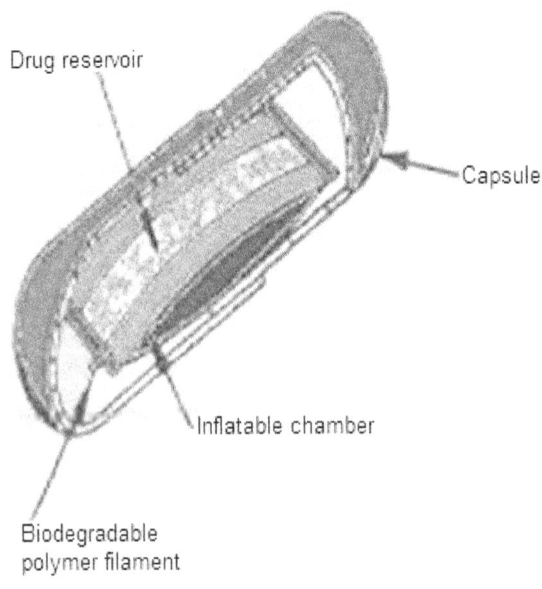

Fig.7.5 Volatile component based effervescent floating GRDDS.

The inflatable chamber also contains a bioerodible polymer filament (copolymer of PVA and PE) that gradually dissolves in the gastric fluid leading the inflatable chamber collapse and spontaneous ejection of the system from stomach.

Another intragastric floating system is based on flotation chamber which entraps an inert, harmless gas/ air, and a microporous vacuum compartment enclosing drug reservoir. The peripheral walls of drug reservoir compartment are sealed to prevent any contact of the undissolved drug with stomach mucosal membrane. Gastric fluid enters through the apertures, dissolves the drug and carries the drug solute to external medium (Fig. 7.6).

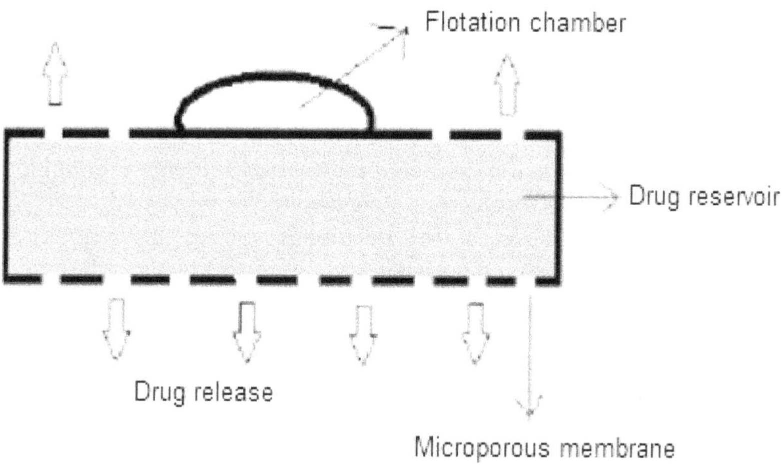

Fig.7.6 Single unit intragastric floating GRDDS with flotation chamber.

(ii) ***Non-Effervescent systems:*** *Hydrodynamically balanced systems: HBS™* These are single-unit dosage forms, containing one or more gel-forming hydrophilic polymers. Hydroxypropylmethylcellulose (HPMC) is the most common used excipient, although hydroxyethylcellulose (HEC), hydroxypropylcellulose (HPC), sodium carboxymethylcellulose (NaCMC), agar, carrageenans or alginic acid are also used. The polymer is mixed with drug and usually administered in a gelatin capsule. The capsule rapidly dissolves in the gastric fluid, and hydration and swelling of the surface polymers produces a floating mass. Drug release is controlled by the formation of a hydrated boundary at the surface. Continuous erosion of the surface allows water penetration to the inner layers, maintaining surface hydration and buoyancy (Fig. 7.7).

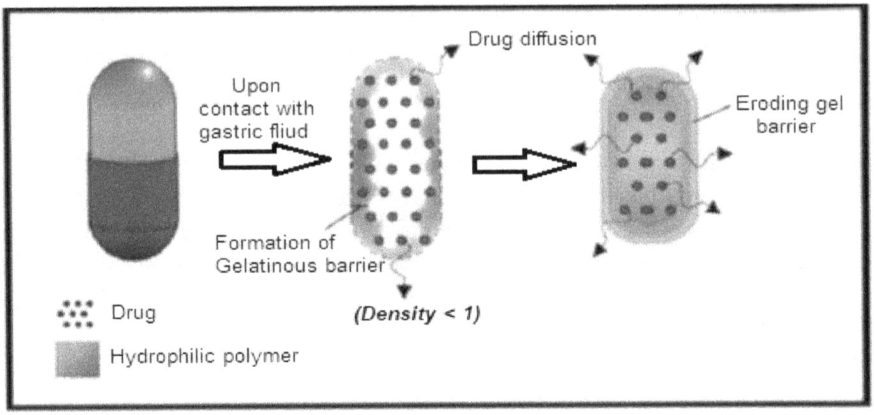

Fig.7.7 Diagrammatic representation of hydrodynamically balanced non-effervescent floating GRDDS.

Incorporation of fatty excipients gives low-density formulations and reduced penetration of water, reducing the erosion. The main limitation is that the effectiveness of the formulation depends on the air sealed in the dry mass centre following hydration of the gelatinous surface layer and hence the characteristics and amount of polymer.

Osmotically driven GRDDS

In such systems a bioerodible capsule consists of inflatable floating support containing osmotically driven DDS. In stomach the capsule quickly disintegrates releasing the intragastric osmotically driven DDS. The system also contains a polymer bag containing a liquid that gassifies at body temperature and also contains a bioerodible plug that erodes after a predicted time to deflate the support (Fig 7.8).

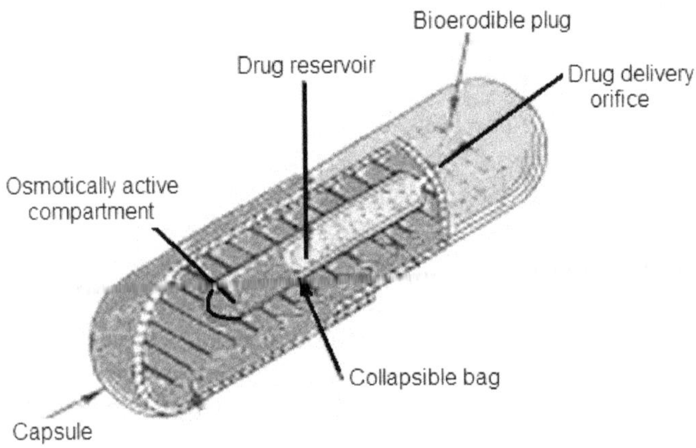

Fig.7.8 Representative design of osmotically driven GRDDS.

Raft-forming systems

Such systems comprise a gel-forming solution (e.g. sodium alginate solution containing carbonates or bicarbonates) swells and forms a viscous cohesive continuous gel layer (called raft) containing entrapped CO_2 bubbles (Fig. 7.9) on contact with gastric fluid.

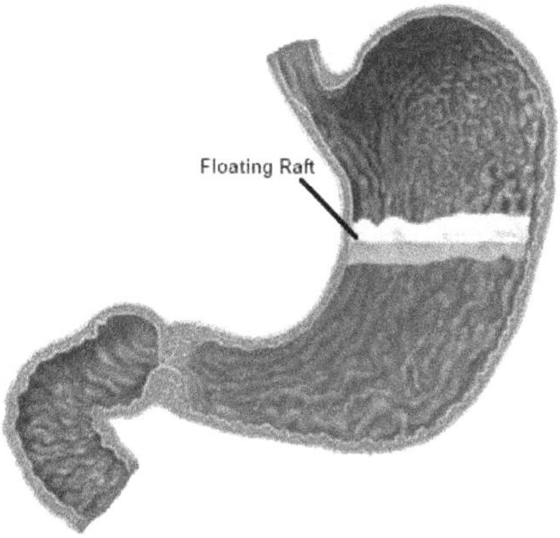

Fig.7.9 Floating raft system.

Various research reports have been made on such systems. An antacid raft-forming floating system was fabricated using sodium alginate as a gel-forming polymer, sodium bicarbonate and acid neutralizer as gas-generating agents. Thus, CO_2 gas is generated lowered the bulk density of the system, and as a result, the raft floats on the gastric fluid. A controlled release floating raft system of mebeverine hydrochloride, was developed that formed a CO_2 entrapped cohesive gel on swelling. The formed raft can remained intact in the stomach for several hours, promoting the sustained release of the drug. As raft-forming systems produce a layer on the top of gastric fluids, they are often used for gastroesophageal reflux treatment. Such rafts are particularly useful for delivering antacid drugs such as aluminum hydroxide, calcium carbonate, and simethicone. However, the mechanical strength of the systems is weak and can be easily disrupted by the MMC.

Multiple unit systems

Besides single unit floating systems, low density multiple unit floating systems namely hollow microspheres or microballoons are immensely popular. Generally, techniques used to prepare hollow microspheres involve simple solvent evaporation or solvent diffusion/evaporation methods. Polycarbonate, Eudragit S, cellulose acetate, calcium alginate, agar and low methoxylated pectin are commonly used as polymers. Buoyancy and drug release are dependent on quantity of polymer, the plasticizer–polymer ratio and the solvent used. At present, hollow microspheres (Fig.7.10) are considered to be one of the most promising buoyant systems because they combine the advantages of multiple unit systems and good floating properties.

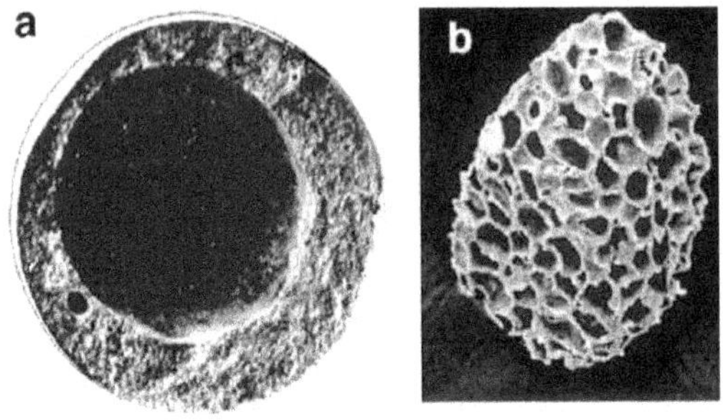

Fig.7.10 SEM images of (a) cross section of microballoon, (2) hollow foam microparticle.

Features of floating GRDDS

There are several advantages attributed to the use of floating DDS including improvement in patient compliance; achievement of better therapeutic effect of drugs with a short half-life; and enhancement of absorption of drugs, which are soluble primarily in the stomach and achievement of site-specific delivery of drug to the stomach. The limitations to the use of these formulations include the requirement for the presence of fluids in the stomach (dosage form is administered typically with a fluid of about 200–250 ml in order to maintain buoyancy effect of the formulation in the stomach. Also, the drugs that cause gastric mucosa irritation and those with solubility and/or stability issues in gastric fluids and those that cause gastric mucosa irritation like biomolecules such as proteins and peptides (which are liable to proteolysis in gastric fluid) are not suitable for incorporation into this type of delivery system. In addition, drugs which are well absorbed along the entire GI tract and undergo significant first pass metabolism are not suitable candidates, since the slow gastric emptying could lead to a reduction in systemic bioavailability.

Bioadhesive GRDDS

Mucoadhesion of dosage forms to the gastric mucosa tends to retain them in the stomach. Mucoadhesion can be achieved by use of mucoadhesive polymers namely, chitosan, thiolated chitosan, Carbopol, methyl cellulose etc. In this approach, drugs are incorporated in a mucoadhesive agent, which can be either natural or synthetic polymers. Bonding established between the polymer and mucosal surface facilitates the mucoadhesion process, which generally involves two steps: the contact stage and the consolidation stage. Several types of dosage forms have been proposed to allow prolonged residence within the stomach based on bioadhesive polymers namely beads, tablets, capsules, microspheres, microparticles, mini-tablets etc. Although the concept of bioadhesion has gained increasing interest in alternative routes of administration (e.g., nasal, buccal, ocular, vaginal and rectal), only a few successful approaches to develop bioadhesive systems with prolonged residence time in the stomach have been reported. The major challenge for such systems is the high turnover rate of the gastric mucus and the resulting limited retention times. Furthermore, it is difficult to specifically target the gastric mucus with bioadhesive polymers. For example, polycarbophil and Carbopol stick to the various surfaces they come into contact with. An advantage of mucoadhesive dosage forms in the stomach (and in general) is the intimate contact with the mucosa leading to short pathways for locally acting drugs, such as antibiotics against *H. pylori*.

Bioadhesive/mucoadhesive microspheres are promising delivery systems that adhere to the mucosal layer, meanwhile releasing their drug contents in a sustained manner. Such microspheres can either consist entirely of a bioadhesive polymer or an outer coating by attaching bioadhesive/ mucoadhesive materials to the microspheres (Figure 7.11).

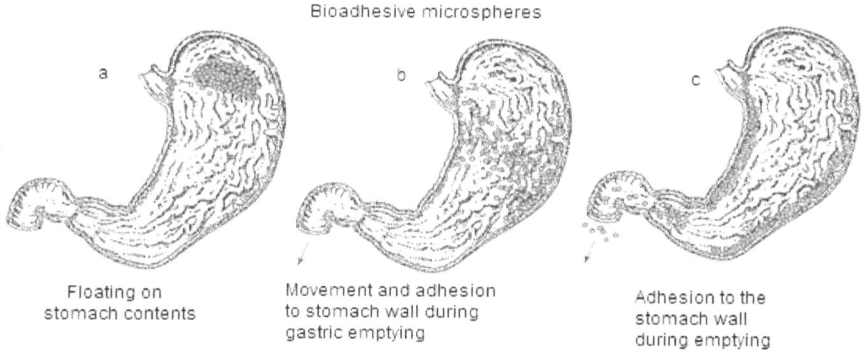

Fig.7.11 Floating and adhesive behaviour of biodhesive floating microspheres.

Bioadhesive microspheres can be modified to adhere to any form of mucosal tissue. They have the added advantage of efficient absorption and improved bioavailability of drug content due to the high surface-to-volume ratio, an intimate contact with the mucosal layer, and they could help target specific absorption sites. Improved bioavailability from mucoadhesive systems has been observed from microspheres containing drugs, such as testosterone and its esters, vasopressin, dopamine, insulin and gentamycin. There are, however, challenges in the development of particles with adequate drug loading for their intended application. Furthermore, in this system, specific targeting might be difficult because composition of the mucus is different according to the region of the mucous membrane. In addition, the constant turnover of the mucus, and high stomach hydration might decrease the bioadhesion of polymers. Moreover, there is high risk of adhesion to the esophagus which may lead to collateral lesions.

Expandable GRDDS

Another approach to retain a dosage form in the stomach is by increasing its size above the diameter of the pylorus, even in the widest state during the housekeeper wave. Due to significant inter-individual variations, the cutoff size cannot be given exactly. Approximately, the dosage form should be > 13 mm; however, even bigger units have been observed to be emptied from the stomach. In order to facilitate swallowing, it is highly desirable to design dosage forms with an initially small size, which, once they are in the stomach, significantly increase in size. The expanded state should be achieved fairly quickly, in order to prevent premature emptying through the pylorus. On the other hand, the systems should also guarantee their clearance from the stomach after predetermined time intervals, in order to avoid accumulation following multiple administrations. Other characteristics of an optimal size-increasing drug delivery system include: no effect on gastric motility and emptying pattern, no other local adverse effects (e.g., on the gastrointestinal wall), and inexpensive industrial manufacture.

The expandable GRDF are usually based on three configurations: (i) a small ('collapsed') configuration which enables convenient oral intake; (ii) expanded form that is achieved in the stomach and thus prevents passage through the pyloric sphincter; and (iii) another small form that is achieved in the stomach when retention is no longer required i.e., after the GRDF has fully released its active ingredient, thereby enabling evacuation. The expansion can be achieved by either swelling or by unfolding in the stomach.

Swelling systems

Such systems are generally prepared from one or more matrix forming polymers chosen from polycarbonates, polyacrylates, polymethacrylates, or polystyrene together with another gel forming, highly swellable hydrocolloid component, which is typically a cellulose compound or a polysaccharide. On coming in contact with gastric fluid, the polymer imbibes water and swells. The extensive swelling of these polymers is due to the presence of physical/chemical cross-links in the hydrophilic polymer network. These cross-links prevent the dissolution of the polymer and hence maintain the physical integrity of the dosage form. Sustained and controlled drug release may be achieved by selection of polymer of proper molecular weight and swelling of the polymer retards the drug release. The release of hydrophilic drugs is mainly governed by diffusion mechanisms while hydrophobic drugs are released by erosion of the external surface of the dosage form. The swollen polymer hinders the exit of dosage form from pylorus (Fig. 7.12).

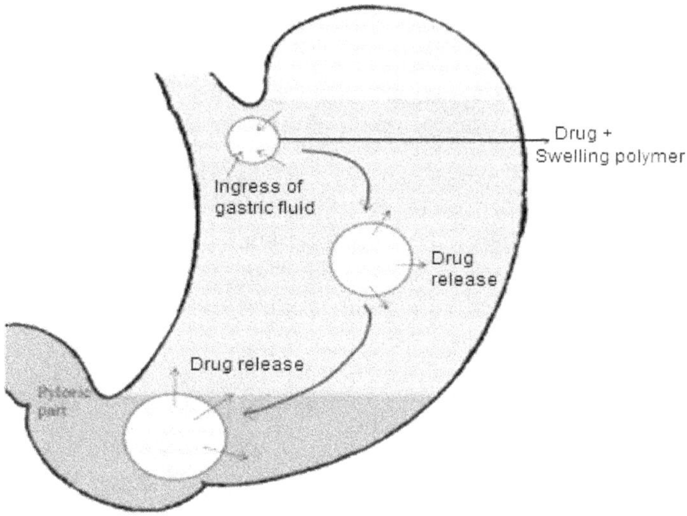

Fig.7.12 GRDDS based on swelling.

Unfolding systems

Unfolding systems are probably the best alternatives to resist to the gastric emptying. Several geometric shapes, such as tetrahedron, ring, cloverleaf, disk, string and pellet/sphere, which can be packed tightly into a gelatin capsule and unfold after dissolution of the capsule shell, have been patented (Fig 7.13).

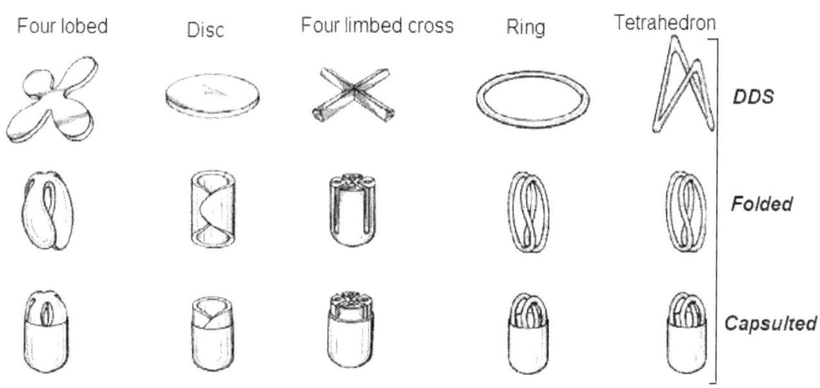

Fig.7.13 Different geometric forms of unfoldable systems that can be capsulated to get unfolded in stomach.

In the stomach the capsule shell dissolves, releasing the GRDDS which unfolds or opens out to achieve its extended configuration. The functionality of these systems is based on dimensions and mechanical shape memory. Many technologies were developed but only few of them have reached the market.

Example of unfolding system is the "Accordion pill®" developed by INTEC Pharma, not yet commercialized. The dosage form is folded in an accordion-like shape in a hard gelatin capsule. After the capsule dissolves in the stomach, the accordion unfolds and can remain in the stomach for approximately 12 h.

Though expandable systems represent an interesting concept and seem to be efficacious; however, permanent retention of rigid, large monolithic forms may interfere with gastric motility, causing possible adverse effects such as bowel obstruction, local damage, intestinal adhesion and gastropathy. Furthermore, such dosage forms are difficult to industrialize and might be expensive.

Others

Magnetic system

In magnetic systems, a dosage form consists of active pharmaceutical ingredient, excipients and a small amount of internal magnet. An extracorporeal magnet is placed over the stomach to control the position of the dosage form containing internal magnet as presented in Figure 7.14. The position and the magnetic field intensity of the extracorporeal magnet can affect the gastroretentive time. In a study on magnetic bioadhesive granules containing ultra-fine ferrite reported retention of all granules in rabbit stomach for more than 2 hours when an external magnetic field intensity of 1700 G was used. Studies have reported improvement in the gastroretentive time and bioavailability by magnetic tablets. In a study in human volunteers using magnetic acyclovir tablets reported an increased gastroretentive time and plasma drug concentration in the presence of an extracorporeal magnet. The difficulty of positioning the external magnet coupled with the inability to hold it in place throughout the drug release make this treatment very unpleasant for the patient. Only a few studies have been conducted on magnetic systems and their clinical significance has yet to be explored. Therefore, future research studies on these systems need to focus more on their clinical significance.

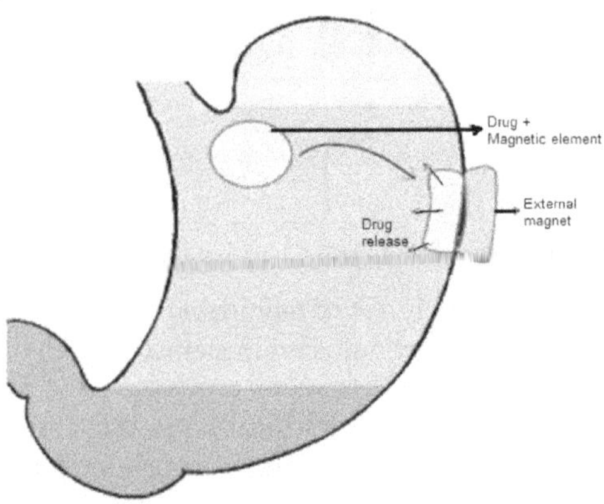

Fig.7.14 GRDDS based on application of magnetic field.

Superporous hydrogels

Based on swelling properties the efficacy of superporous hydrogel systems is mainly governed by polymer formulation. The gastric retention is a result of the mechanical properties of the dosage form. The polymers used in such systems increase the dimensions of the dosage form, to be larger than 7 - 12 mm (the pylorus diameter). Most of the hydrophilic polymers swell by osmotic absorption of water, leading to a three dimensional network.

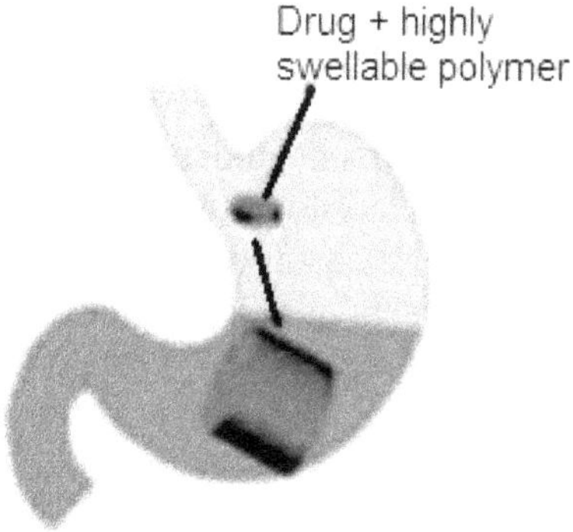

Fig.7.15 GRDDS based on superporous hydrogel.

Figure 7.15 depicts the schematic concept of the superporous hydrogel system. The conventional hydrogel system is a slow process and takes several hours to reach equilibrium; thus, the dosage form can be easily evacuated from the stomach. On the contrary, the superporous hydrogel systems swell up to 100 times or more, and gain enough mechanical strength to withstand pressure by gastric contraction, thereby increasing the gastroretentive time. Highly swellable polymers, such as croscarmellose sodium and sodium alginate are used in these systems. However, these systems can be highly sensitive to pH, and swelling can be reversible due to changes in pH and poor mechanical strength of the structure. Those which are able to swell substantially without disruption of the overall structure are called hydrogels, and if the water content absorbed exceeds 95% of the total weight, this is called a superabsorbent hydrogel.

When administered the water absorption propagates through the spaces in the 3D structure of polymer. The spaces termed as effective pore size can be from 10 nm to 10 micrometers in diameter. The process is very slow and the dosage form needs some time (min to hours) to reach the equilibrium. During this time, the dosage form may be evacuated prematurely leading to the all or none effect. Efforts are being made to create an effective pore size larger than 10 micrometers in order to speed up the water absorption process but these products generally exhibit poor mechanical properties. For improved superporous hydrogels, to be useful there is a need to swell fast to a large size and at the same time maintain high mechanical strength by adding a composite material during the synthesis.

In situ gelling

In situ gelling GRDDS are polymeric formulations that are sol forms before entering in the body, but change to gel forms under physiological conditions. Examples of natural polymers capable of in situ gelling are pectin, xyloglucan, gellan gum, chitosan and alginic acid. The system may be classified into (i) physically induced *in-situ* gelling systems and (ii) chemically induced *in-situ* gel systems, and (iii) *in-situ* gel formation based on physiological stimuli. Physically induced in situ gel formation occurs when the polymer absorbs water from the surrounding environment and expands to give the desired space. Chemically induced *in-situ* gel systems are formed by ionic crosslinking using ion sensitive polysaccharides such as sodium alginate, iota carrageenan, gellan gum and pectin. These polymers undergo a phase transition in the presence of various ions such as K^+, Ca^{2+}, Mg^{2+}, Na^+. Once administered they form a gel inside the stomach under certain conditions involving the use of a gelling agent which can form a system that contains the dispersed drug and other excipients. An intra-gastric floating in situ gelling system of an amoxicillin was developed using gellan as the gelling polymer and calcium carbonate as the gas-releasing agent. Such system is capable of dose size reduction.

Ion-exchange resin systems

The ion-exchange resin system consists of the water insoluble cross-linked polymer (resin) that can be either cationic or anionic. In general, it is designed to release the drug in a controlled manner. The suitable resins can be chosen according to the drug properties. In case of GRDDS, drugs should be released in the stomach and hence this system is applicable to cationic drugs. Therefore, cationic resin can be selected. A specific amount of resin is poured on a known drug concentration and mixed homogeneously for a certain period. The drug ions from the solution get adsorbed onto the resin matrix and displace cations from the resin. Such loaded drug resin complexes are called resinates. When the resinates come into contact with the hydrogen ions in the acidic environment of the stomach, hydrogen ions are exchanged with the drug ions present in the resinates matrix. As a consequence, the drug ions are released into the gastric fluid while the resin particles are eliminated through the large intestine. The release rate of the drug from resins depends on inherent properties of the resins such as the particle size, cross-linking density, type of ionogenic group. Moreover, it also depends on the nature of the drugs, ionic environment and test solution. When an ion exchange resin is highly cross-linked, the drug loading efficiency gets decreased. The degree of drug resin complexation can be calculated by dry weight resin capacity measurement methods. It is determined by weighing a dry resin, rewetting it in drug solution, and displacing completely from the resin. The displaced ions can be assayed giving the degree of drug resin complexation. Even though this system alone may not be suitable to increase the gastroretentive time, the ion exchange resin can be combined with floating delivery systems or bioadhesive systems to prolong the gastroretentive time. Some of its limitations may be difficulty in estimating the amount of bound resin with drug, and safety issues concerning its ingestion.

Combination of different systems

Even though various GRDDS technologies have been extensively explored to achieve successful gastroretentive systems, most have their own limitations. The variation in gastroretentive time, especially in the fed and fasted states, is still one of the main challenges faced by many formulation scientists. No single approach might be the best for resolving the problems. I Therefore, it is desirable to explore suitable GRDDS that can overcome the limitations of a single approach. Using combination approaches such as expandable and effervescent floating systems, mucoadhesive and floating systems, swellable and floating systems, and mucoadhesive and high-density system may be useful strategies for minimizing the variability of GRT. In practice, systems such as the gas-generating devices combine different gastroretentive properties or concepts. They increase in size to prevent transit and at the same time they float due to their low density (as described above). For systems where dual mode of action is claimed, bioadhesion is often claimed in combination with floating or even swelling behavior.

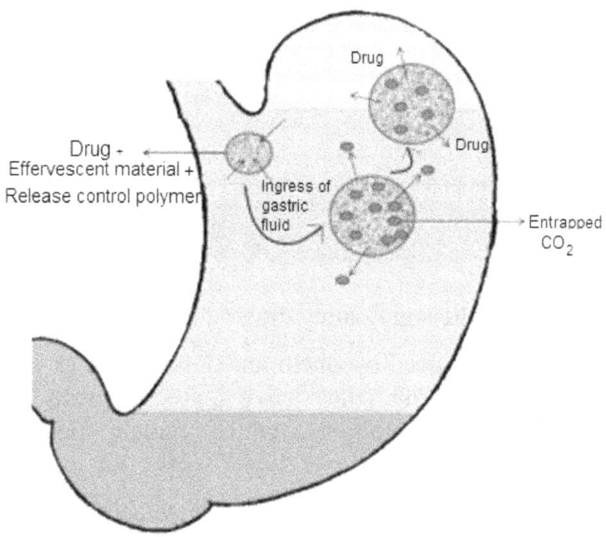

Fig.7.16 GRDDS based on combination of polymer swelling and effervescence.

Moreover, dual-working systems are less affected by the physiological condition of the stomach such as the fasting and fed states and these systems can ensure delayed gastric emptying. Therefore, future works on GRDDS should be focused on combinations of different mechanisms in order to prolong gastric retention of dosage forms even in the fasted state.

Table 7.1 complies certain commercial gastroretentive drug delivery systems.

Technology	Company	Product	Active Pharmaceutical ingredient
Bioadhesive tablets	Lupin, India	Xifaxan	Rifaximin
Effervescent floating system	Ranbaxy, India	Zanocin OD Riomet OD	Oflaxacin Metformin HCl
Polymer-based swelling technology: AcuForm_	Depomed, Inc., USA	Gabapentin GR ProQuin_ XR	Gabapentin Ciprofloxacin
Minextab Floating_ system	Galenix, France	Cafeclor LP Tramadol LP	Cefaclor Tramadol
Gastroretention with osmotic system Floating, CR capsule	GlaxoSmithKline Roche, UK	Coreg CR Madopar	Carvedilol Levodopa and benserazide
Floating liquid alginate	Pierre Fabre Medicament, France	Topalkan	Aluminum magnesium antacid
Coated multi-layer floating and swelling system	Sun Pharma, India	Baclofen GRS	Baclofen

7.2 TIMELINE

1968 Early studies on floating drug delivery systems

1975 HBS introduced by Sheth and Tossounian as single-unit dosage forms, containing the active ingredient with one or more gel forming hydrocolloids, which remain floating on stomach contents.

1980 Madopar LP, based on Hydrodynamically balanced system, was marketed by Roche

1980s Introduction of floating alginate beads

1984 The mucoadhesive/bioadhesive system was first introduced by Park and Robinson

1994	A patent was assigned to Reckitt and Colman Products that described a raft-forming formulation using triclosan.
2000	Novel superporous hydrogels were invented by Omidian et al.
2019	Development of magnetic gastroretentive delivery system for acyclovir by 3D printing

7.3 CHAPTER AT A GLANCE

Term	Description
High density/ non-floating system	Formulated by coating the drug on a heavy core or mixing it with inert materials, density exhibited higher than the density of gastric content. GI transit time of pellets can be enhanced from an average of 5.8 to 25 h.
Low density/ floating system	Less density than gastric fluids and so remain buoyant in the stomach without affecting gastric emptying rate for a prolonged period. Can be classified into effervescent and non-efferverscent systems
Effervescent systems	Comprises of the swellable polymers like chitosan, and effervescent agents like sodium bicarbonate, disodium glycine carbonate, cytroglycine, citric acid and tartaric acid
Gas generating system	Uses effervescent reactions between carbonate/bicarbonate salts and citric/tartaric acid to liberate CO_2, which gets entrapped in the gellified hydrocolloid layer of the systems thus decreasing its specific gravity and making it to float
Volatile liquid containing system	Gastric residence time can be sustained by adding an inflatable chamber, containing a liquid such as ether, cyclopentane, that gasifies at body temperature to cause the inflatation of the chamber in the stomach
Air trapped flotation chamber based GRDDS	Drug reservoir is encapsulated within the microporous compartment containing pores. The floating chamber comprising entrapped air provides delivery system the ability to remain buoyant over the gastric content.
Non-effervescent systems	Formulated using highly swellable or gel forming cellulose type hydrocolloids, matrix forming polymers and polysaccharides
Hydrodynamically balanced system	Formulated using highly swellable or gel forming cellulose type hydrocolloids, matrix forming polymers and polysaccharides

Table *contd...*

Term	Description
Osmotically driven GRDDS	Formulated using osmotic agents
Raft forming systems	A gel-forming solution swells and forms a viscous cohesive gel containing entrapped CO_2 bubbles on contact with gastric fluid
Multiple unit systems Microballoons/ micro-beads/ microspheres	The air entrapped in microparticle/ porous structure confers buoyancy to the microparticles. However a minimal gastric content is needed to maintain buoyancy.
Bioadhesive/ mucoadhesive system	Gastric retention increased by adhering the bioadhesive system to the gastric mucosal membrane, thus improving bioavailability
Expandable GRDDS	A formulation could withstand the gastric emptying when it is larger in size than the pyloric sphincter. For achieving this, three configurations are required: one for oral administration, an expandable gastric form and a part enabling gastric evacuation following complete drug release.
Swelling (plug) system	Systems which upon swallowing undergo swelling up to an extent which prevents their exit from the pylorus and hence can be retained for prolonged period of time
Unfolding system	Undergo unfolding and enlarge in size, remain lodged at the pyloric sphincter avoiding its exit from the stomach
Magnetic system	Dosage form comprises a small magnet and another magnet is applied on the abdomen over the position of stomach
Superporous hydrogel	A kind of swelling systems with a pore size >100 µm, that swell within a min due to rapid water uptake by capillary wetting through numerous interconnected open pores
In situ gelling	Systems which upon swallowing undergo gel formation
Combination of different systems	Such systems combine different gastroretentive properties or concepts

EXERCISES

Multiple choice Questions

1. Drug candidates not suitable for GRDDS
   (a) Drugs which have site-specific absorption in the stomach, or upper part of intestine.
   (b) Drugs those cause gastric mucosa irritation.
   (c) Drugs required to exert local therapeutic action in stomach.
   (d) Drugs poorly soluble or insoluble in intestinal fluids

2. It is advisable not to administer floating dosage forms to bedridden patients prior to
   (a) Breakfast (b) Bedtime
   (c) Lunch (d) None of the above

3. Which of the following is not a non-effervescent type of GRDDS?
   (a) Hydrodynamically balanced system (b) Volatile liquid based
   (c) Osmotically driven (d) Raft forming

4. High density GRDDS systems have a density close to
   (a) 2.5 g/cm^3 (b) 3.5 g/cm^3
   (c) 2.0 g/cm^3 (d) None of the above

5. For designing gas generating systems, the stoichiometric ratio of citric acid and sodium bicarbonate is in general
   (a) 0.76:1 (b) 0.8:1
   (c) 0.66:1 (d) 1:1

6. Gastric residence time can be sustained by adding an inflatable chamber, containing a liquid such as
   (a) Acetone (b) Chloroform
   (c) Ether (d) All

7. Incorporation of fatty acids in HBS reduces
   (a) Density of the formulation (b) Penetration of water
   (c) Erosion (d) All of the above

8. Which of the following is not a formulation component of the osmotically driven GRDDS?
   (a) Inflatable floating support (b) A bioerodible plug
   (c) Osmotically active compartment (d) Microporous membrane
9. For retention of expandable systems in the stomach the dosage form should be more than
   (a) 13 mm (b) 12 mm
   (c) 11mm (d) 10 mm
10. Identify the type of GRDDS depicted in the given image

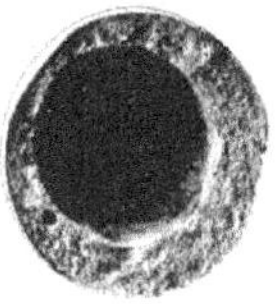

   (a) Mini tablet (b) Microsphere
   (c) Microballoon (d) Foam porous particle

Short Answer Questions

1. The expandable systems are usually based on three configurations. Comment.
2. With the help of neat diagram explain the osmotically driven GRDDS.
3. Give a brief account of unfolding systems.
4. What do you understand by magnetic GRDDS?
5. What are the limitations of GRDDS?

Long Answer Questions

1. Define GRDDS. Classify them. Give the advantages and disadvantages of GRDDS.
2. Write a descriptive note on effervescent or gas- based GRDDS.
3. Explain MMC. Give its significance in designing GRDDS. Which drug candidates are suitable and unsuitable for GRDDS.
4. Explain the factors affecting the efficacy of GRDDS.
5. Write notes on (i) Superporous hydrogels, and (ii) Bioadhesive GRDDS.

Answer Key MCQs

(1) – (b), (2) – (d), (3) – (b), (4) – (a), (5) – (d), (6) – (c), (7) – (d), (8) – (d), (9) – (a), (10) – (c).

BIBLIOGRAPHY

1. Crowley PJ, Martini LG. Formulation design: new drugs from old, (2004) Drug Discov. Today: Therapeutic strategies, 1, 537-542.
2. Reddy LH, Murthy RS. Floating dosage systems in drug delivery, (2002) Crit. Rev. Ther. Drug Carrier Syst. 19, 553-585.
3. Hou SY et al. Gastric retentive dosage forms, (2003) Crit. Rev. Ther. Drug Carrier Syst. 20, 459-497.

Chapter 8

NASOPULMONARY DRUG DELIVERY SYSTEM

♦ LEARNING OBJECTIVES ♦

***After completing this lesson, the Reader should be able to understand*:**

- **Nasal administration as a successful delivery route**
- **Nasal drug delivery devices**
- **Pulmonary drug delivery as a route of choice in certain cases**
- **Pulmonary drug delivery devices**

8.1 INTRODUCTION

The efficacy of a treatment mostly depends on the techniques by which the drug is delivered and the optimum concentration of the drug in body. The efficacy of the drug and its treatment can be achieved by controlling the pharmacokinetics, pharmacodynamics, immunogenicity, and biorecognition. These new strategies based on interdisciplinary approaches are often called novel/advanced drug delivery systems. Different drug delivery/drug targeting systems already exist and currently under development can be efficiently used to minimize the drug degradation and loss, to prevent harmful side effects and to increase drug bioavailability. For over 20 years, the potential benefit of nanotechnology is appreciated by most of the researchers and it is providing vast improvements in drug delivery and drug targeting. New advancements in the drug delivery strategies are minimizing toxicities and improving the efficacy of the treatments.

The widespread interest in intranasal route for therapeutic purposes other than the topically nasal drug delivery arises from the particular anatomical, physiological and histological characteristics of the nasal cavity, which provides potential for rapid systemic drug absorption and quick onset of action. In addition, intranasal absorption avoids the gastrointestinal and hepatic presystemic metabolism, enhancing drug bioavailability in comparison with that obtained after gastrointestinal absorption. Growing attention has been given to the potential of a pulmonary route as an non-invasive administration for systemic delivery of therapeutic agents (mainly peptides and proteins) based on the fact that the lungs could provide a large absorptive surface area (up to 100 m^2), extremely thin (0.1 – 0.2 μm) absorptive mucosal membrane and good blood supply. Although recent advances show great promise, but pulmonary delivery of peptides and proteins is complicated by the complexity of the anatomic structure of the human respiratory system and the effect of disposition exerted by the respiration process.

NASAL DELIVERY

For many years drugs have been administered nasally for both topical and systemic action. Topical administration includes the treatment of congestion, rhinitis, sinusitis and related allergic or chronic conditions, and has resulted in a variety of different medications including corticoids, antihistamines, anti-cholinergic and vasoconstrictors. In recent years, increasing investigations of the nasal route have focused especially on nasal application for systemic drug delivery. Nasal drug delivery is a useful delivery method for drugs that are active in low doses and show minimal oral bioavailability such as proteins and peptides. Many drugs have been shown to achieve better systemic bioavailability through nasal route than by oral administration. Drug candidates ranging from small metal ions to large macromolecular proteins have been tested in various animal models. It has been documented that nasal administration of certain hormones and steroids has resulted in a more complete absorption. Intranasal delivery is currently being employed in treatments for migraine, smoking cessation, acute pain relief, osteoporosis, nocturnal enuresis and vitamin-B12 deficiency. Other examples of therapeutic areas under development or with potential for nasal delivery include cancer therapy, epilepsy, anti-emetics, rheumatoid arthritis and insulin-dependent diabetes.

Advantages

1) Drug degradation that is observed in the gastrointestinal tract is absent.
2) Hepatic first pass metabolism is avoided.
3) Rapid drug absorption and quick onset of action can be achieved.
4) The bioavailability of small and large drug molecules can be improved by means of absorption enhancer or other approach.
5) Polar compounds exhibiting poor oral absorption may be particularly suited for this route of delivery.
6) Nasal route is an alternative to parenteral route, especially, for protein and peptide drugs.
7) Convenient for the patients, especially for those on long term therapy, when compared to parenteral medication.

Limitations

1) Nasal cavity provides smaller absorption surface area when compared to GIT.
2) There is a risk of local side effects and irreversible damage of the cilia on the nasal mucosa, both from the substance and from constituents added to the dosage form.
3) Relatively inconvenient to patients when compared to oral delivery systems since there is a possibility of nasal irritation.
4) There could be a mechanical loss of the dosage form into the other parts of the respiratory tract like lungs because of the improper technique of administration.

Anatomy and Physiology of Nasal Cavity

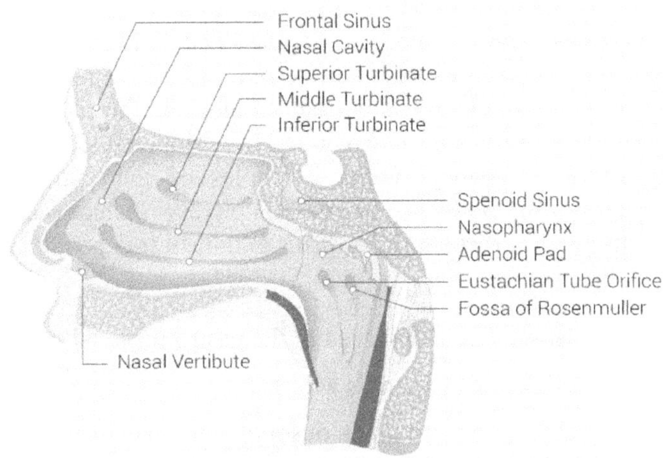

Fig.8.1 Descriptive diagram of human nasal cavity.

The nasal cavity is divided into two halves by the nasal septum and extends posterior to the nasopharynx, while the most anterior part of the nasal cavity, the nasal vestibule, opens to the face through the nostril. There are three distinct functional areas in the nasal cavity, the vestibular, olfactory and respiratory zones. The vestibular area (approximately 0.6 cm^2) serves as a first barrier against airborne particles with low vascularization comprised of stratified squamous and keratinized epithelial cells with nasal hairs. The olfactory area (around 15 cm^2) enables olfactory perception and is highly vascularized. The respiratory area (approx. 130 cm^2) serves with its mucus layer produced by highly specialized cells as an efficient air- cleansing system. The surface of this zone is enlarged by the division of the cavity by lateral walls into three nasal conchae or turbinates (Fig. 8.1) and by the magnification of the mucosa by microvilli and cilia. The zone is highly vascularized.

The posterior region of the nasal cavity is the nasopharynx. Its upper part consists of ciliated cells; the lower part contains squamous epithelium. The area is also part of the mucosal immune system. Due to the rich vascularization, the olfactory and in particular the respiratory zone may serve as an efficient absorption surface for topically applied drugs. The olfactory region with its vicinity to the cerebrospinal fluid and direct nervous interface to the brain has attracted research interest for nose- to- brain delivery.

The respiratory epithelium as well as other parts of the nasal cavity and airways is lined by superficial epithelium consisting primarily of two types of cells: mucus- producing goblet cells (20%) and ciliated cells (80%). The various cell types of the epithelium are joined together by tight junctions. Mucus continuously produced by goblet cells traps inhaled particulate and infectious debris while the propulsive force (about 1,000 strokes/min) generated by ciliated cells transports the mucus towards the nasopharynx and the gastrointestinal tract for elimination. This effective cleansing mechanism is called mucociliary clearance (MCC). The MCC time is approximately 20 min but is subject to great intersubject variability. The MCC is dependent on the function of the cilia and the characteristics of the covering mucus, which can be influenced by acute or chronic illnesses like common cold or allergic rhinitis. Many substances can influence the MCC of the airways, either by stimulation or inhibition. A stimulatory effect of drugs on the MCC is of clinical importance, because these substances can possibly be used to improve pathological conditions of the MCC. Components (drug, excipients) of nasally administered formulations with a too pronounced MCC- impairing activity may limit their use.

FACTORS INFLUENCING NASAL DRUG ABSORPTION

Several factors affect the systemic bioavailability of drugs which are administered through the nasal route. The factors can be affecting to the physiochemical properties of the drugs, the anatomical and physiological properties of the nasal cavity and the type and characteristics of selected nasal drugs delivery system. These factors play key role for most of the drugs in order to reach therapeutically effective blood levels after nasal administration. The factors influencing nasal drug absorption are summarized in Figure 8.2 and described thereafter.

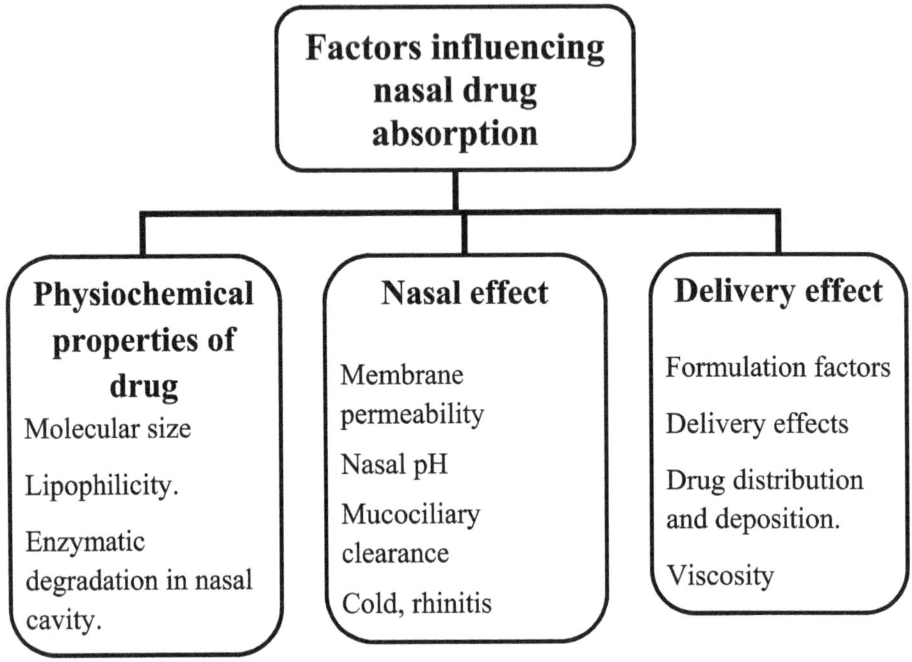

Fig.8.2 Factors affecting nasal drug absorption.

1) Physiochemical properties of drug

Molecular size

The molecular size of the drug influence absorption of the drug through the nasal route. The lipophilic drugs have direct relationship between the molecular weight and drug permeation whereas water soluble compounds depict an inverse relationship. The rate of permeation is highly sensitive to molecular size for compounds with molecular weight ≥ 300 Daltons but less than 500 daltons. Box 1 illustrates the selection criteria for drug candidates suitable for nasal delivery.

Lipophilicity

By increasing lipophilicity, the permeation of the compound normally increases through nasal mucosa. Lipophilic drugs like buprenorphine, naloxone, testosterone and 17a-ethinyl- estradiol are almost completely absorbed when administered intranasally. The pharmacokinetic profiles of lipophilic drugs are often identical to those obtained after an intravenous injection and the bioavailability approaches 100%. An example is the nasal administration of Fentanyl where the t_{max} for both intravenous and nasal administration was same and very rapid (≤ 7 min) and the bioavailability was nearly 80%. The nasal absorption of polar drugs and especially large molecular weight polar drugs such as peptides and proteins is limited due to low membrane permeability.

Box 1

SELECTION OF DRUG CANDIDATE FOR NASAL DELIVERY

The biopharmaceutical drug classification system reveals that drug candidates that fit into class I (high permeability, high solubility) have the highest potential for nasal delivery.

To further refine the selection criteria for small molecules in aqueous solution, one may be guided by the Rule of Five defined by Lipinski et al. Establish the following rule of thumb:

- Drug characteristics: molecular weight <500 Da, log P <5;
- Dose per spray puff (left and right nostril): potency < 5 mg/dose;
- Volume maximally 100 μl/spray puff: solubility > 50 mg/ml;
- Drug in solution: pH approximately 5.5, osmolality <500 mOsm/kg.

Nasal membrane permeability is the most important factor, which affects the absorption of the drug through the nasal route. The large molecular weight drugs like peptides and proteins have low membrane permeability as discussed earlier. Water-soluble high molecular weight drugs cross the nasal mucosa mainly by passive diffusion through the aqueous pores (i.e. tight junctions).

Nasal pH

The nasal pH plays an important role in the efficiency of nasal drug absorption. Small water-soluble compounds such as benzoic acid, salicylic acid, and alkaloid acid show extensive nasal absorption at the pH values at which these exist in non-ionized form. However, at pH values where these compounds are partially ionized, substantial absorption was found. This means that the non-ionized lipophilic form crosses the nasal epithelial barrier via transcellular route, whereas the more lipophilic ionized form passes through the aqueous paracellular route.

Mucociliary clearance (MCC)

MCC accounts for a substantial difference in bioavailability following nasal delivery. If the formulation irritates the nasal mucosa, this mechanism will cause the irritant to be rapidly diluted, followed by increased clearance, and swallowed. The result is a much shorter duration inside the nasal cavity and therefore less nasal bioavailability. This is especially the case for drugs that are not easily absorbed across the nasal membrane. It has been shown that for both liquid and powder formulations, that are not mucoadhesive, the half life of clearance is of the order of 15–20 min. It has further been suggested that the deposition of a formulation in the anterior part of the nasal cavity can decrease clearance and promote absorption as compared to deposition further back in the nasal cavity. The use of bioadhesive excipients in the formulations may overcome rapid mucociliary clearance

Cold, rhinitis

Rhinitis is a most common nasal disease that influences the bioavailability of the drug. Rhinitis is mainly classified into allergic rhinitis and common cold. The symptoms of common cold are hyper secretion, itching and sneezing mainly caused by the viruses, bacteria or irritants. Allergic rhinitis is the allergic airway disease, which affects 10% of population. It is caused by chronic or acute inflammation of the mucous membrane of the nose. These conditions affect the absorption of drug through the mucus membrane due the inflammation.

2) **Delivery factors:** Factors that affect the delivery of drug across nasal mucosa such as surfactants, dose, pH, osmolarity, viscosity, particle size and nasal clearance, drug structure can be used as advantage to improve absorption.

Formulation (concentration, pH, osmolarity)

Concentration gradient plays very important role in the absorption / permeation process of drug through the nasal membrane due to nasal mucosal damage. For example nasal absorption of L-tyrosine increased with an increase in drug concentration. On the other hand absorption of salicylic acid was found to decline with concentration. The pH of the formulation and nasal surface, can affect drug's permeation. To avoid nasal irritation, the pH of the nasal formulation should be adjusted to 4.5–6.5. Furthermore, lysozyme is found in nasal secretions, which is responsible for destroying certain pathogenic bacteria at acidic pH. If the instilled formulation is alkaline, lysozyme will get inactivated making the nasal tissue susceptible to microbial infection.

The osmolarity of the dosage form affects the nasal absorption of the drug. Thus the concentration of sodium chloride in the formulation affects nasal absorption. In a study maximum absorption was achieved by 0.462 M sodium chloride concentration; higher concentration not only increased bioavailability but also led to the toxicity to the nasal epithelium.

Drugs distribution and deposition

The drug distribution in the nasal cavity is one of the important factors, which affects the efficiency of nasal absorption. The mode of drug administration could affect the distribution of drug in nasal cavity, which in turn will determine the absorption efficiency of a drug. The absorption and bioavailability of the nasal dosage forms mainly depends on the site of disposition. The anterior portion of the nose provides a prolonged nasal residential time for disposition of formulation, it enhances the absorption of the drug. While the posterior chamber of nasal cavity when used for the deposition of dosage form; it is eliminated by the mucociliary clearance process and hence shows low bioavailability. The site of disposition and distribution of the dosage forms are mainly depends on delivery device, mode of administration, physicochemical properties of drug molecule.

Viscosity

A higher viscosity of the formulation increases contact time between the drug and the nasal mucosa thereby increasing the time for permeation. At the same time, highly viscous formulations interfere with the normal functions like ciliary beating or mucociliary clearance and thus alter the permeability of drugs.

NASAL DOSAGE FORMS

Only a few nasal delivery systems are currently on the market to deliver therapeutics into the nasal cavities, i.e. nasal drops as multiple or single-dose formulation, aqueous nasal sprays, a nasal gel pump, pressurized MDIs and dry powder inhalers. The selection of dosage form depends upon the drug being used, proposed indication, patient population and marketing preferences. Some of these delivery systems and their important features are summarized below:

a) ***Nasal Drops***

Nasal drops are one of the most simple and convenient systems developed for nasal delivery. The main disadvantage of this system is the lack of dose precision and therefore nasal drops may not be suitable for prescription products. It has been reported that nasal drops deposit human serum albumin in the nostrils more efficiently than nasal sprays.

b) ***Nasal Sprays***

Both solution and suspension formulations can be formulated into nasal sprays. Due to the availability of metered dose pumps and actuators, a nasal spray can deliver an exact dose from 25 to 200 μL. The particle size and morphology (for suspensions) of the drug and viscosity of the formulation determine the choice of pump and actuator assembly. Solution and suspension sprays are preferred over powder sprays because powder results in mucosal irritation.

c) ***Nasal Gels***

Nasal gels are high-viscosity thickened solutions or suspensions. Until the recent development of precise dosing devices, there was not much interest in this system. The advantages of a nasal gel include the reduction of post-nasal drip due to high viscosity, reduction of taste impact due to reduced swallowing, reduction of anterior leakage of the formulation, reduction of irritation by using soothing/emollient excipients and target delivery to mucosa for better absorption.

d) ***Nasal Powders***

This dosage form may be developed if solution and suspension dosage forms cannot be developed e.g., due to lack of drug stability. The advantages to the nasal powder dosage forms are the absence of preservative and superior stability of the formulation. However, the suitability of the powder formulation is dependent on the solubility, particle size, aerodynamic properties and nasal irritancy of the active drug and/or excipients. Local application of drug is another advantage of this system but nasal mucosa irritancy and metered dose delivery are some of the challenges for formulation scientists and device manufacturers.

STRATEGIES TO IMPROVE NASAL ABSORPTION

Bioavailability of nasally administered drugs is particularly restricted by low drug solubility, rapid enzymatic degradation in nasal cavity, poor membrane penetration and rapid MCC. Thus several approaches have been suggested to overcome these limitations. Various strategies employed to improve bioavailability of the drug in the nasal mucosa are aimed:

1. To improve the nasal residence time
2. To enhance nasal absorption (Use of nasal enzyme inhibitors, permeation enhancers)
3. To modify drug structure to change physicochemical properties (prodrug approach, structural modification).

Any one or combination of above approaches is used to enhance the absorption and bioavailability of the formulations. Several methods used to facilitate nasal absorption of the drugs include:

(i) Nasal enzyme inhibitors: Nasal metabolism of drugs can be eliminated by using the enzyme inhibitors. For the formulation of proteins and peptides enzyme inhibitors like peptidases and proteases are used. The absorption enhancers like salts and fusidic acid derivatives also shows enzyme inhibition activity to increase the absorption and bioavailability of the drug. The other enzyme inhibitors commonly used for the enzymatic activity are tripsin, aprotinin, borovaline, amastatin, bestatin and boroleucin inhibitors.

(ii) Permeation enhancers: The permeation enhancers are primarily used for the enhancement of absorption of the active medicament. Generally, the absorption enhancers act *via* one of the following mechanisms:

(iii) Inhibit enzyme activity: reduce mucus viscosity or elasticity; decrease mucociliary clearance; open tight junctions; and solubilize or stabilize the drug. The mechanism of action of permeation enhancer is increasing the rate at which drug passes through the nasal mucosa. Many enhancers act by altering the structure of epithelial cells in some way, but they should accomplish this while causing no damage or permanent change to nasal mucosa. Various types of penetration enhancers for organic drugs include surfactants, bile salts, chelators, fatty acid salts, phospholipids, glycyrrhetenic acid derivatives, cyclodextrins and glycols.

(iv) **Prodrug approach:** Prodrug approach is mainly meant for optimizing favorable physicochemical properties such as solubility, taste, odor, stability, etc. Prodrug approach is intended for improving the nasal bioavailability especially for the proteins and peptides. The aim is to enhance the membrane permeability along with increased enzymatic stability. The synthesized prodrug undergoes enzymatic transformation to release the active medicament, when it crosses the enzymatic and membrane barrier. The absorption of peptides like angiotensin II, bradykinin, caulein, carnosine, enkephalin, vasopressin and calcitonin can be improved by preparing enamine derivatives. The nasal bioavailability of poorly soluble L-Dopa was enhanced using this concept. The aspartate ester prodrug of acyclovir was more permeable and less labile to enzymatic hydrolysis than its parent drug.

(v) **Structural modification:** The chemical modification of drug molecule has been commonly used to modify the physicochemical properties of a drug such as molecular size, molecular weight, pKa and solubility to improve the nasal absorption of drug. Example, chemical modification of salmon calcitonin to ecatonin (C-N bond replaces the S-S bond) showed better bioavailability than salmon calcitonin.

(vi) **Particulate drug delivery:** Microspheres, nanoparticles and liposomes can be used as carriers to encapsulate an active drug in order to maximize therapeutic efficacy. Overall, this can result in increased absorption efficacy and stability and reduced toxicity of the active ingredient. Microspheres mainly increase the absorption and bioavailability by adhering to the nasal mucosa and increase the nasal residence time of drug. The microspheres prepared by using polymers like dextran, chitosan, biodegradable starch microspheres improve the bioavailability of various drugs. Liposomes are amphiphilic in nature are well characterized for favorable permeation of drugs through the biological membranes, so the water soluble drugs have been delivered to nasal drugs. Cationic liposomes are having good permeation capacity than negatively charged anionic liposomes. Particulate systems can be designed to be mucoadhesive to increase the retention time and facilitate sustained release.

APPLICATION DEVICES

Numerous delivery devices are available for intranasal administration. Devices vary in accuracy of delivery, dose reproducibility, cost and ease of use. Currently, metered- dose systems provide the greatest dose accuracy and reproducibility. Differences also exist in force of delivery, spray patterns and emitted droplet size. The latter is of the utmost importance for drug deposition within the nasal cavity. The challenge is to optimize deposition while limiting the fraction of small particles able to bypass the nose and enter the lungs. Several companies have proposed new delivery technologies, which can provide a more uniform particle size distribution and therefore improve the nasal deposition pattern.

(A) *Devices for Liquid Dosage forms*

Liquid preparations are the most widely used dosage forms for nasal administration of drugs. They are mainly based on solutions, suspensions and emulsions. Their humidifying effect is convenient and useful, since many allergic and chronic diseases are often connected with drying of mucous membranes. Microbiological instability, irritation and allergic rhinitis are the major drawbacks associated with the water-based dosage forms because these formulations require preservatives that impair the mucociliary function. Short residence time of the formulation in the nasal cavity is yet another disadvantage of liquid formulations. The devices used to deliver liquid dosage forms are described below.

1. ***Rhinyle catheter and squirt tube***

   Catheters are used to deliver the drops to a specified region of nasal cavity easily. Place the formulation in the tube and one end of the tube is positioned in the nose, and the solution is delivered into the nasal cavity by blowing through the other end by mouth. The method is mainly used for experimental studies in animals; but can also be done in humans without local anesthetics if care is taken to minimize contact with the sensitive mucosal membranes. This method is, however, not suitable for self-administration.

2. ***Squeeze bottle***

   Squeezed nasal bottles are mainly used as delivery device for decongestants. These are smooth plastic bottles with a simple jet outlet. On pressing the plastic bottle the air inside the container is pressed out of the small nozzle, thereby atomizing a certain volume. By releasing the pressure again air is drawn inside the bottle. This procedure often results in contamination of the liquid by microorganisms and nasal secretion sucked inside. Dose accuracy and deposition of liquids delivered via squeezed nasal bottles are strongly dependent on the mode of administration. Whether the bottle is pressed vigorously or smoothly, it influences the dose as well as the droplet size of the formulation. Thus the dose is hard to control. Therefore squeezed bottles with vasoconstrictors are not recommended to be used by children.

3. ***Metered-dose pump sprays***

   Most of the pharmaceutical nasal preparations on the market containing solutions, emulsions or suspensions are delivered by metered-dose pump sprays. Nasal sprays, or nasal mists, are used for the nasal delivery of a drug or drugs, either locally to generally alleviate cold or allergy symptoms such as nasal congestion or systemically. Although delivery methods vary, most nasal sprays function by instilling a fine mist into the nostril by action of a hand-operated pump mechanism. The pumps typically deliver 100 μl (25–200 μl) per spray, and they offer high reproducibility of the emitted dose and plume geometry in *in vitro* tests. Metered- dose pump sprays include the container, the pump with the valve and the actuator. The dose accuracy of metered-dose pump sprays is dependent on the surface tension and viscosity of the formulation. Traditional spray pumps replace the emitted liquid with air, and preservatives are therefore required to prevent contamination. However, driven by the studies suggesting possible negative effects of preservatives, pump manufacturers have developed different spray systems that avoid the need for preservatives. For solutions with higher viscosity, special pump and valve combinations are on the market.

4. ***Single- and duo-dose spray devices***

   Metered-dose spray pumps require priming and some degree of overfill to maintain dose conformity for the labeled number of doses. They are well suited for drugs to be administered daily over a prolonged duration, but due to the priming procedure and limited control of dosing, they are less suited for drugs with a narrow therapeutic window. For expensive drugs and vaccines intended for single administration or sporadic use and where tight control of the dose and formulation is of particular importance, single-dose or duo-dose spray devices are preferred.

5. ***Nasal pressurized metered-dose inhalers (pMDIs)***

   Most drugs intended for local nasal action are delivered by spray pumps, but some have also been delivered as nasal aerosols produced by pMDIs. Following the ban on CFC propellants, the pMDI products for both pulmonary and nasal delivery were removed from the US market in 2003. The use of the CFC based pMDIs for nasal products was limited due to complaints of nasal irritation and dryness. Furthermore, the particles from a pMDI are released at a high speed (5,200 vs. 1,500 cm/s at a distance 1–2 cm from the actuator tip) and the expansion of a compressed gas, causes an comfortable “cold Freon effect”. The issues related to the high particle speed and “cold Freon effect” have been reduced with the hydrofluoroalkane (HFA)-based pMDI for nasal use offering lower particle speeds and the first nasal pMDI using HFA as propellant to deliver the first generation topical steroid beclomethasone dipropionate was approved for allergic rhinitis in the USA. Like spray pumps, nasal pMDIs produce a localized deposition on the anterior non-ciliated epithelium of the nasal vestibule and in the anterior parts of the narrow nasal valve, but due to quick evaporation of the spray delivered with a pMDI, "drip-out" may be less of an issue.

6. ***Powered nebulizers and atomizers***

   Nebulizers use compressed gasses (air, oxygen, and nitrogen) or ultrasonic or mechanical power to break solutions and suspensions into small aerosol droplets that can be directly inhaled into the mouth or nose. The smaller particles and slow speed of the nebulized aerosol are preferable. Nasal inhalation from a nebulizer shows improved deposition to the upper narrow part of the nose when compared to a metered-dose spray pump, but around 33 - 56 % of the delivered dose gets deposited in the lungs. This may result in coughing and increased dose for inhaled medications. Some nebulizers and atomizers are tabulated in Table 8.1.

(B) ***Devices for powder dosage forms***

Dry powders are less frequently used in nasal drug delivery. Major advantages of this dosage form are the lack of preservatives and the improved stability of the formulation. Compared to solutions, the administration of powders could result in a prolonged contact with the nasal mucosa. Powders tend to stick to the moist surface of the nasal mucosa before being dissolved and cleared. The use of bioadhesive excipients or agents that slow ciliary action may decrease clearance rates and improve absorption. A number of factors like moisture sensitivity, solubility, particle size, particle shape, and flow characteristics will impact deposition and absorption. The function of nasal powder devices is usually based on one of three principles:

1. **Powder sprayers** with a compressible compartment to provide a pressure that when released create a plume of powder particles similar to that of a liquid spray. Unidose™ Xtra nasal spray device is a simple, single unit dose device that does not require priming. Featured with simple push button operation it operates at low actuation force. Zolmitriptan powder cyclodextrin formulation (uses µco™ powder carrier system) is an example of nasal powder spray for enhanced absorption. Another example is nasal powder of granisetron for the indication of delayed chemotherapy-induced nausea and vomiting based on the same formulation technology and delivered with the Fit-lizer™ device that is light weight and patient friendly device that offers complete and consistent delivery.

Table 8.1 Summary of commercial nebulizers and atomizers.

Device, Manufacturer	Intended application	Principle
VibrENT pulsation membrane nebulizer®, Pharma GmbH	For delivery to the nose and sinuses in patients with chronic rhinosinusitis	Utilizes a pulsating aerosol generated via a perforated vibrating membrane. The pulsation in combination with small particles is assumed to offer better penetration to the sinuses, and instruction on specific breathing technique during delivery is advocated to minimize inhalation
Bi-Directional™, OptiNose	For delivery to the nose and sinuses	Utilizes an exit resistor to create positive pressure in the nose and sinuses Prevents lung deposition of formulation
Aeroneb Solo vibrating mesh nebulizer, Aerogen, Ireland	For delivery to nose	Designed to minimize lung inhalation Produced more deposition in terms of volume of liquid (27 % vs. 9 %) in the nasal cavity. The much higher fraction found in the nasal cavity is probably a result of the shorter nebulizing time
ViaNase atomizer, Kurve Technology Inc., USA	Capable of targeting the sinuses	Atomizes liquids by producing a vortical (derived from vortex) flow on the droplets as they exit the device.
Impel nitrogen-driven atomizer, Impel Inc.	Enable drug delivery to the upper parts of the nose in order to achieve nose to brain delivery	A nasal atomizer driven by highly pressurized nitrogen gas (is under development).

2. **Dry powder inhalers (Breath-actuated inhalers)** where the subject uses his own breath to inhale the powder into the nostril from a blister or capsule. Dry powder inhalers (DPIs) are devices through which a dry powder formulation of an active drug is delivered for local or systemic effect via the nasal route. These are bolus drug delivery devices that contain solid drug, suspended or dissolved in a non-polar volatile propellant or in dry powder inhaler that is fluidized when the patient inhales. The medication is commonly held either in a capsule for manual loading or a proprietary form from inside the inhaler. Once loaded or

actuated, the operator puts the mouthpiece of the inhaler into their mouth and takes a deep inhalation, holding their breath for 5-10 seconds. The dose that can be delivered from inhalers is typically less than a few tens of milligrams in a single breath since larger powder doses may lead to provocation of cough. There are a variety of such devices namely (i) Rhinocort Turbuhaler®, Astra Zeneca, multi-dose inhaler device modified for nasal inhalation of budesonide, and (ii) Twin-lizer™, Nippon Shinyaku Co., Ltd, Japan, a topical steroid (dexamethasone cipecilate) delivered with a powder-based inhalation device for allergic rhinitis

3. **Nasal insufflators** describe devices consisting of a mouthpiece and a nosepiece that are fluidly connected. Delivery occurs when the subject exhales into the mouthpiece to close the velum, and the airflow carries the powder particles into the nose through the device nosepiece similar to the rhinyle catheter described above. Insufflators can be constructed by using a straw or tube which contains the drug substance and sometimes it contains syringe also. The achieved particle size of these systems is often increased compared to the particle size of the powder particles due to insufficient deaggregation of the particles and results in a high variation for initial deposition areas. Many insufflator systems work with pre-dosed powder doses in capsules. Trimel has acquired a device originally developed by a Danish company (Direct Haler). There are two versions of this device that looks like a small drinking straw. One version is intended for pulmonary drug delivery where subjects inhale through the small tubular device and one for nasal drug delivery where subjects blow into one end of the tube while the other end is inserted into the vestibule of the nostril. The device can in principle be viewed as a powder version of the rhinyle catheter for liquid delivery. OptiNose has developed a breath-powered Bi-Directional™ nasal delivery technology for liquid and powder medications which utilizes the exhaled breath to deliver the drug into the nose. Importantly, the breath-powered Bi-Directional™ technology can be adapted to any type of dispersion technology for both liquids and powders.

(C) *Nasal Gels*

Nasal gels are high-viscosity thickened solutions or suspensions. Until the recent development of precise dosing devices, there was not much interest in this system. The advantages of a nasal gel include the reduction of post-nasal drip due to high viscosity, reduction of taste impact due to reduced swallowing, reduction of anterior leakage of the formulation, reduction of irritation by using soothing/emollient excipients and target delivery to mucosa for better absorption. The deposition of the gel in the nasal cavity depends on the mode of administration, because due to its viscosity the formulation has poor spreading abilities. Without special application techniques it only occupies a narrow distribution area in the nasal cavity, where it is placed directly. Recently, the first nasal gel containing Vitamin B12 for systemic medication has entered the market.

APPLICATIONS OF NASAL DELIVERY

1. **Delivery of non-peptide pharmaceuticals: e.g.** progesterone, estradiol, propranolol, nitroglycerin, sodium chromoglyate, adrenal corticosteroids, sex hormones (17ß-estradiol, progesterone, norethindrone, and testosterone), vitamin B, cardiovascular drugs (nitroglycerine, isosorbide dinitrate), sympathomimetics (ephedrine, epinephrine, phenylephrine), parasympathomimetics (nicotine, metacholine), parasympatholytics (scopolamine, atropine, ipatropium), prostaglandins, central nervous systems stimulants (cocaine, lidocaine), narcotics and antagonists (bupemorphine, naloxane), histamine and antihistamines (disodium cromoglycate, meclizine), antimigrane drugs (dierogotamine, ergotamine), cephalosporins, antivirals (phenyl-p-guanidine benzoate, enviroxime), and inorganic compounds (colloidal gold, colloidal carbon, colloidal silver).
2. **Delivery of peptide-based pharmaceuticals:** Examples are insulin, calcitonin, pituitary hormones etc.
3. **Delivery of drugs to brain through nasal cavity: Drugs to treat** Parkinson's disease, Alzheimer's disease or pain, neurotrophic factors such as NGF, IGF-I, FGF and ADNF, proteins such as AVP, CCK analog, MSH/ACTH and insulin.
4. **Delivery of vaccines through nasal route**: The diseases like anthrax and influenza are treated by nasal vaccines prepared by using the recombinant Bacillus anthracis protective antigen (rPA) and chitosan respectively. Nasally administered vaccines, especially if based on attenuated live cells or adjuvanted by means of an immunostimulator or a delivery system, can induce both mucosal and systemic immune responses.
5. **Delivery of diagnostic drugs:** Pancreatic disorders of the diabetic patients are diagnosed by using 'Secretin' and the secretory function of gastric acid is determined by Pentagastrin.

Table 8.2 Marketed nasal spray solutions for systemic drug delivery.

Drug substance (Brand name)	Indication	Manufacturer
Protein and peptide drugs		
Salmon calcitonin (Karil)	Osteoporosis	Novartis Pharma
Desmopressin acetate (Minirin)	Antidiuretic hormone	Zydus Pharma, India
Buserelin (Suprefact)	Prostrate cancer	Sanofi-Aventis, Germany
Nafarelin acetate (Synarel)	Endometriosis	Pfizer, US
Oxytocin (Syntocinon)	Lactation induction	Novartis Pharma
Protirelin (Antepan, Relefact)	Thyroid diagnostics	Aventis Pharma
Non-peptide drugs		
Zolmitriptan (AscoTop)	Migraine	Astra Zeneca
Sumatriptan (Imigran)	Migraine	Glaxo SmithKline
Dihydroergotamine (Migranal)	Migraine	Novartis Pharma
Estradiol (Aerodiol)	Hormone replacement	Servier

PULMONARY DELIVERY

Pulmonary delivery of drugs has become an attractive target and of tremendous scientific and biomedical interest in the health care research as the lungs is capable of absorbing pharmaceuticals either for local deposition or for systemic delivery. The respiratory epithelial cells have a prominent role in the regulation of airway tone and the production of airway lining fluid. In this respect, growing attention has been given to the potential of a pulmonary route as a non-invasive administration for systemic and local delivery of therapeutic agents, because the high permeability and large absorptive surface area of lungs, (approximately 70-140m^2 in adult humans having extremely thin absorptive mucosal membrane) and good blood supply. The alveolar epithelium of the distal lung has been shown to be an absorption site for most of the therapeutics and various macromolecules. Further advantages over peroral applications are the comparatively low enzymatic activity, rapid absorption of drug and the capacity for overcoming first-pass metabolism. It has been already reported that, the local respiratory disorders and some systemic diseases can be well treated by delivering the drugs through pulmonary route. This includes the topical treatment of asthma, local infectious diseases, pulmonary hypertension, systemic use of insulin, human growth hormones, and oxytocin. Presently this is true for many biotherapeutics currently injected intravenously, such as growth hormones, glucagons, or insulin, each of which could possibly be delivered to humans by inhalation were the efficiency of inhalation therapy is greater.

Transepithelial Transport of Drugs

The human respiratory system is a complex organ system having a close structure-function relationships. This system mainly comprise of two vital regions: the conducting airways and the respiratory region. The airway is further divided into nasal cavity, and associated sinuses, and the nasopharynx, oropharynx, larynx, trachea, bronchi, and bronchioles. The respiratory region consists of respiratory bronchioles, alveolar ducts, and alveolar sacs. The transepithelial transport of drugs along the respiratory epithelium from these two regions is characterized by large quantitative differences. The drug transport in upper airways is limited due to smaller surface area and lower regional blood flow. Furthermore, this region possesses a high filtering capacity and removes up to 90% of delivered drug particles. Further inhaled substances deposit on the mucus layer, which coats the walls of the conducting airways. Mucus is secreted by goblet and submucosal gland cells and forms a gel-like film consisting of mucin as the major component. Ciliated cells are also present in this region they cause propulsion of mucus upward and out of the lung, thus the lung will be cleared of foreign substances. In contrast, the smaller airway and alveolar space accounts for more than 95% of the lung's surface area and is directly connected to the systemic circulation via the pulmonary circulation. Apart from this, morphology of the major alveolar epithelial cells, the pulmonary blood-gas barrier system, and size of pores and tight junction depth of alveolar and endothelial cells govern the transepithelial drug transport.

Mechanisms and Ways of Pulmonary Drug Administration

Through pulmonary route, the drug can be administered by two primary modes: first, intranasal administration, and second, oral inhalative administration. By oral inhalative administration far better results can be expected as it allows administering very small particles with a concentration loss of only 20% in comparison with 85% by nasal route. Oral inhalative administration can again be classified as intratracheal instillation and intratracheal inhalation. In the intratracheal instillation, a small amount of drug solution or dispersion is delivered into the lungs by a special syringe. This provides a fast and quantifiable method of drug delivery to the lungs. The localized drug deposition is achieved with a comparatively small absorptive area. So, the instillation process is much simple, non-expensive, and has non-uniform drug distribution. However, intratracheal instillation is not a physiological route for application, and results obtained from these studies may not be transferable to aerosol applications in humans. On the contrary, inhalation method uses aerosol technique by which we can get more uniform distribution with great penetration. However, this method is more costly and difficult to measure the exact dose in lungs. The deposition of drug by aerosol administration in the pulmonary airway mainly takes place by three mechanisms:- gravitational sedimentation, inertial impaction, and diffusion. If the drug particle size is comparatively bigger, then, deposition takes place by first two mechanisms where, either sedimentation occurs due to gravitational force or inertial impaction occurs due to hyperventilation. When the particle size is smaller they deposit mainly by diffusion mechanism, which in turn is based on the Brownian motion. Other factors affecting deposition are size of the particles or droplets, the geometry, the surface electrical charges, shape of the particulate matter and the mass median aerodynamic diameter.

Drug Delivery Devices

For pulmonary route, drug delivery devices play an important role equivalent to that of formulation aspects. It is difficult to administer a formulation through pulmonary route without suitable drug delivery devices. The drug delivery devices are (1) Metered dose Inhalers, (2) Dry Powder Inhalers, and (3) Nebulizers: Jet Nebulizers, Ultrasonic Nebulizers.

1. ***Metered Dose Inhalers (MDI)*:** A metered-dose inhaler (MDI) is a complex system designed to provide a fine mist of medicament, generally with an aerodynamic particle size of less than 5 microns, for inhalation directly to the airways. They consist of a micronized form of the drug in a propellant under pressure with surfactants to prevent clumping of drug crystals. When the device is actuated, the propellant gets exposed to atmospheric pressure, which leads to aerosolization of the drug. As it travels through the air, the aerosol warms up leading to evaporation of the propellant that reduces the particle size to the desirable range. The fraction of drug to the airways ranges from 5 to 15 %. It is used for treatment of respiratory diseases such as asthma and chronic obstructive pulmonary diseases. The drug can be given in the form of suspension or solution. Many metered-dose inhalers are now formulated using hydro fluoroalkane instead of chlorofluorocarbons (CFC's) as the propellants for the asthma medication. The breath-activated metered-dose inhaler releases a mist of medicine when a person inhales. This type of inhaler has less propellant than a metered-dose inhaler. Example Autohaler®.

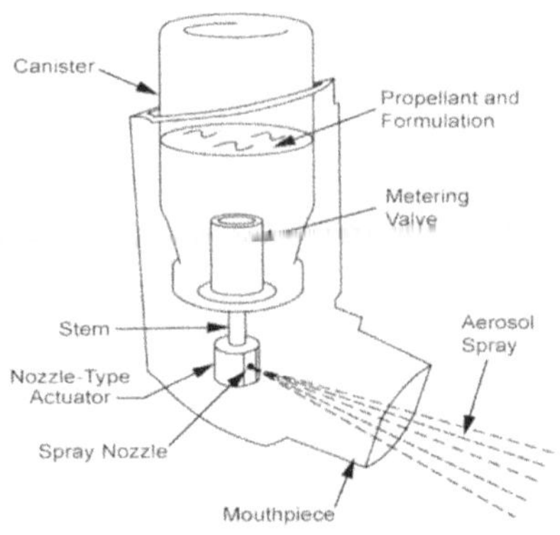

Fig.8.2 A pressurized metered dose inhaler.

Frequently spacers are used in MDIs. A spacer is a device used to increase the ease of administering aerosolized medication from a MDI. It adds space in the form of a tube or chamber between the mouth and canister of medication. Most spacers have a one-way valve that allows the person to inhale the medication while inhaling and exhaling normally; these are often referred to as valved holding chambers (VHC). AeroChamber®, InspirEase® and Volumatic® are examples of a spacer.

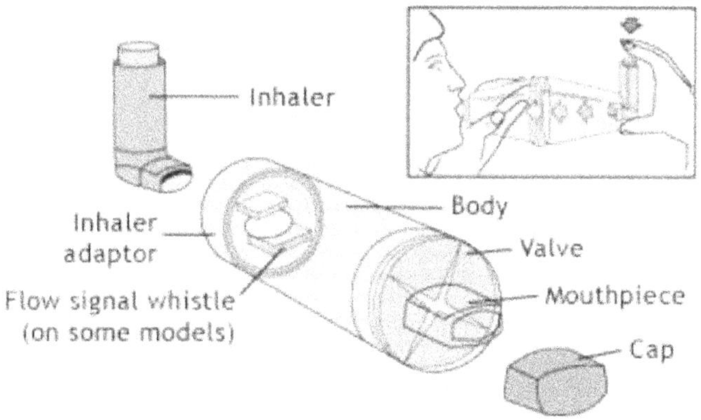

Fig.8.4 MDI with spacer.

Using an inhaler without a spacer requires coordinating several actions in a definite order (pressing down on the inhaler, breathing in deeply as soon as the medication is released, holding breath & exhaling). Not everyone is able to do it perfectly. Use of a spacer, particularly a valved holding chamber, avoids such timing issues. Valved holding chambers are particularly useful for children, people with severe shortness of breath, and those with cognitive impairment (elderly). Spacers slow down the speed of the aerosol erupting from the inhaler, facilitating greater amount of drug entering into the lungs.

1. ***Dry Powder Inhalers (DPIs)***

New inhalers have been developed because of difficulty of using the conventional metered dose inhaler (MDI) and because of the impending ban on CFC's. DPIs are bolus drug delivery devices that contain solid drug in a dry powder mix that is fluidized when the patient inhales. Dry powder formulations either contain the active drug alone or have a carrier powder (e.g. lactose) mixed with the drug to increase flow properties of drug. DPIs are a widely accepted inhaled delivery dosage form, particularly in Europe, where they are currently used by approximately 40% of asthma patients. Lack of requirement of propellant is an advantage of DPIs over MDIs. Dry powder inhalers (DPI's) in general are easier to use than the MDI and cause fewer irritant effects. Unlike the MDI few patients develop a poor inhalation technique with continued use of DPI's. Comparisons of multidose DPI's have shown that they achieve a similar degree of bronchodilatation to the MDI. The fraction of the drug delivered to the site of action by a DPI varies from 9% to 30% and varies among different commercially available products (Fig 8.5).

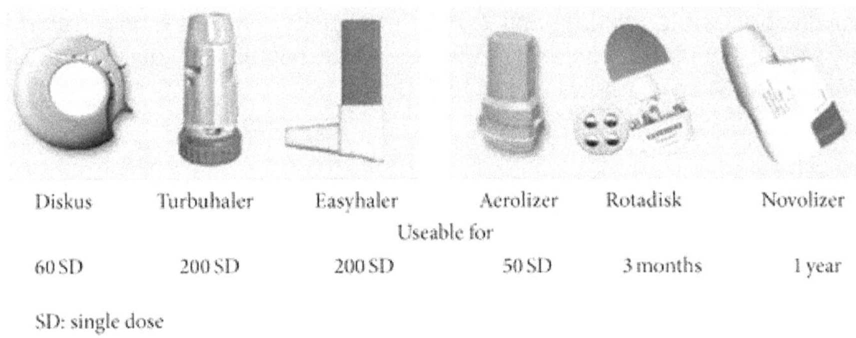

Fig.8.5 Examples of DPIs.

Currently, there are two types of DPIs,

***Unit-Dose Devices*:** Single-dose powder inhalers are devices in which a powder contained capsule is placed in a holder. The capsule is opened within the device and the powder is inhaled.

***Multi-dose Devices*:** Multi-dose device uses a circular disk that contains either four or eight powder doses on a single disk. The doses are maintained in separate aluminium blister reservoirs until just before inspiration.

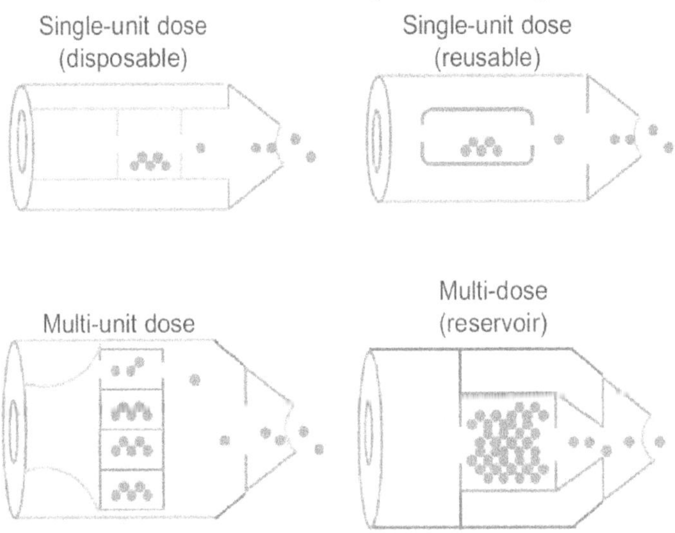

Fig.8.6 Diagrammatic representation of Single and Multiunit dose devices for DPI.

DPI's cannot be used with spacers; this may be a disadvantage in patients who inhale large doses of steroids.

Many conventional techniques have been reported to produce DPI formulations. However, these methods have number of limitations, such as particle size, size distribution, shape and poor control over powder crystallinity. These problems can be rectified by specialized milling techniques. Jet-milling of drug under nitrogen gas with new nanojet milling instrument is the most suitable method for creating nanoparticles meant for pulmonary drug delivery. Here, some of the important techniques are discussed in brief (Table 8.3).

Table 8.3 Techniques for particle engineering for pulmonary delivery.

Technique	Process highlight	Features/ applications
Spray drying	In this process, the feed solution is supplied at room temperature and pumped to the nozzle where it is atomized by the nozzle gas. The atomized solution is then dried by preheated drying gas in a special chamber to remove water moisture from the system, thus forming dry particles.	Efficiently produces respirable colloidal particles in the solid state above 2-μm size. Results in uniform particle morphology. Suitable for thermolabile materials, such as proteins and peptides, because mechanical high- energy input is avoided in this process. Better control on particle formation and hence can be easily translated to large scale production.

Table *contd...*

Technique	Process highlight	Features/ [illegible]
Spray freeze drying method	It involves spraying the drug solution into liquid nitrogen as a freezing medium followed by lyophilization.	Produces lig[illegible] particles and high fine particle fraction with improved aerosol performance and almost 100% yield. Thermolabile proteins and peptides, such as insulin and plasmid DNA can be formulated as DPI. Is an expensive process.
Supercritical fluid technology	The basic feature of this process is the controlled crystallization of drugs from dispersion in supercritical fluids (CO_2). Used for production of microparticles, nanoparticles, liposomes, and inclusion complexes.	Used for the production of particulate pulmonary drug delivery systems containing proteins and peptides. Used to improve the formulation properties of certain drug candidates.
Solvent precipitation method	Involves sono crystallization and micro-precipitation by opposing liquid jets. Inhalable	Crystalline drug particles with narrow size distribution could be prepared by direct controlled crystallization. Recently,

Table *contd....*

	particles can be produced by rapid precipitation from aqueous solutions using anti-solvents.	ultrasonic radiation has been applied to control the precipitation. Various anti-asthmatic drugs are prepared using the sonocrystallization technique.
Double emulsion/solvent evaporation technique	Method involves preparation of oil/water emulsion with subsequent removal of the oil phase through evaporation. The organic solvent diffuses out of the polymer phase and into the aqueous phase, and is then evaporated, forming drug loaded polymeric nanoparticles.	By this method, biodegradable polymers have been intensively investigated as carriers for respiratory solid drug nanoparticles.
Particle replication in non-wetting templates (PRINT)	Is top-down particle fabrication technique. This technique is able to produce uniform-sized organic micro and nanoparticles with complete control of size, shape, and surface functionality.	Helps in loading of small organic therapeutics, proteins, peptides, oligonucleotides, siRNA contrast agents, radiotracers, and flurophores.

2. ***Nebulizers***: Nebulizers are widely used as aerosolize drug solutions or suspensions for delivery to the respiratory tract and are particularly useful for the treatment of hospitalized patients. The device delivers the drug in the form of mist. Pressurized room air is used to create a mist of the drug solution, which is inhaled for approximately 5-10 minutes. To deliver a drug by nebulization, the drug must first be dispersed in a liquid (usually aqueous) medium. After application of a dispersing force (either a jet of gas or ultrasonic waves), the drug particles are contained within the aerosol droplets, which are then inhaled. There are two basic types: (1) air jet, and (2) ultrasonic nebulizer. In air jet nebulizer compressed air is forced through an orifice, an area of low pressure is formed where the air jet exists. A liquid may be withdrawn from a perpendicular nozzle (the Bernoulli's effect) to mix with the air jet to form droplets. A battle within the nebulizer is often used to facilitate the formation of aerosol cloud. Carrier gas (oxygen) may be used to generate the air jet.

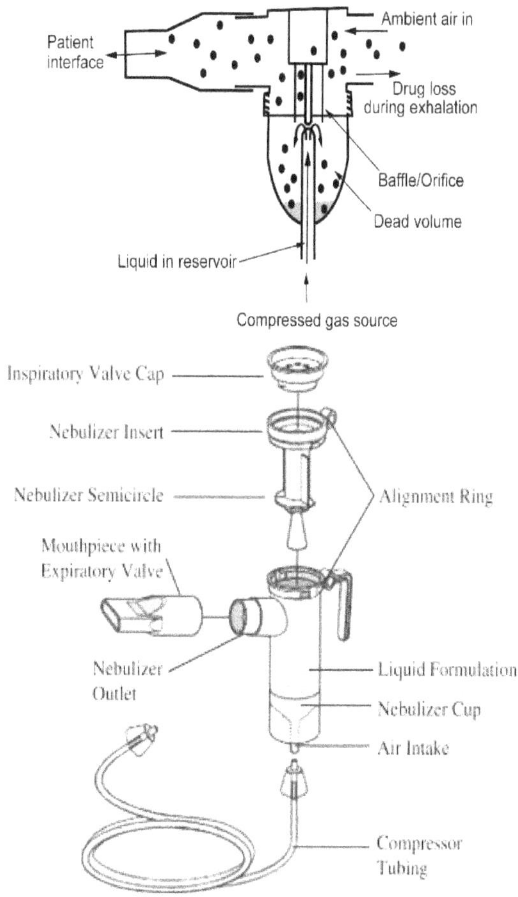

Fig.8.7 Jet nebulizer: (a) flow diagram of working principle, (b) whole assembly.

Jet nebulizers are based on the venturi principle, whereas ultrasonic nebulizers use the converse piezoelectric effect to convert alternating current to high-frequency acoustic energy. There are several advantages to jet nebulization, including the fact that effective use requires only simple, tidal breathing, and that dose modification and dose compounding are possible. Disadvantages include the duration of treatment time and equipment size.

In ultrasonic nebulizers, ultrasound waves are formed in an ultrasonic nebulizer chamber by a ceramic piezoelectric crystal that vibrates when electrically excited. It utilizes ultrasonic power in order to produce micron-scaled inhalable particles; ultrasonic nebulizers break down the drug solution into small droplets via piezoelectric vibration. There is a baffle within the inhaler, as well as jet nebulizers, to remove large droplets and return them to the main chamber of device (Fig. 8.8).

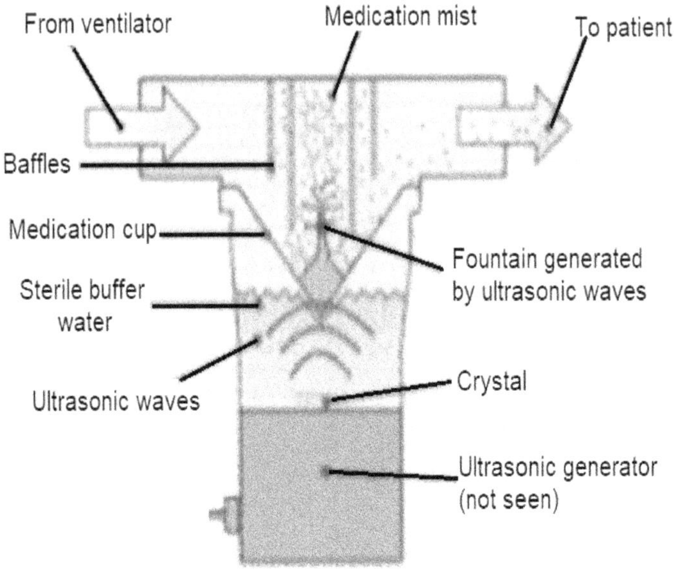

Fig.8.8 Diagrammatic representation of working principle of ultrasonic nebulizer.

Ultrasonic nebulizers produce a more uniform particle size than jet nebulizers, but are less widely used due to cost. Up to 10 times the amount of drug is required in a nebulizer to produce the same degree of bronchodilation achieved by a metered-dose inhaler.

Box 2

Sodium Chloride Nebulizer Solution

1. It is used to thin mucus so it can be taken from the body by coughing.
2. It is used to mix with other drugs for use in a special machine (**nebulizer**).

Applications of Pulmonary Delivery

1. Treatment of chronic diseases through pulmonary route: Antitubercular chemotherapy is mainly due to multidrug administration for longer period, which causes patient non-compliances in addition to high cost of treatment and systemic toxicity. These reasons along with many other drawbacks associated with conventional methods of tuberculosis treatment demands the development of novel lung-targeted drug delivery approaches. Antitubercular drugs have been successfully entrapped and delivered in biodegradable and biocompatible polymers.

2. Delivery of peptides: Systemic delivery of insulin.
3. Glucocortcoids such as budesonide, triamcinolone acetonide, and fluticasone, have a high degree of hepatic first-pass inactivation can be administered by inhalation in patients with asthma allergic rhinitis and advanced chronic obstructive pulmonary disease.
4. Nebulizers are a very suitable method of treatment for lung infestations of yeast, fungi or bacteria as they fill the air with a very fine mist of macromolecules of essential oils.

8.2 TIMELINE

1025 AD	The Persian physician, Avicenna described nasal inhalation as an administration mode in his influential medical encyclopedia entitled *Canon of Medicine*,
600 BC	The inhalation of therapeutic aerosols for the treatment of asthma is described in the writings of the influential Indian physicians, Charaka and Sushruta,
1764	Inhalation of balsamic vapors for the treatment of asthma was prescribed
1778	First inhaler device based on clever valve design.
1852	The first known DPI was invented by Boston physician Ira Warren
1890s	Wyeth Pencil Inhaler was commercialized as a portable and convenient treatment of various ailments, including catarrh, bronchitis, and croup
1899	A patent by Helbing and Pertch described a propellant-based liquid aerosol generator that used ethyl or methyl chloride (now considered toxic via inhalation) as the propellant to atomize the liquid.
1930	A nebulizer, the Pneumostat, using compressed air to power the atomization, was developed in Germany.
1956	Riker Laboratories, Inc., (now 3 M Drug Delivery Systems) introduced the first pressurized metered dose inhaler (MDI).
Early 80s	Introduction of nasal route as a promising systemic delivery alternative to other conventional drug delivery routes
1980s	MDIs had become the preferred delivery system for the delivery of therapeutic aerosols to the lung. Spray drying technique was explored as an alternative means of producing fine particles for pulmonary delivery.

1990s	Spray freeze drying method was explored for pharmaceutical applications.
Late 19th Century	Glass nebulizers were invented as the first inhaler devices
1973 to 2013	Many US patent on "metered dose inhaler" or "dry powder inhaler" described.

8.3 CHAPTER AT A GLANCE

Term	Description
Mucociliary clearance	Mucus continuously produced by goblet cells traps inhaled particulate and infectious debris while the propulsive force generated by ciliated cells transports the mucus towards the nasopharynx and the gastrointestinal tract for elimination
Factors affecting nasal absorption	Physicochemical properties of drugs, Nasal effect, Delivery effect.
Nasal dosage forms	Drops, sprays, gels, powders
Methods used to facilitate nasal absorpton	Nasal enzyme inhibitors, permeation enhancers, prodrug approach, structural modification, particulate drug delivery.
Rhinyle catheter and squirt tube	Catheters are used to deliver the drops to a specified region of nasal cavity easily
Squeeze bottles	These are smooth plastic bottles with a simple jet outlet. On pressing the plastic bottle the air inside the container is pressed out of the small nozzle, thereby atomizing a certain volume. Generally used for decongestants
Metered dose pump sprays	Used to produce nasal sprays, or nasal mists, for the nasal delivery of a drug (s) for local or systemic use.
Powder sprayers	These are devices with a compressible compartment to provide a pressure that when released create a plume of powder particles similar to that of a liquid spray
Nasal insufflators	These are devices consisting of a mouthpiece and a nosepiece that are fluidly connected. Delivery occurs when the subject exhales into the mouthpiece to close the velum, and the airflow carries the powder particles into the nose through the device nosepiece.

Table *contd...*

Term	Description
Nasal gels	Nasal gels are high-viscosity thickened solutions or suspensions for nasal administration
Pulmonary drug delivery modes	Intranasal administration and oral inhalative administration
Metered dose inhaler	A metered-dose inhaler (MDI) is a complex system designed to provide a fine mist of medicament, generally with an aerodynamic particle size of less than 5 microns, for inhalation directly to the airways.
Spacer	A spacer is a device used to increase the ease of administering aerosolized medication from a MDI
Dry powder inhalers (DPIs)	DPIs are bolus drug delivery devices that contain solid drug in a dry powder mix that is fluidized when the patient inhales.
Nebulizer	Nebulizers are devices used with a facemask or mouthpiece to deliver the drug from a reservoir solution. They are of two types: Jet nebulizer and ultrasonic nebulizer.

EXERCISES

Multiple choice Questions

1. Select the incorrect answer. Pulmonary drug delivery is a significant non-invasive drug delivery route as it
   (a) Provides large absorptive surface area
   (b) Has large number of enzymes
   (c) Is rich blood supply
   (d) Has extremely thin mucosa
2. Which of the following is not an advantage of nasal drug delivery route?
   (a) Drug degradation that is observed in the gastrointestinal tract is absent.
   (b) Hepatic first pass metabolism is avoided.
   (c) Rapid drug absorption and slow onset of action can be achieved.
   (d) Improves bioavailability of small and large drug molecules

3. Which of the following nasal region serves as efficient absorption surface for topically applied drugs?
   (a) Respiratory zone (b) Nasopharynx
   (c) Vestibular region (d) Nasal cavity
4. Mucociliary clearance is not dependent on
   (a) Function of the cilia (b) Allergens
   (c) Stimulatory drugs (d) Size of nasal cavity
5. The drug candidates having maximum potential for nasal delivery are those belonging to
   (a) BCS class I (b) BCS class II
   (c) BCS class III (d) BCS class IV
6. Identify the devices for nasal powder dosage form
   (a) Powder sprayers
   (b) Breath actuated inhalers
   (c) Nasal insufflators
   (d) All of above
7. Which of the following is not a characteristic of MDI?
   (a) Produces a fine mist of medication
   (b) Produces aerodynamic particle size of < 5 microns
   (c) Uses propellant
   (d) Actuated by breath
8. Which of the following is example of spacer used in MDIs?
   (a) AeroChamber (b) InspirEase
   (c) Volumatic (d) All of the above
9. Pick the incorrect advantage of DPIs over MDIs
   (a) Does not require propellant
   (b) Achieve higher degree of bronchodilation
   (c) Easier to use
   (d) Cause fewer irritant effects
10. Ultrasonic nebulizers break down the drug solution into small droplets via
   (a) Venturi principle (b) Valve assembly
   (c) Piezoelectric vibration (d) Oscillation

Short Answer Questions

1. With the help of neat diagram explain the working of pressure based MDI for pulmonary delivery.
2. What are the disadvantages of nasal drug delivery?
3. Enlist the methods used for making particles for DPI. Explain any two.
4. What are the criteria for selecting drug candidate for nasal delivery?
5. Give the applications of pulmonary drug delivery.

Long Answer Questions

1. Explain the factors affecting nasal drug absorption.
2. Give descriptive account of nebulizers for pulmonary delivery.
3. In context to nasal drug delivery devices give an account of Rhinyle catheter, squeeze bottle and
4. Explain the following pulmonary drug delivery devices: (i) Metered dose inhalers, and (ii) Nebulizers.
5. Give detailed account of Dry powder inhalers used for nasal and pulmonary routes.

Answer Key MCQs

(1) – (b), (2) – (c), (3) – (a), (4) – (d), (5) – (a), (6) – (d), (7) – (d), (8) – (d), (9) – (b), (10) – (c).

BIBLIOGRAPHY

1. Groneberg DA, Witt C, Wagner U, Chung KF, Fischer A. Fundamentals of pulmonary drug delivery. Resp Med. 2003;97:382–87.
2. Scheuch G, Siekmeier R. Novel approaches to enhance pulmonary delivery of proteins and peptide. J Physio Pharmacol. 2007;58:615–25.
3. Chan HK. Inhalation drug delivery devices and emerging technologies. Expert Opin Ther Patents. 2003;13:1333–43.
4. www.aptar.com

Chapter 9

TARGETED DRUG DELIVERY

♦ **LEARNING OBJECTIVES** ♦

***After completing this lesson, the Reader should be able to understand*:**

- **Basic concepts of drug targeting.**
- **Approaches for drug targeting.**
- **Advantages and disadvantages of targeted drug delivery.**
- **Preparations and applications of various carriers for targeted drug delivery.**

9.1 INTRODUCTION

It is of paramount importance in therapeutics to address the issues of the drug development involving the delivery of specific drugs to their site of action in therapeutically acceptable doses. Though, high throughput screening has led to the discovery of several new drug molecules ranging from small molecule drugs to macromolecules like proteins and peptides; the physicochemical properties of the drug candidates, their unapproachability and/or availability at a sub-optimal concentration at the target sites limit their successful clinical application. To overcome these hurdles, drug delivery systems (DDS) are employed which could either be a formulation or a device that facilitates the administration of a drug to the body with improved pharmacokinetics, efficacy, and overall safety. Targeting the drugs and the drug delivery systems involves the improvement of the specificity of the system towards the pharmacologically relevant target in the body. Targeted drug delivery systems (TDDS) involve the administration of the DDS to the patient, delivery of the DDS at the target (pathological or biological) site, release of the active ingredients in/around the target and avoiding non-specific toxicity in normal cells. The above concept of targeted drugs or "magic bullet" was first conceived by Paul Ehrlich in the early twentieth century and since then several strategies have developed to achieve targeting.

An ideal targeted drug delivery system is supposed to perform the following functions:

- Facilitate the therapeutic substance to reach the site of action from the site of administration where the target site can be an organ, tissue, cell, or even specific cell organelles.
- Release the therapeutic payload in its active form in/around the target site presenting effective therapeutic levels at the site of action.
- Protect the payload from the detrimental environmental factors such as pH, enzymes, etc.
- Avoid toxicity or adverse reactions of the payload on non-specific normal cells and facilitating the administration of lower doses to achieve clinical benefits.

Today, the pharmaceutical scientist has several options to render the DDS for carrying out the above-mentioned functions:

- Direct targeting to site of action, e.g., topical applications for skin diseases.
- Use of external stimuli, e.g., ultrasound.
- Chemical modification of the drug to make its physicochemical properties ideal for the delivery which includes the prodrug approach.
- Use of nanocarriers like liposomes, polymeric micelles, polymeric nanoparticles, solid lipid nanoparticles which can be functionalized further with the attachment of targeting ligands, antibodies, etc.

9.2 BASIC CONCEPTS OF DRUG TARGETING

The drugs or drug carrier systems can be divided into two broad categories for the targeting potential.

(i) **Passive targeting:** This is otherwise called as physiology-based targeting because it is based on the natural physiology of the human body. Hormones, neurotransmitters, growth factors, etc. have a natural tendency to go and target the receptors at their sites of action, e.g., insulin and insulin receptors. This concept can be applied to the drugs too. Accumulation of drugs/drug-carrier systems at the intended site of action by the action of physicochemical and physiological factors is called as passive targeting. Passive targeting also benefits from the presence of internal stimuli, such as pH difference (e.g., low pH in the tumor microenvironment), redox systems (e.g., exploiting high glutathione in cancer), etc in the diseased tissues.

Certain tissues under diseased conditions present opportunities in terms of modified physiologies which can be exploited by passively targeting nanocarriers. A presence of leaky vasculature with large gaps in the blood vessel's epithelial layers has been observed in cases of inflamed tissues in inflammatory bowel disease and inflammatory rheumatoid arthritis and in tumor tissues. In such areas with increased vascular permeability, particles like micelles, liposomes, and other drug carriers with particle size ranging from 10-500 nm can extravasate and accumulate inside the interstitial space. If these carriers are loaded with a certain drug, they can bring these drugs into the "leaky" zones where the drug can be released as a result of the normal degradation of the carrier. Such spontaneous and passive drug delivery is also called as an 'enhanced permeability and retention' (EPR) effect. The evident requirement for this type of targeted delivery is that the drug carrier used should demonstrate the ability to circulate long in the blood to provide a sufficient level of target accumulation.

The nanocarriers are largely subjected to clearance by the reticuloendothelial system (RES) comprising of macrophages and mononuclear phagocytes. This fact can be used to passively target the macrophages and even lymph nodes and spleen to treat infections that affect the RES (e.g., leishmaniasis and malaria). Often modifications (e.g., attachment of polyethylene glycol; PEG) are made on nanocarriers to make them long-circulating, avoiding the RES and granting them time to accumulate at target sites in high amounts (long-circulating nanocarriers). However, passive targeting has a great potential for unintended organ accumulation as a major limitation in this strategy.

(ii) Active targeting: Active targeting is also called as ligand-mediated targeting. Ligands, which are specific to surface substances or receptors that are overexpressed in damaged organs, tissues, cells, or subcellular domains should be chosen properly for the intended purpose. Compared to passive targeting, this targeting strategy has a superior control on accurate drug delivery. Appropriate modifications and functionalization on the drugs or drug carriers afford them affinity towards specific receptors/markers on cells, tissues, or organs. Factors such as the disease, the intended target organ, and a larger presence of targetable components on the target organ/cell (e.g., transferrin receptors in the tumor) than in normal cells are taken into consideration while deciding on the targeting moiety to be attached to the therapeutic substances. Modifications on the drugs or drug carriers can involve the use of ligands such as peptides, antibodies, sugars, lectins, etc. Thus, on the administration to the body, the targeting moieties will enable the drug/drug-carriers to efficiently reach only the intended sites of action and avoid non-specific accumulations and related side effects.

Active targeting can further be divided into three different targeting levels.

First-order targeting: This is the distribution of the drug to capillary beds of target sites- organ or tissue, for example, in case of lymphatic tissue, peritoneal cavity, pleural cavity, cerebral ventricles, eyes, joints, etc.

Second-order targeting: This is the targeting of drugs to specific sites such as the tumor cells, for example, to Kupffer cells in the liver.

Third-order targeting: It is the type of drug targeting wherein the drug is intracellularly localized at the target site via endocytosis or through the receptor-based ligand-mediated entry.

9.3 APPROACHES FOR DRUG TARGETING

The drug targeting approaches may be studied under physical targeting, chemical targeting, and biological targeting.

(i) **Physical targeting:** Physical targeting refers to systems that localize therapeutic substances to the target site owing to their size, composition, and structure that are not specifically designed for the biological receptor. This approach of targeting is based on the non-specific accumulation of payloads in a certain area of the body compared to other regions. Sometimes, external stimuli are also applied to localize the therapeutic agent to the target site. The external stimuli include applied heat, light, magnetic field, ultrasound, etc.

(ii) **Chemical targeting:** Chemical targeting refers to the localization of the therapeutic payload to the target site through site-specific prodrugs. Sometimes, chemical and enzymatic reactions allow for drug localization.

(iii) **Biological targeting:** Biological targeting refers to localization of the payload to the target site through the utilization of antibodies, peptides, proteins, etc that have an affinity to the receptor sites, organs, or other biological targets in a specific manner.

9.4 ADVANTAGES AND DISADVANTAGES

The various advantages of targeted drug delivery are as follows:

- It facilitates simplified drug administration protocols.
- Maximize the therapeutic index.
- The reduction in the dose needed to achieve therapeutic benefit and subsequent reduction in the cost of clinical management.

- Drug concentration at the desired target site can be sharply increased without distribution to other non-target sites (healthy tissues) leading to minimization of overall toxicities and adverse effects associated with drug therapy.

The various disadvantages of targeted drug delivery are outlined below.

- Rapid clearance of targeted systems.
- Immune reactions against intravenous administered carrier systems.
- Insufficient localization of targeted systems into tumor cells.
- Diffusion and redistribution of released drugs.
- Need sophisticated technology for the design of targeted systems.
- Specialized skills may be needed for manufacturing, storage, and administration.
- Stability of few targeted drug delivery systems are often very challenging.
- Targeted drug delivery systems are usually expensive compared to conventional dosage forms.

9.5 LIPOSOMES

Since long nanocarriers have been used for targeting of drugs. The various nanocarriers include nanoparticles (NPs), dendrimers, liposomes, niosomes, solid lipid nanoparticles, micelles, cyclodextrins, monoclonal antibodies, etc. Depending on the desired application or targeted site, these nanocarriers can be administrated through oral, topical, and parenteral routes. The following sections briefly discuss about liposomes for targeted drug delivery.

The term liposome is derived from Greek words: 'Lipos' meaning fat and 'Soma' meaning body. Liposomes are colloidal, concentric bilayered lipid vesicles where the aqueous compartment is entirely enclosed by a bilayer membrane, usually composed of lipids of either natural or synthetic origin. The size of liposomes varies in the range of 50-1000 nm for drug delivery applications. The essential components of liposomes include phospholipids (mainly phosphatidylcholine) and cholesterol where cholesterol acts as a fluidity buffer. Solutes in the core, such as drugs, cannot overcome the hydrophobic barrier. However, the bilayer allows for the absorption of hydrophobic molecules and therefore, liposomes are known to be amphiphilic carriers. Liposomes differ in composition, size, number of layers, etc. These can either have a single bilayer, known as "unilamellar" or multiple bilayers, termed as "multilamellar". Unilamellar vesicles are further grouped into small unilamellar vesicles (SUVs) and large unilamellar vesicles (LUVs) according to their size. Drugs held and delivered by liposomes have significantly improved pharmacokinetic properties such as the therapeutic index.

Interestingly, these lipoidal vesicles improve the pharmacokinetic properties of few drugs via the reduction in drug elimination and hence, increasing circulation time. For this, liposomes are coated with polyethylene glycol, besides other polymers, resulting in an increased half-life. The encapsulation of drugs by liposomes leads to the prevention of their untimely degradation. These can amplify target-specificity once they are associated with ligands or antibodies.

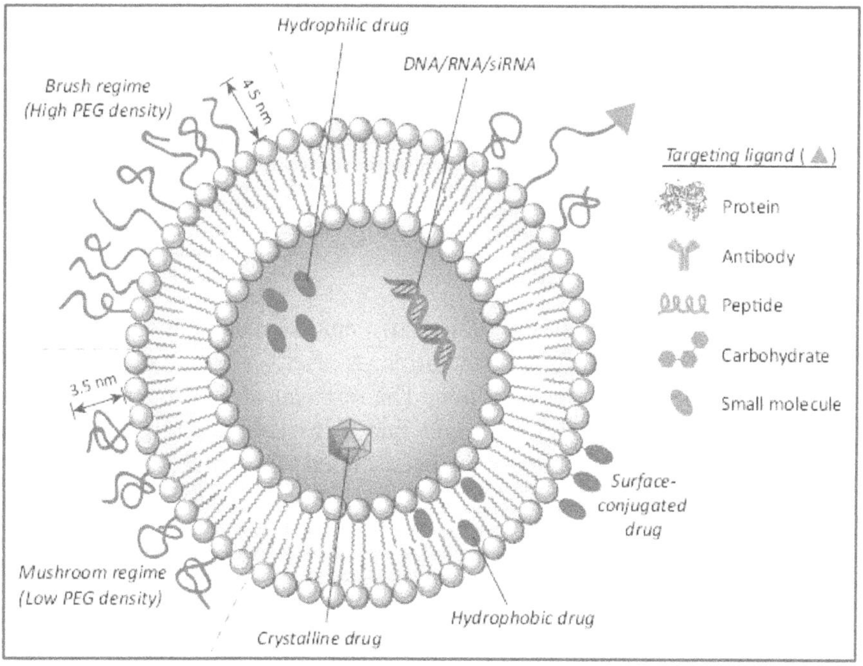

Fig.9.1 Schematic diagram of a liposome. Liposomes can be surface functionalized through PEGylation and to promote receptor-mediated endocytosis by using targeting ligands such as antibodies, peptides, proteins, carbohydrates, and various other small molecules. Polyethylene glycol (PEG) density determines its structure at the liposome surface, with densities below 9% adopting a mushroom-like globular structure and those above 9% adopting a more rigid, extended, brush-like morphology. Adapted from reference [1].

(i) Preparation of liposomes: Various methods have been reported for fabrication of liposomes. The recently reported methods can be categorized as conventional, which mostly involve approaches that are easy to use at laboratory scale, and novel methods that appear to be more useful for up-scale production but require some special equipment.

Conventional methods-

The preparation of liposomes share the common fundamental steps like (1) lipids dissolution in organic solvents, (2) drying of the resultant solution,

(3) hydration of dried lipid (using various aqueous media), and (4) separation of the formed liposomes. The various conventional methods for liposome fabrication discussed as follows.

Film hydration

This method is also termed as Bangham method. It is the simplest and oldest method used in liposome technology. In this method, lipids are firstly dissolved in a suitable organic solvent and dried down to yield a thin film at the bottom of the flask. The obtained lipid film is hydrated using an appropriate aqueous medium to produce liposomal dispersion. The hydration condition affects the structural organization of the formed liposomes. Gentle hydration of the lipid film forms giant unilamellar vesicles (GULV), whereas hash hydration gives rise to multilamellar vesicles (MLV) with poor size homogeneity. The most commonly used sizing methods include sonication that leads to the production of small unilamellar vesicles (SUV).

Reverse phase evaporation

This method involves the formation of w/o emulsion using the hydrophilic and lipophilic components of the formulation. A brief sonication of this mixture is required for system homogenization. The removal of the organic phase under reduced pressure yields a milky gel that turns subsequently into liposomal suspension. The liposomes can be isolated from the dispersion using centrifugation, or dialysis.

Solvent injection

This method involves a quick injection of the lipid solution (in ethanol or diethyl ether) into an aqueous medium. The process is performed either at room or at a higher temperature (e.g., 60°C), depending on whether the organic solvent is water-miscible or not. The liposomes prepared by the solvent injection process are mostly polydispersed and highly contaminated by organic solvents, especially ethanol due to the formation of azeotrope mixture with water.

Detergent removal

In this method, phospholipids are dissolved in an aqueous solution containing detergents at critical micelle concentrations. Subsequent to the removal of detergent, the reaction medium frees individual phospholipid molecules that self-assemble into bilayered structures. Detergent removal is mostly achieved by means of a dialysis bag, polystyrene-based absorbent beads, or gel permeation chromatography. Dilution of the resultant mixture with some appropriate aqueous medium forms the liposomes.

Heating method

This method is very popular due to its green chemistry approach. No organic solvents are used in this method and hence is considered a green environment-friendly method. In this method, lipids are hydrated for 1 hour and heated for another hour above the transition temperature of the phospholipids in the presence of a hydrating agent (glycerin or propylene glycol 3%). When cholesterol is part of the formulation, the reaction medium is heated up to 100°C because of its high melting point. The resultant liposomes can be readily used without any further sterilization treatments because the processing condition already uses a high temperature. In addition, there is no need for further removal of the hydrating agents employed, since these represent physiologically acceptable ingredients that are well-established for pharmaceutical applications.

Novel methods of liposome synthesis-

Microfluidic channel method

This novel method makes use of microscopic channels (in the size range of 5–500 µm). In this method, lipids are dissolved in an appropriate organic solvent (ethanol or isopropanol) and the resultant solution is propelled perpendicularly or in the opposite direction to the aqueous medium within the micro-channels. The continuous axial mixing of the organic and aqueous solutions leads to liposomes formation because of local diffusion of phospholipids in the aqueous phase, which encourages the self-assembly process. The disadvantages of these methods include the imperative use of organic solvent and drastic agitation, as well as difficulty for large scale production.

Supercritical fluid method

This is another green synthesis approach. This technique makes use of a supercritical fluid, such as carbon dioxide (CO_2) maintained under supercritical conditions (supercritical temperature and pressure). In this state, CO_2 is an excellent green solvent for lipids. The high-performance liquid chromatography (HPLC) pump provides a continuous flow of the aqueous phase into a view cell that contains the supercritical lipid solution, allowing the phase transition of the dissolved phospholipids. Upon a sudden decrease in pressure, CO_2 gets completely removed and phospholipids self-assemble into a bilayered vesicular system. The supercritical fluidic method affords large unilamellar vesicles (100–1200 nm) with 5-fold higher encapsulation efficiency than the equivalent conventional method.

(ii) **Applications of liposomes:** Liposomes have shown the ability to improve the physicochemical features of the cargoes and facilitates their transport to the sites of interest. The concepts of liposomal encapsulation have been applied in several fields of life science. Liposomes are frequently used for the delivery of drugs, genes, vaccines. Liposomal formulations have been used to address a wide range of pathological conditions through different administration routes, including dermal, transdermal, oral, pulmonary, and parenteral routes. The clinical areas commonly explored in liposome delivery include skin disorders, cancers, and infectious diseases.

Till date, the major applications of liposomes include enhanced drug solubilization (e.g. amphotericin B, minoxidil), protection of sensitive drug molecules (e.g. cytosine arabinose, DNA, RNA, antisense oligonucleotides, ribozymes), enhanced intracellular uptake (all agents, including antineoplastic agents, antibiotics and antivirals) and altered pharmacokinetics and biodistribution of the encapsulated drug.

Liposomal drugs are among the first nanotechnology products used as therapeutic agents to get the approval of the FDA for clinical use. DOXIL® (doxorubicin liposomes) was approved in 1995 as a medicament for Kaposi's sarcoma. Many different liposome formulations of various anticancer agents were shown to be less toxic than the free drug so that most of the medical applications of liposomes that have reached the preclinical stage are in cancer treatment

While usually liposomes are digested by phagocytic cells in the body after intravenous administration, they are ideal vehicles for the targeting of drug molecules into these macrophages. Amphotericin B has been successfully delivered through liposomes for antifungal therapy.

9.6 NIOSOMES

Niosomes are vesicles composed of non-ionic surfactants, amphiphilic compounds with an overall neutral charge. They are liposome-like vesicles formed from the hydrated mixtures of cholesterol, charge inducing substance, and nonionic surfactants such as monoalkyl or dialkyl polyoxyethylene ether. Basically, these vesicles do not form spontaneously. Thermodynamically stable vesicles form only in the presence of proper mixtures of surfactants and charge inducing agents. In this closed bilayer structure, hydrophobic parts of the molecule are oriented away from the aqueous solvent whereas the hydrophilic head comes in contact with the aqueous solvent. It resembles phospholipid vesicles in liposomes and hence, enables entrapment of hydrophilic drugs. The low cost, stability, and resultant ease of storage of nonionic surfactants have led to the exploitation of these compounds as alternatives to phospholipids.

The unique structure of niosomes allows the development of effective novel drug delivery systems with the ability to load both hydrophilic and lipophilic drugs. Hydrophilic drugs and lipophilic drugs are entrapped into the aqueous core and membrane bilayer of noisome respectively. These vesicles can be formulated either unilamellar or multilamellar in structure. Moreover, niosomes possess great stability, cost-effectiveness, and simple methodology for the routine and large-scale production without the use of hazardous solvents.

The advantages of niosomes, compared to other micro and nanoencapsulation technologies can be summarized as follows:

- Compared to phospholipid molecules used in liposome formulations, the surfactants used in the formation of niosomes are more stable;
- Simple methods are required for manufacturing and large–scale production of niosomes;
- As the excipients and types of equipment used for production are not expensive, the noisome manufacturing process is cost-effective;
- Niosomes possess longer shelf-life than liposomes and most other nanocarrier systems;
- Unlike liposomes, they are stable at room temperature and less susceptible to light.

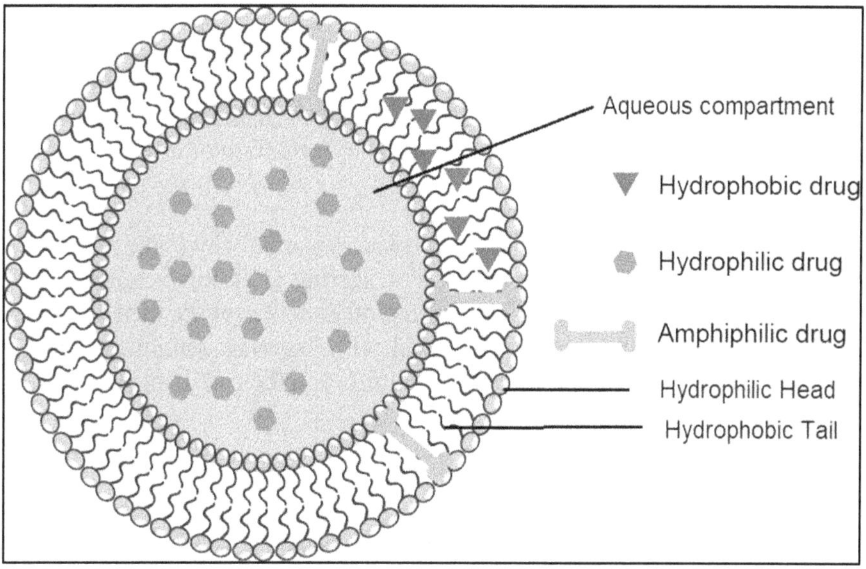

Fig 9.2 Schematic representation of a niosome.

(i) Preparation of niosomes:

Film hydration method

Thin-film hydration method is a simple and well-known preparation method. In this method, the surfactants, cholesterol, and some additives such as chargedmolecules are dissolved in an organic solvent in a round bottomed flask. Then the organic solvent is removed using a rotary vacuum evaporator to obtain thin film on the inside wall of the flask. An aqueous solution of drug is added and the dry film is hydrated above the transition temperature of the surfactant for specified time with constant shaking. Multilamellar niosomes are formed by this method.

Ether injection method

In this method, the surfactants with additives are dissolved in diethyl ether and injected slowly through a needle in an aqueous drug solution maintained at a constant temperature, which is above the boiling point of the organic solvent. The organic solvent is evaporated using a rotary evaporator. During the vaporization the formation of single layered vesicles occurs.

Reverse phase evaporation

In this method, niosomal ingredients are dissolved in a mixture of ether and chloroform and added to aqueous phase containing the drug. The resulting mixture is sonicated in order to form an emulsion and the organic phase is evaporated. Large unilamellar vesicles are formed during the evaporation of the organic solvent.

Microfluidization method

This method is based on submerged jet principle. In this method, the drug and the surfactant fluidized streams interact at ultrahigh velocities, in precisely defined micro channels within the interaction chamber. The high speed impingement and the energy involved leads to formation of niosomes.

Heating method

In this method, surfactants and cholesterol are separately hydrated in buffer and the solution is heated to about 120°C with stirring to dissolve cholesterol. The temperature is reduced and surfactants and other additives are then added to the buffer in which cholesterol is dissolved while stirring continues. Niosomes form at this stage, are left at room temperature, and then are kept at 4-5°C under nitrogen atmosphere until use.

Bubble method

In this method, surfactants, additives, and the buffer are added into a glass flask with three necks. Niosome components are dispersed at 70°C and the dispersion is mixed with homogenizer. After that, immediately the flask is placed in a water bath followed by the bubbling of nitrogen gas at 70°C. Nitrogen gas is passed through a sample of homogenized surfactants resulting in formation of large unilamellar vesicles

(ii) Applications of niosomes:

- Niosomes have been used as drug carriers in the transdermal delivery of many drug candidates.

- Niosomes in sub-micron size are used for parenteral administration.
- Enhanced oral absorption of many drugs (e.g. methotrexate) following niosomal formulation has been reported.
- Niosomes are also used in radiopharmaceutical applications.
- Gene delivery
- Drug targeting to the reticuloendothelial system (RES), blood-brain barrier, etc.
- Antineoplastic treatment-Niosomes can alter the metabolism prolong the circulation and half-life of the drug, decreasing the side effects of the drugs. Niosomes decrease the rate of proliferation of tumors and higher plasma levels by slower elimination.
- Leishmaniasis treatment-Niosomal formulations have been successfully demonstrated activity against Leishmaniasis.
- Niosomes have shown promise for the delivery of peptide drugs protecting them from gastrointestinal adversities.
- Niosomes have been used for studying immune response.
- Niosomes can be used as carriers for hemoglobin.
- These vesicular systems are also used as sustained drug delivery platforms.

9.7 NANOPARTICLES

The National Nanotechnology Initiative (NNI) defines nanoparticles as structures with all three dimensions within the nanoscale (1-100 nm). Pharmaceutical nanoparticles are defined as solid, submicron-sized (less than 100 nm in diameter) drug carrier that may or may not be biodegradable. In drug delivery science relatively large (size >100 nm) nanoparticles may be needed for loading a sufficient amount of drug onto the particles. The drug it self may be size reduced to nanoscale for delivery and are called nanocrystals, nanomorphs or pure drug nanoparticles. But in most of the delivery systems, nanocarriers are used for drug loading and subsequently delivered. These drug loaded nanocarrier systems are also called as nanoparticles. In the present context we consider nanoparticles as polymeric nanoparticles such as nanospheres and nanocapsules. Nanospheres are matrix system in which drug is uniformly dispersed in a polymeric matrix, while nanocapsules are the system in which the drug is surrounded by a unique polymeric membrane.

The submicron size of nanoparticles offers a number of distinct advantages over microparticles, including relatively higher intracellular uptake compared with microparticles. In terms of intestinal uptake, apart from their particle size, nanoparticle nature and charge properties influence the uptake by intestinal epithelia. Uptake of nanoparticles prepared from hydrophobic polymers seems to be higher than that of particles with more hydrophilic surfaces. Generally, nanoparticles based in hydrophobic polymers such as poly(styrene), uncharged and positively charged, provide an affinity to follicle-associated epithelia as well as to absorptive enterocytes, whereas negatively charged poly (styrene) nanoparticles show only low affinity to any type of intestinal tissues. In contrast, nanoparticles based on hydrophilic polymers, negatively charged, show a strong increase in bioadhesive properties and are absorbed by both M cells and absorptive enterocytes. A combination of both nanoparticle surface charges and increased hydrophilicity of the matrix material seem to affect the gastrointestinal uptake in a positive sense.

(i) Preparation of nanoparticles:

The processes involved in nanoparticles preparation are bottom up, top-down, combination and chemical reaction processes. Bottom up process involves precipitation starting from molecular solution. In this process nucleation inhibitors are often used to control the size of the nanoparticles. The top-down process involves comminution of larger particles down to nanoparticles. Combination processes (top-down and bottom up) are also used to further fine tune the particle size. The chemical reaction process (usually polymerization reaction) forms nanoparticles directly.

The various methods of nanoparticle synthesis are discussed as follows.

Emulsification/solvent evaporation

Emulsification-solvent evaporation involves two steps. The first step requires emulsification of the polymer solution into an aqueous phase. During the second step polymer solvent is evaporated, inducing polymer precipitation as nanospheres. A polymer organic solution containing the dissolved drug is dispersed into nanodroplets, using a dispersing agent and high-energy homogenization, in a nonsolvent or suspension medium such as chloroform or ethyl acetate. The polymer precipitates in the form of nanospheres in which the drug is finely dispersed in the polymer matrix network. The solvent is subsequently evaporated by increasing the temperature under pressure or by continuous stirring. However, this method can only be applied to liposoluble drugs, and limitations are imposed by the scale-up of the high energy requirements in homogenization. Frequently used polymers are PLA, PLGA, ethylcellulose, cellulose acetate phthalate, poly(E-caprolactone), etc.

Solvent displacement and interfacial deposition

Solvent displacement and interfacial deposition are similar methods based on spontaneous emulsification of the organic internal phase containing the dissolved polymer into the aqueous external phase. Solvent displacement forms nanospheres or nanocapsules, whereas interfacial deposition forms only nanocapsules. Solvent displacement involves the precipitation of a preformed polymer from an organic solution and the diffusion of the organic solvent in the aqueous medium in the presence or absence of a surfactant. The polymer, generally PLA, is dissolved in a water-miscible solvent of intermediate polarity, leading to the precipitation of nanospheres. This phase is injected into a stirred aqueous solution containing a stabilizer as a surfactant. Polymer deposition on the interface between the water and the organic solvent, caused by fast diffusion of the solvent, leads to the instantaneous formation of a colloidal suspension. To facilitate the formation of colloidal polymer particles during the first step of the procedure, phase separation is performed with a totally miscible solvent that is also a nonsolvent of the polymer. The solvent displacement technique allows the preparation of nanocapsules when a small volume of nontoxic oil is incorporated in the organic phase.

Interfacial deposition is a process used for the production of nanocapsules; however, this is not a polymerization technique but an emulsification/ solidification technique. In interfacial deposition, a fifth compound is introduced, of oil nature, miscible with the solvent of the polymer but immiscible with the mixture. The polymer deposits on the interface between the finely dispersed oil droplets and the aqueous phase, forming nanocapsules. An aqueous solution is used as the dispersing medium. The main difference is that polymers such as PLA are dissolved together with the drug in a solvent mixture (eg, benzyl benzoate, acetone, and phospholipids). This mixture is injected slowly into a stirred aqueous medium, resulting in the deposition of the polymer in the form of nanoparticles. Polymer deposition occurs at the interface between water and benzoyl nanodroplets, forming nanocapsules with a shell-like wall.

Emulsification/solvent diffusion

In this method, the encapsulating polymer is dissolved in a partially watersoluble solvent such as propylene carbonate and saturated with water to ensure the initial thermodynamic equilibrium of both liquids. In fact, to produce the precipitation of the polymer and the consequent formation of nanoparticles, it is necessary to promote the diffusion of the solvent of the dispersed phase by dilution with an excess of water when the organic solvent is partly miscible with water or with another organic solvent in the opposite case. Subsequently, the polymer-water saturated solvent phase is emulsified in an aqueous solution containing stabilizer, leading to solvent diffusion to the external phase and the formation of nanospheres or nanocapsules, according to the oil-to-polymer ratio. Finally, the solvent is eliminated by evaporation or filtration, according to its boiling point.

Salting out with synthetic polymers

Salting -out is based on the separation of a water-miscible solvent from aqueous solution via a salting-out effect. The salting-out procedure can be considered as a modification of the emulsification/solvent diffusion. Polymer and drug are initially dissolved in a solvent such as acetone, which is subsequently emulsified into an aqueous gel containing the salting-out agent (electrolytes, such as magnesium chloride, calcium chloride, and magnesium acetate, or non-electrolytes such as sucrose) and a colloidal stabilizer such as polyvinylpyrrolidone or hydroxyethylcellulose. This oil/water emulsion is diluted with a sufficient volume of water or an aqueous solution to enhance the diffusion of acetone into the aqueous phase, thus inducing the formation of nanospheres.

Polymerization method

In this technique, the monomer units are allowed to polymerize in an aqueous solution of the drug candidate. The drug may be loaded by adsorption on the surface of polymeric nanoparticle after its formation in the aqueous phase post-polymerization. The nanoparticle suspension is then purified by centrifugation to separate the stabilizers and surfactants used for the polymerization reaction.

(ii) Applications of nanoparticles:

Nanoparticles find diverse applications in drug delivery science and technology. The major applications of nanoparticles in drug delivery are discussed below.

- Nanoparticles have a large surface area and hence they improve the solubility and hence bioavailability of drugs with poor aqueous solubility.
- Improved bioavailability may lead to a reduction of dose size and hence reduction in dose-dependent toxicities.
- Nanoparticles have been used for the treatment of various cancers. They offer less toxic and more target-specific therapies towards cancer cells. Nanoparticle targeting to the cancer cells is both active and passive.
- Targeted drug delivery for other drugs as well.
- Alternative drug and vaccine delivery mechanisms (e.g. inhalation, oral in place of injection).
- Nanoparticles have been used for controlled delivery of drug substances. Various stimuli responsive drug delivery systems have been developed for nanoparticles. E.g. mesoporous silica based nanosystems.

9.8 MONOCLONAL ANTIBODIES

Monoclonal antibodies (mAbs) are purified antibodies produced by a single clone of cells. They are engineered to recognize and bind to a single specific antigen. Accordingly, when administered, mAbs home in on a particular circulating protein or on cells that bear the correct antigenic signature on their surfaces. It is the specificity of mAbs that has made them valuable tools for health professions.

They imitate the natural antibodies in the body. Monoclonal antibodies are engineered by either "hybridoma technology" or "antibody libraries". Monoclonal antibodies that possess a high binding affinity, as well as specificity towards any target antigen, are generally produced using antibody libraries. For example, antibody libraries with applications in gene therapy can select mAbs mediating phage-endocytosis by the body cells. Therapeutic monoclonal antibodies have mainly found use as naked antibodies. However, now these are utilized in targeted drug delivery owing to the fact that targeted drug delivery systems can overcome the side-effects caused by conventional chemotherapy of cancer. Drugs can be conjugated with the monoclonal antibodies and further can be targeted.

Four major antibody types that have been developed are murine, chimeric, humanized and human. Antibodies of each type are distinguished by suffixes on their name. Initial therapeutic antibodies were murine analogues (suffix -omab). These antibodies have a short half-life in vivo and limited penetration into tumor sites. Chimeric and humanized antibodies have generally replaced them in therapeutic antibody applications. To reduce murine antibody immunogenicity, murine molecules were engineered to remove immunogenic content and to increase immunologic efficiency. This was initially achieved by the production of chimeric (suffix -ximab) and humanized antibodies (suffix -zumab). These mAbs exhibit reduced immunogenicity, and thus increased serum half-life.

Humanized antibodies are produced by grafting murine hypervariable regions on amino acid domains into human antibodies. This results in a molecule of approximately 95% human origin. Human monoclonal antibodies (suffix -umab) are produced using transgenic mice or phage display libraries by transferring human immunoglobulin genes into the murine genome and vaccinating the transgenic mouse against the desired antigen, leading to the production of appropriate monoclonal antibodies.

(i) Preparation of monoclonal antibodies:

Hybridoma technology

Monoclonal antibodies are typically produced by fusing myeloma cells with the spleen cells from a rat that has been immunized with the desired antigen. The production process of monoclonal antibodies using hybridoma technology involves various steps as follows.

Step-1: Immunization of mice and isolation of splenocytes-Mice are immunized with an antigen and then their blood is screened for antibody production. The antibody producing splenocytes (e.g. B lymphocytes) are then isolated for in vitro hybridoma production.

Step-2: Preparation of myeloma cells-Myeloma cells are immortalized cells that, once fused with spleen cells, can result in hybridoma capable of unlimited growth. Myeloma cells are prepared for fusion.

Step-3: Fusion-Myeloma cells and isolated splenocytes are fused together to form hybridomas in the presence of polyethylene glycol (PEG). PEG helps in fusion of cell membranes. Unfused myeloma cells cannot grow and thus cannot replicate their DNA. Unfused spleen cells cannot grow indefinitely because of their limited life span. Only fused hybrid cells, referred to as hybridomas, are able to grow indefinitely that make it immortal (similar to a cancer cells).

Step-4: Clone screening and picking-Clones are screened and selected on the basis of antigen specificity and immunoglobulin class.

(ii) Applications of monoclonal antibodies:

The first FDA-approved therapeutic mAbs, Orthoclone OKT3, was approved in 1986 to limit organ transplant rejection. Since 1986, more than 70 mAbs, serving either therapeutic or diagnostic purposes, have been approved. Most of the mAbs currently in the clinic have been developed for the treatment of diseases as cancer, followed by autoimmune diseases, genetic diseases, infectious diseases, asthma, cardiovascular, etc.

- The treatment for cancer involves monoclonal antibodies that bind only to cancer cell-specific antigens and induce immunological responses against the target cancer cells. mAbs approved by the FDA include: Bevacizumab, Cetuximab, Panitumumab, Trastuzumab, etc.
- Monoclonal antibodies used for autoimmune diseases include infliximab and adalimumab, which are effective in rheumatoid arthritis, Crohn's disease and ulcerative Colitis by their ability to bind to and inhibit TNF-α.
- Basiliximab and daclizumab inhibit IL-2 on activated T cells and thereby help prevent acute rejection of kidney transplants.
- Omalizumab inhibits human immunoglobulin E (IgE) and is useful in moderate-to-severe allergic asthma.
- Monoclonal antibodies have been widely used in the field of diagnosis for the detection of hormones, vitamins, cytokines, allergens, numerous tumor markers, and a wide range of markers associated with many diseases, including microbial infections.

9.9 CHAPTER AT A GLANCE

Term	Description
Passive targeting	Accumulation of drugs/drug-carrier systems at the intended site of action by the action of physicochemical and physiological factors is called as passive targeting.
Active targeting	Ligand mediated targeting
First-order targeting	This is the distribution of the drug to capillary beds of target sites- organ or tissue, for example, in case of lymphatic tissue, peritoneal cavity, pleural cavity, cerebral ventricles, eyes, joints, etc.
Second-order targeting	This is the targeting of drugs to specific sites such as the tumor cells, for example, to Kupffer cells in the liver.
Third-order targeting	It is the type of drug targeting wherein the drug is intracellularly localized at the target site via endocytosis or through the receptor- based ligand-mediated entry.
Approaches for drug targeting	Physical targeting, Chemical targeting and Biological targeting
Liposomes	Liposomes are colloidal, concentric bilayered lipid vesicles where the aqueous compartment is entirely enclosed by a bilayer membrane, usually composed of lipids of either natural or synthetic origin.
Liposome preparation methods	Film hydration, Reverse phase evaporation, Solvent injection, Detergent removal, Heating method, Microfluidic channel method, Supercritical fluid method.
Niosomes	Niosomes are vesicles composed of non-ionic surfactants, amphiphilic compounds with an overall neutral charge.
Niosome preparation methods	Film hydration, Reverse phase evaporation, Ether injection method, Heating method, Microfluidization method, Bubble method.
Nanoparticles	Nanoparticles are defined as solid, submicron-sized (less than 100 nm in diameter) drug carrier that may or may not be biodegradable. In drug delivery science relatively large (size >100 nm) nanoparticles may be needed for loading a sufficient amount of drug onto the particles.

Nanoparticle preparation methods	Emulsification/solvent evaporation, Solvent displacement and interfacial deposition, Emulsification/solvent diffusion, Salting out with synthetic polymers, Polymerization method.
Monoclonal antibodies (mAbs)	Monoclonal antibodies (mAbs) are purified antibodies produced by a single clone of cells which are engineered to recognize and bind to a single specific antigen.
Monoclonal antibody preparation	Hybridoma technology

EXERCISES

Multiple choice Questions

1. The EPR Effect is exemplified by-
   (a) Active targeting
   (b) Passive targeting
   (c) Chemical targeting
   (d) Colon targeting
2. Tumor cell targeting is an example of-
   (a) First order targeting
   (b) Second order targeting
   (c) Third order targeting
   (d) None
3. Which of the following statement best explains biological targeting?
   (a) Localization of the payload using carriers like antibodies.
   (b) Localization of payloads to the biological targets by using external stimuli.
   (c) Localization of payload is based on the physicochemical properties of the drug.
   (d) None of the above

4. Use of site specific prodrugs are examplefied in-

   (a) Physical targeting (b) Chemical targeting

   (c) Biological targeting (d) None

5. The film hydration method in liposome preparation is also known as-

   (a) Bangham method (b) Pasteur method

   (c) Kelvin method (c) Swiss method

6. PEGylation of liposomes results in-

   (a) Improved clearance

   (b) Improved circulation time

   (c) Reduced toxicities

   (d) Reduced absorption

7. Non-ionic surfactant based nanovesicles are called as-

   (a) Liposomes (b) Polymerosomes

   (c) Niosomes (d) Lysosomes

8. Comminution of particles for preparation of nanoparticles is-

   (a) a top-down method (b) a bottom-up method

   (c) a hybridoma technology (d) None

9. Which of the following monoclonal antibodies carry a suffix of "umab"?

   (a) Murine (b) Chimeric

   (c) Humanized (d) Human

10. What is the functional role of PEG in hybridoma technology?

    (a) Used for immunization of mice

    (b) helps fusion of cell membranes

    (c) Used for tumor cell targeting

    (d) Improve the solubility of solutes

Short Answer Questions

1. What are the functions of an ideal targeted drug delivery system?
2. Differentiate between passive and active targeting.

3. Present a note on the various advantages and disadvantages of targeted drug delivery systems.
4. What do you understand by hybridoma technology?
5. What are the therapeutic applications of liposomes?

Long Answer Questions

1. Discuss in brief about the concept of drug targeting and approaches for targeted drug delivery.
2. Illustrate any two methods for synthesis of nanoparticles. Add a note on advantages of nanoparticles in drug delivery.
3. What are liposomes? Describe any two method for preparation of liposomes.
4. How are niosomes different from liposomes? Describe any two methods for preparation of niosomes.
5. What are therapeutic monoclonal antibodies? How are they prepared? Add a note on their applications.

Answer Key MCQs

(1) – (b), (2) – (b), (3) – (a), (4) – (b), (5) – (a), (6) – (b), (7) – (c), (8) – (a), (9) – (d), (10) – (b)

BIBLIOGRAPHY

1. Pattni BS, Torchilin VP. Targeted Drug Delivery Systems: Strategies and Challenges. In: Devarajan P., Jain S. (eds) Targeted Drug Delivery: Concepts and Design. Advances in Delivery Science and Technology. 2015, Springer, Cham.

2. Mills JK, and Needham D. Targeted drug delivery. Expert Opinion on Therapeutic Patents, 1999, 9 (11): 1499-1513.

3. Pérez-Herrero E, Fernández-Medarde A. Advanced targeted therapies in cancer: Drug nanocarriers, the future of chemotherapy. Eur J Pharm Biopharm. 2015,93:52-79.

4. Biffi S, Voltan R, Bortot B, Zauli G, Secchiero P. Actively targeted nanocarriers for drug delivery to cancer cells. Expert Opin Drug Deliv. 2019, 16(5):481-496.

5. Nelson PN, Reynolds GM, Waldron EE, Ward E, Giannopoulos K, Murray PG. Monoclonal antibodies. Mol Pathol. 2000, 53(3):111-7.

□□□

Chapter 10

OCULAR DRUG DELIVERY SYSTEMS

♦ LEARNING OBJECTIVES ♦

***After completing this lesson, the Reader should be able to understand*:**

- **The barriers to ocular drug delivery.**
- **Strategies to overcome the ocular barrier.**
- **Various novel ocular formulations and drug delivery systems including inserts.**

10.1 INTRODUCTION

In the past two decades, the arena of ocular drug delivery technologies has dynamically advanced and resulted in newer therapeutic interventions for chronic ocular disorders. The primary objectives of any ocular drug delivery system are to maintain therapeutic drug concentrations at the target site, reduce dosing frequency and to improve drug permeability in the ocular tissue. At the same time, the drug delivery system should cause no or minimal adverse ocular reactions and aim to achieve better patient compliance.

Ocular pathological disorders are generally described as anterior segment and posterior segment disorders. Clinicians treat anterior segment disorders like dry eye disease, cataract and allergic conjunctivitis by topical eye drops. The major disadvantage of topically applied ophthalmic formulations is relatively low ocular bioavailability. This can be accounted to high tear- fluid turnover rates and high nasolacrimal drainage. Novel ocular drug delivery approaches including nanomicelles, nanoparticles, drug eluting contact lenses, ocular inserts and ocular devices that allow enhanced percorneal residence and enhance bioavailability of the therapeutic agents.

Ocular pathological conditions involving the posterior segment generally result in vision loss due to damage to the retina. Hyperglycemia for a prolonged period of time can cause damage to the retinal endothelial cells causing back of the eye disorders like diabetic retinopathy (DR), diabetic macular edema (DME) and retinal vein occlusion (RVO). Novel ocular drug delivery technologies like nanoformulations, implants and other ocular devices allow enhanced drug residence time at the target tissue along with improvements of pharmacological response. Developments in novel drug delivery technologies can ultimately improve pharmacological action of drugs at the target tissue by elevating the concentrations and ocular bioavailability of the required therapeutic agent. To understand the drug delivery approaches to treat ocular diseases, it is very important to briefly review the barriers to ocular drug delivery.

10.2 BARRIERS TO OCULAR DRUG DELIVERY

The structure of eye can be divided into two main parts: anterior segment and posterior segment (see Fig 10.1). Anterior segment of the eye occupies approximately one-third while the remaining portion is occupied by the posterior segment. Tissues such as cornea, conjunctiva, aqueous humor, iris, ciliary body and lens make up the anterior portion. Back of the eye or posterior segment of the eye include sclera, choroid, retinal pigment epithelium, neural retina, optic nerve and vitreous humor. The anterior and posterior segment of eye is affected by various vision threatening diseases. Diseases affecting anterior segment include, but not limited to glaucoma, allergic conjunctivitis, anterior uveitis and cataract. While, age-related macular degeneration (AMD) and diabetic retinopathy are the most prevalent diseases affecting posterior segment of the eye.

Human ocular anatomy possesses static and dynamic ocular barriers to prevent toxic chemical substances including therapeutic molecules to reach various tissues of the eye. Ocular barriers of anterior and posterior segments retard the passive absorption of various therapeutic agents and thus reduce the ocular bioavailability of various drugs. Both static (corneal epithelium, corneal stroma, corneal endothelium, blood aqueous barrier) and dynamic barriers (tear dilution, conjunctival and retinal-blood barriers) hinder drug absorption affecting drug bioavailability of topical formulation (<5%). The globular shape of human eye, and precorneal factors such as blinking and continuous tear turn over reduce absorption of topically applied formulations. Lipophilic corneal epithelia allow absorption of hydrophobic drugs but acts as a barrier for paracellular diffusion of hydrophilic drugs due to tight junctions. Corneal epithelia efficiently prevent absorption of drugs with size exceeding 10 Å. Therefore, drug absorption requires overcoming corneal epithelia efficiently. Decrease in transcorneal diffusion of drug through aqueous humor and expression of efflux transporters on the plasma membrane of corneal cells are major restrictions for drug delivery to the targeted ocular tissues. The use of prodrugs, permeation enhancers and recent use of nanomicelles can enhance permeability of the drug through the corneal barriers.

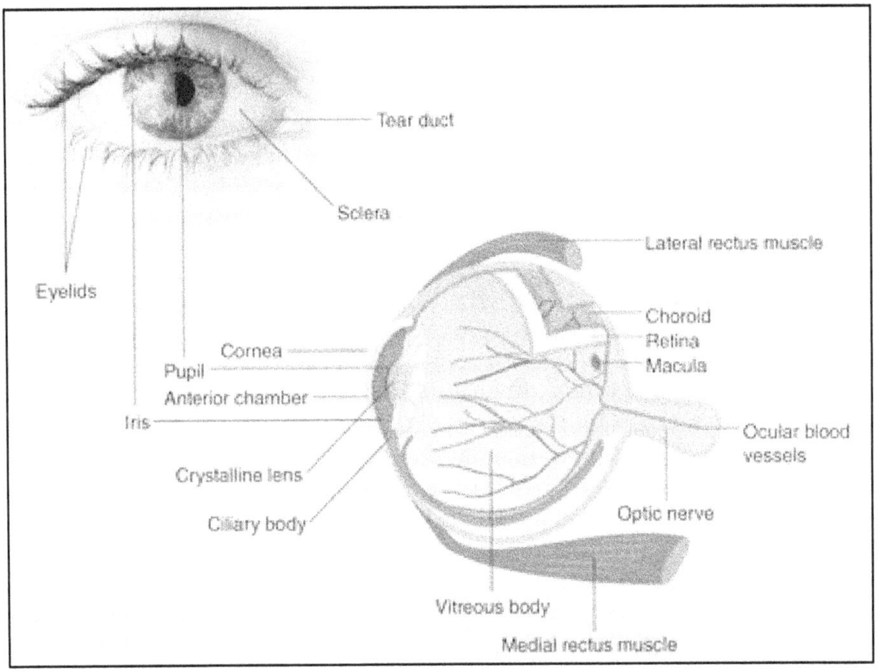

Fig.10.1 Schematic diagram showing the anatomy of human eye.

While in the posterior segment of the eye, the scleral, choroidal and retinal epithelial and the blood retinal barrier accounts for limiting ocular drug bioavailability. The sclera provides higher trans scleral permeability than the cornea for hydrophilic compounds diffusing through the collagen network. Permeation through the sclera is largely dependent on molecular weight, molecular radius and charge. Macromolecules exhibit lower penetration through scleral pores than small molecules. The choroid is a vascular natured dynamic barrier, which impedes drug delivery by trans-scleral pathway. The retina is a significant limiting factor for diffusion of molecules with larger radius and molecular weight greater than 76 kDa. The inner limiting membrane (ILM) of retina severely confines passaging of macromolecules over 150 kDa molecular weight. Moreover, the ILM progressively restricts molecules with larger radius. Retinal pigmented epithelium and choriocapillaries collaboratively produce Bruch's membrane. The thickness of Bruch's membrane increases with age inhibiting drug transport into tissues and draining hydrophobic drugs through systemic circulation. The blood retinal barrier (BRB) comprises two subdivisions, an outer blood retinal barrier (oBRB) and an inner blood retinal barrier (iBRB). Both the oBRB and iBRB are permeation barriers between the blood and the retina having tight junction proteins between the cells. BRB also exhibits efflux transporters, which reduces bioavailability of several therapeutic agents. Blood aqueous barrier consists of an epithelial and an endothelial barrier. The permeability of drugs through the blood aqueous barrier is determined by osmotic pressure and physicochemical characteristics of drug molecules.

Strategies to overcome the barriers

Drug solubility & penetration enhancement- Many ocular drugs have low aqueous solubility; this can be improved using hydrotropic compounds, cyclodextrins, dendrimers, micelles, etc. Inclusion of penetration enhancers within a formulation improves drug partitioning into tissue. Benzalkonium chloride is a preservative used in ocular formulation with penetration enhancement effects. Other penetration enhancers include cetylpyridinium chloride, ethylenediaminetetraacetic acid [EDTA], polyoxyethylene strearyl ether and polyethoxylated castor oil, bile salts, boric acid, Gelucire®, etc.

Drug retention strategies- Viscosity-enhancing polymers, in situ gels and bioadhesives allow eye drop formulation to resist precorneal losses and they retain intimate contact with ocular tissue longer giving the dose form more time to penetrate ocular membranes.

Drug delivery from ocular inserts are a means to place the dose form in immediate contact with ocular mucosa, this strategy allows controlled and sustained drug release for an extended period. Ocular implants are implantable devices designed to penetrate the ocular membranes or reside entirely within the eye. This strategy overcomes all external barriers and can offer short term medication or deliver medication for several years when treating chronic conditions.

10.3 NOVEL OCULAR DRUG DELIVERY STRATEGIES

The eye offers multiple entry routes through which ocular drugs may be delivered. Delivery to the anterior segment of the eye may be achieved through topical and subconjunctival routes, or injected intracamerally. Posterior segment delivery can be achieved topically, systemically, and periocularly (i.e., through sub-Tenon's), via the suprachoroidal space, and via intraocular (i.e., intravitreal) injections. Success of therapeutic drug delivery depends on the delivery site, tissue barriers, drug type, and delivery method adopted. To enhance the drug bioavailability, ophthalmic formulation requires a higher precorneal residence time and an enhanced drug penetration. Therefore, a drug delivery system offering longer retention and a sustained release of the drug molecule to pass through these barriers is essential. Several nanocarriers, such as nanoparticles, nanosuspensions, liposomes, nanomicelles and dendrimers have been developed for ocular drug delivery. Some of them have shown promising results for improving ocular bioavailability. The following sub section describes various novel ocular formulations and drug delivery systems.

(i) **Nanomicelles:** Nanomicelles are prepared with amphiphilic molecules (surfactants/polymers) and are the carriers to to formulate drugs in to clear aqueous solutions with high drug loading capabilities. The nanomicelles can significantly improve the corneal permeation of the therapeutic agents. Various polymeric materials like polyhydroxy ethyl aspartamide, poly (ethylene oxide)-poly (propylene oxide)-poly (ethylene oxide) copymer, polyehthylene glycol-block-poly-α,β-aspartic acid, poly(ethylene glycol)-b-poly(l-lysine), etc have been used to formulate nanomicelles. Various drugs like voclosporin, dexamethasone, rapamycin, etc have been delivered through these novel nanotechnology platform. Cequa® is preservative free, clear and sterile nanomicellar formulation of a highly hydrophobic drug Cyclosporine-A.

(ii) **Nanoparticles:** Nanoparticles are promising candidate for ocular drug delivery owing to their small size leading to reduced tissue irritation and sustained release property. To prevent rapid elimination from the precorneal pocket following topical ocular administration, nanoparticles with mucoadhesive properties have been developed. Polyethylene glycol (PEG), chitosan and hyaluronic acid are commonly employed to improve precorneal residence time of nanoparticles. Chitosan is positively chatged and hence it binds to the negatively charged surface of the cornea improving the residence time of the chitosan coated nanoparticles. Reduced zeta potential of polymeric nanoparticles results in better and longer interaction between the nanoparticles and eye surface leading to enhanced therapeutic effect for prolonged period. Nanoparticle size is also critical for its residence time in the ocular tissue. Very small nanoparticles (<20 nm) are rapidly cleared from ocular tissue following periocular administration. The optimal size range for improved ocular residence is proposed to be 200-2000 nm.

For ophthalmic delivery, nanoparticles are generally composed of lipids, proteins, natural or synthetic polymers such as albumin, sodium alginate, chitosan, poly (lactide-co-glycolide) (PLGA), polylactic acid (PLA) and polycaprolactone. Drug loaded nanoparticles can be nanocapsules or nanospheres. In nanocapsules, drug is enclosed inside the polymeric shell while in nanospheres; drug is uniformly distributed throughout polymeric matrix.

(iii) **Nanosuspensions:** Nanosuspensions are colloidal dispersion of submicron drug particles stabilized by polymer(s) or surfactant(s). It is emerged as promising strategy for delivery of hydrophobic drugs. For ocular delivery, it provides several advantages such as sterilization, ease of eye drop formulation, less irritation, increase precorneal residence time and enhancement in ocular bioavailability of drugs which are insoluble in tear fluid. The efficacy of nanosuspensions in improving ocular bioavailability of glucocorticoids has been demonstrated in several research studies.

(iv) **Liposomes:** Liposomes are lipid vesicles with one or more phospholipid bilayers enclosing an aqueous core. For ophthalmic applications, liposomes represent ideal delivery systems due to excellent biocompatibility, cell membrane like structure and ability to encapsulate both hydrophilic and hydrophobic drugs. Liposomes have demonstrated good effectiveness for both anterior and posterior segment ocular delivery. The positively charged liposomes i.e., cationic liposomes have better efficacy in ocular delivery than negatively charged and neutral liposomes due to superior binding with negatively charged surface of cornea. Didodecyldimethylammonium bromide, stearylamine, and N-[1-(2,3-dioleoyloxy)propyl]-N,N,N-trimethylammonium chloride are commonly employed for fabricating cationic liposomes.

Visudyne® and Tears again® are the examples of commercially available ocular liposomal formulations for the treatment of age related macular degeneration (AMD) and Dry Eye syndrome, respectively.

(v) **Dendrimers:** Dendrimers are nanosized, highly branched, star shaped polymeric carrier systems. These branched polymeric systems are available in different molecular weights with terminal end amine, hydroxyl or carboxyl functional group. The terminal functional group may be utilized to conjugate targeting moieties. The highly branched structure of dendrimers allows incorporation of wide range of drugs, hydrophobic as well as hydrophilic.

Poly (amidoamine) (PAMAM) dendrimers are widely employed in ocular drug delivery with improved ocular residence time and bioavailability.

(vi) **In situ gels:** In-situ hydrogels are the polymeric solutions which undergo sol-gel phase transition to form viscoelastic gel in response to some environmental stimuli which include temperature, pH and ions. The examples of few thermosensitive polymers for ocular delivery include poloxamers, polycaprolactone, polyethylene glycol, poly (lactide), poly (glycolide), poly (N-isopropylacrylamide) and chitosan. These thermosensitive polymers form temperature dependent micellar aggregates which gellify after a further temperature increment due to aggregation or packing. For drug delivery, these polymers are mixed with drugs in the solution state and solution can be administered which forms an in situ gel depot at physiological temperature. These thermosensitive gels demonstrated promising results for enhancing ocular bioavailability for both anterior and posterior segment. The advantages of thermosensitive gels in ocular drug delivery include sustained drug release, prolong contact time of drugs with the cornea, reduced dosing frequency, reduced side effects and higher ocular bioavailability over aqueous drops.

(vii) **Drug eluting contact lenses:** Contact lenses are thin, and curved shape polymeric disks which are designed to cover the cornea. After application, contact lens adheres to the film of tears over the cornea due to the surface tension. Drug loaded contact lens have been developed for ocular delivery of numerous drugs such as β-blockers, antihistamines and antimicrobials. It is postulated that in presence of contact lens, drug molecules have longer residence time in the post-lens tear film which ultimately led to higher drug flux through cornea with less drug inflow into the nasolacrimal duct. Usually, drug is loaded into contact lens by soaking them in drug solutions. These soaked contact lenses demonstrated higher efficiency in delivering drug compared to conventional eye drops. The materials used for fabrication of the contact lenses include poly (hydroxyethyl methacrylate) (PHEMA) (e.g. methafilcon, polymacon), silicone hydrogel (e.g. lotrafilcon A, lotrafilcon B, senofilcon A, comfilcon A), PVA hydrogel, etc.

Fig.10.3 A soft contact lense.

(viii) **Microneedles:** Microneedle based technique is an emerging and minimally invasive mode of drug delivery to posterior ocular tissues to treat age related macular degeneration, diabetic retinopathy and posterior uveitis. This new microneedle based administration strategy may reduce the risk and complications associated with intravitreal injections such as retinal detachment, hemorrhage, cataract, endophthalmitis and pseudo endophthalmitis. Moreover, this strategy may help to circumvent blood retinal barrier and deliver therapeutic drug levels to retina/choroid. Microneedles are custom designed to penetrate only hundreds of microns into sclera, so that damage to deeper ocular tissues may be avoided. These needles help to deposit drug or carrier system into sclera or into the narrow space present between sclera and choroid called "suprachoroidal space" (SCS). Puncturing of sclera and depositing drug solution or carrier systems in sclera or SCS may facilitate diffusion of drug into deeper ocular tissues, choroid and neural retina.

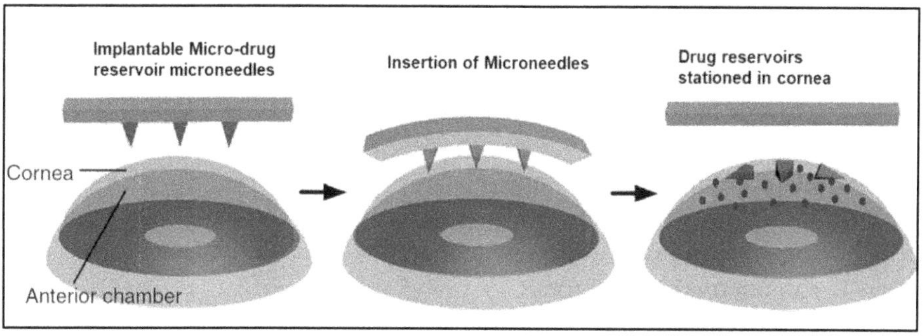

Fig.10.3 Microneedle based ocular drug delivery.

(ix) **Ocular inserts:** Ocular inserts are sterile, multi-layered, drug-impregnated devices placed into the cul-de-sac or conjunctival sac and, in some cases, directly on the cornea of the eye for the prolonged release of medication. These systems can be insoluble devices that need to be removed after a given period of time or they can be designed to dissolve, erode or biodegrade at the ocular surface. The ocular inserts have been classified on the basis of solubility as Soluble inserts and Insoluble inserts. The insoluble inserts are to be removed from the eyes after depletion of the drug dose. On the other hand, soluble inserts usually erode or dissolve over the period of drug delivery and thereby need not to be removed.

The advantages of ocular inserts include improved ocular residency time, sustained drug delivery, accurate dosing, no or minimal preservative usages, reduced systemic absorption, improved patient compliance due to reduced frequency of drug administration, reduced incidences of side effects, targeting possibilities to internal scleral tissue through the conjunctival-scleral route, increased self-life compared to aqueous solution type dosage forms. The key disadvantages of the ocular inserts are due to the solid characteristic of the dosage form and hence they are felt as a foreign body by the patient. The disadvantages include patient discomfort, feel of movement around the eye, occasional removal due to rubbing of the eyes while sleeping, interference with vision and difficulty in placing the insert in the eye. Few examples of recently commercialized ocular insert products are Vitrasert® (ganciclovir 4.5mg), Retisert® (fluocinolone 0.59 mg), Ozurdex® (dexamethasone 0.7 mg), Iluvien® (fluocinolone acetonide 0.19mg), etc.

Advantages of ocular inserts	***Disadvantages of ocular inserts***
• Improved ocular residency time • Sustained drug delivery • Accurate dosing • No or minimal preservative usages • Reduced systemic absorption • Improved patient compliance due to reduced frequency of drug administration • Reduced incidences of side effects • Targeting possibilities to internal scleral tissue through the conjunctival-scleral route • Increased self-life compared to aqueous solution type dosage forms	• Patient discomfort • Feel of movement around the eye • Occasional removal due to rubbing of the eyes (e.g. while sleeping) • Interference with vision and difficulty in placing the insert in the eye

Soluble inserts

Soluble ophthalmic drug inserts (SODI) were developed by Moscow Helmholtz Ophthalmological Institute in collaboration with the All-Union Research Institute for Medical Equipment, Russia during 1971. A new soluble copolymer of acrylamide, N-Vinyl pyrrolidone and ethyl acrylate (0.25:0.25:0.5) was used for the fabrication of the insert. The thin film inserts are designed in oval shape to fit to the structure of eye weighing about 15 mg. The SODI is inserted into the upper conjunctival sac which subsequently softens in 10-15 seconds and conforms to the shape of the eyeball. The incorporated drug is released upon gradual dissolution of the insert providing option for once-a -day therapy. These systems may exhibit zero-order release kinetics provided the system maintains a constant surface geometry and the loaded drug is poorly soluble. SODI has been used for delivery of neomycin, kanamycin, sulphamethoxy pyridazine, idoxuridine, atropine, pilocarpine, dexamethasone, and other drugs used in ophthalmology.

Insoluble inserts (Ocusert®)

The Ocusert®, pilocarpine ocular therapeutic system, was developed by Alza Corporation and first marketed in the U.S. in 1974. These inserts are considered as the first successful product for delivery of pilocarpine for the treatment of ocular hypertension. Ocusert® consists of a pilocarpine–alginate reservoir sandwiched between thin ethylene vinyl acetate (EVA) films and are designed to deliver pilocarpine at either 20 μg/h or 40 μg/h for 7 days. The insert is encircled with a retaining annular ring made up of the same material impregnated with TiO_2 (see Fig. 10.3). The annular ring helps in positioning the insert in the eye. Zero-order drug release is achieved by diffusion of drugs from the reservoir through the release controlling polymer (e.g. EVA). Flux enhancers like di (2-ethyl hexyl) phthalate are used in the reservoir to modulate drug release rates. The dimensions of the elliptical device are (for the 20 μg/h system): major axis-13.4 mm, minor axis-5.7 mm, thickness-0.3 mm. The major limitation of insoluble inserts is that the inserts are to be removed from the eyes after depletion of the drug dose. Some other disadvantages of this system include unreliable control of intraocular pressure, leakage, folding, difficulty inserting the devices and ejection or irritation.

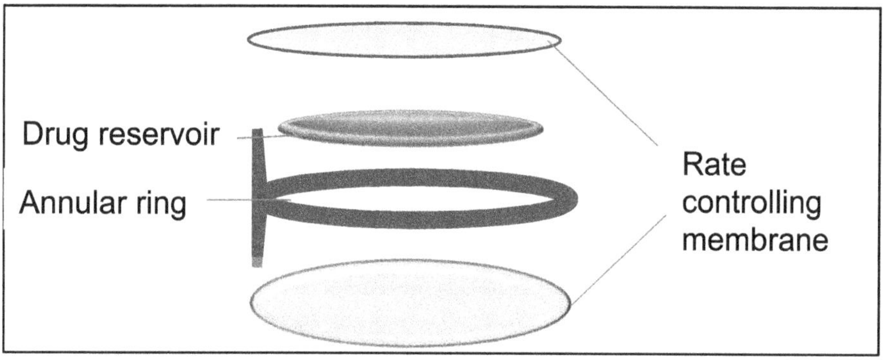

Fig.10.4 Schematic diagram of Ocusert type ocular insert system.

10.4 TIME LINES

19th century	Development of paper ocular patches.
1771	Development of SODI® by Russian scientists.
1974	Development of Ocusert® in US.
1981	Development of Artificial tear insert.
1995	Vitrasert® approved
2005	Retisert® approved
2009	Ozurdex® approved
2011	Iluvien® approved

10.5 CHAPTER AT A GLANCE

Term	Description
Anterior segment disorders	Glaucoma, allergic conjunctivitis, anterior uveitis and cataract
Posterior segment disorders	Age-related macular degeneration (AMD). diabetic retinopathy, diabetic macular edema (DME) and retinal vein occlusion (RVO)
Static ocular barriers	Corneal epithelium, corneal stroma, corneal endothelium and blood aqueous barrier
Dynamic ocular barriers	Tear dilution, conjunctival and retinal-blood barriers
Strategies to overcome the ocular barrier	Drug solubilization, penetration enhancement, drug/dosage form retention
Ocular inserts	Sterile, multi-layered, drug-impregnated devices placed into the cul-de-sac or conjunctival sac and, in some cases, directly on the cornea of the eye for the prolonged release of medication.

EXERCISES

Multiple choice Questions

1. Which of the following is an anterior segment ophthalmic disorder-
   (a) Diabetic retinopathy
   (b) Age related macular degeneration
   (c) Glaucoma
   (d) All of the above
2. Which of the following is a posterior segment ocular disorder -
   (a) Retinal vein occlusion (b) Glaucoma
   (c) Cataract (d) None
3. Corneal epithelia restricts absorption of-
   (a) Lipophilic compounds. (b) Hydrophilic drugs.
   (c) small molecules (d) None of the above

4. Bruch's membrane is produced by-
   (a) Retinal pigmented epithelium and choriocapillaris
   (b) Villi and microvilli
   (c) EVA copolymer
   (d) None
5. The functional role of Benzalkonium chloride in ocular preparations is -
   (a) Preservative
   (b) Preservative and permeation enhancer
   (c) Flux enhancer
   (c) Mucoadhesive
6. Which of the following is a commercial nanomicelle ocular formulation?
   (a) Cequa (b) Ocusert
   (c) Visudyne (d) Vitrasert
7. Cationic liposomal formulations are more effective in ocular drug delivery because-
   (a) they permeate well through the ocular membranes
   (b) they bind well with the corneal epithelia
   (c) they improve the shelf life of the formulation
   (d) All of the above
8. Which of the following material is very often used for fabrication of dendrimers?
   (a) Hydroxypropyl methylcellulose (b) Carbopol
   (c) Starch (d) Poly (amidoamine)
9. Which of the following material is common in contact lenses manufacturing?
   (a) Eudragit (b) Avicel
   (c) poly (hydroxyethyl methacrylate) (d) TiO_2
10. The drug release controlling membrane used in Ocusert® is made up of-
   (a) Ethylene vinyl acetate (b) Ethyl cellulose
   (c) Titanium dioxide (d) Acrylamide

Short Answer Questions

1. What are the barriers to ocular drug delivery?
2. What are the limitations of conventional ophthalmic dosage forms?.
3. Write a short note on liposomal ocular drug delivery.
4. Write a note on SODI®?
5. What are the advantages of ocular inserts?

Long Answer Questions

1. Discuss in brief about the various barriers to ocular drug delivery and strategies to overcome the barriers.
2. Illustrate the nanotechnology based platforms for ocular drug delivery.
3. What are the barriers to ophthalmic drug delivery? Discuss how therapeutic contact lenses overcome the said barriers?
4. What are the limitations of conventional ophthalmic drug delivery? Add a note on microneedles.
5. Discuss in brief about various types of ocular inserts. Add a note on the advantages of the same.

Answer Key MCQs

(1) – (c), (2) – (a), (3) – (b), (4) – (a), (5) – (b), (6) – (a), (7) – (b), (8) – (d), (9) – (c), (10) – (a)

BIBLIOGRAPHY

1. Vyas SP and Khar RK. Controlled Drug Delivery -concepts and advances, Vallabh Prakashan, New Delhi, First edition 2002.
2. Morrison PWJ, & Khutoryanskiy VV. Advances in ophthalmic drug delivery. Ther. Deliv. 2014, 5(12): 1297–1315.
3. Marco Fabrizio Saettone, Lotta Salminen. Ocular inserts for topical delivery. Adv Drug Deliv Rev. 1995, 16:95-106.

□□□

Chapter 11

INTRAUTERINE DRUG DELIVERY SYSTEMS

♦ LEARNING OBJECTIVES ♦

After completing this lesson, the Reader should be able to understand:

- **The various types of intrauterine devices.**
- **Advantages and disadvantages of intrauterine devices.**
- **Applications of intrauterine devices.**

11.1 INTRODUCTION

Intrauterine drug delivery system or simply, intrauterine Device (IUD) is a small object that is inserted by a trained professional through the cervix and placed in the uterus to prevent pregnancy or any other gynaecological disorder. The IUD is not noticeable during intercourse and can last from 1-10 years. At present, apart from oral contraceptive agents, IUDs are considered as the most effective methods for long-acting reversible contraception (LARC). The IUDs provide localized therapeutic effects in the uterine cavity. The IUDs can be either medicated or non medicated. The first plastic or non-medicated IUDs were the Lippes loop introduced during 1962 and were associated with a high discontinuation rate due to side effects related to its large surface area and size. The earlier IUDs made of inert plastic materials have largely been superseded in modern practice by products which release copper or levonorgestrel, modifications which substantially enhance the already high efficacy. Further, T-shaped IUDs are associated with less distortion of the endometrial cavity. The various advantages and disadvantages of the IUDs are as follows.

Advantages

- Highly effective in preventing pregnancy.
- Inexpensive.
- Does not interrupt sex.
- Does not require partner's involvement.
- Can be used for a long period of time.
- Can be used as an emergency method of birth control.
- Provides long-term contraception for 3 to 5 years.
- It is a reversible method of contraception.
- It is convenient and associated with user/patient compliance.
- Copper IUDs are associated with decreased risk for endometrial cancer and invasive cervical cancer.

Disadvantages

- The IUD could increase the likelihood of developing pelvic inflammatory disease leading to infertility.
- May increase the possibilities of ectopic pregnancy.
- Can cause heavier and painful menstruation.
- Cramping and discomfort during and 24-48 hours after insertion
- There are risks during insertion and removal.
- 2-10 % of IUDs fall out.
- Increased risk of miscarriage, if an IUD is left in the uterus during a pregnancy.
- An IUD, in rare cases, may attach to or perforate the wall of the uterus.

11.2 MEDICATED INTRAUTERINE DEVICES

The non-medicated IUDs (e.g. Lippes loop) were partially effective in preventing pregnancies due to their mechanical effect on the endometrium which were largely influenced by the size and surface area of the IUDs (See Fig 11.1). These devices are made of plastic or stainless steel only. The greater the contact area with the endometrium the more effective is the contraception. However, the large sized IUDs were associated with bleeding, cramping, frequent expulsion due to irritation and discomfort. Efforts to minimize these side effects of non-medicated IUDs led the researchers to develop medicated IUDs with variation in shape, size and incorporation of pharmacological agents. The medicated IUDs essentially contain pharmacological agents (e.g. copper, hormones, etc) and are either frameless or framed. The first medicated framed IUD was developed by Zipper et al during 1968 with copper as anti-fertility agent. The same year progestin releasing framed IUDs were also reported.

It has been found that as the myometrial fibres contract, the endometrial cavity assumes the shape of capital letter "T". Hence, it can be concluded that an IUD in the shape of "T" can easily conform to the shape and size of the endometrial cavity with significantly reduced incidences of pain and bleeding. Furthermore, the incidences of expulsion of "T" shaped IUDs were reduced due to the fact that the "T" shape conforms well to the uterine cavity and displacement or rotation of the device is restricted (See Fig 11.2).

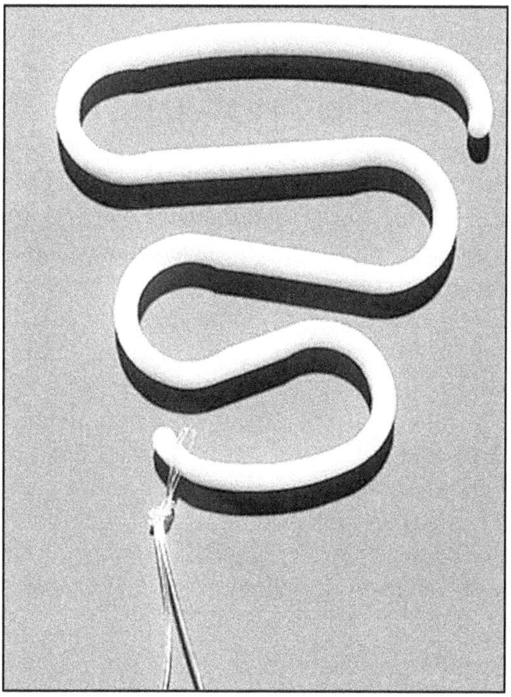

Fig.11.1 Schematic diagram of a Lippes loop type IUD.

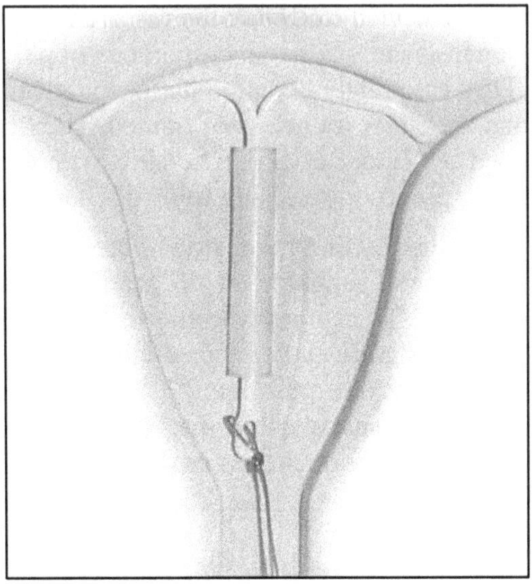

Fig.11.2 Schematic diagram showing placement of "T" shaped IUD in uterine.

(i) **Copper based framed intrauterine devices:** The plastic IUDs (e.g. Lippes loop) had major drawbacks like incompatibility issues and heavy bleedings. This led to the development of copper-based IUDs. Copper and some other metals like zinc, cadmium, etc., have been known to have contraceptive activities. The daily dose of copper for contraception is approximately 9.87 μg. Most copper devices consist of a plastic core that is wrapped in a copper wire (e.g., Nova T, CuT 380A, CuT-380Ag, Multiload 375, etc). The first developed framed copper containing IUD used a "T"-shaped polyethylene device with 30 mm^2 copper wire (Cu T-30). Later devices with larger copper surface areas were developed (e.g., 200 mm^2 and 300 mm^2) with better anti-fertility efficacy (see Fig 11.3). ParaGard® is a commercial brand of copper bearing IUD containing 244.7 mg of copper wire with a total exposed surface area of about 380 mm^2. The mechanism of actions of copper as anti-fertility agent are as follows.

- Copper prevents sperm from reaching the egg and fertilizing it and may also prevent implantation.
- It enhances the spermatocidal and spermatodepressive action of IUDs.
- Cupric ion is a competitive inhibitor of steroidal hormone receptor.
- Copper wire is blastocystocidal. Copper enters the lysosomes of blastocyst and cause cellular autolysis and cell death.
- Hence the mechanism of action of copper bearing IUDs include a combination of ionization and chelation.

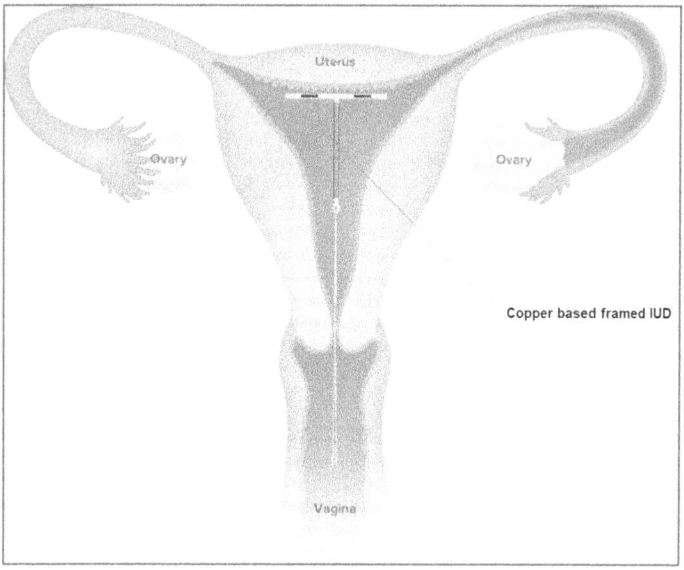

Fig.11.3 Copper based framed IUD placed in the uterus.

(ii) Copper based frameless IUDs: Although incompatibility problems and the effect of T-shaped IUDs on menstrual bleeding are significantly reduced compared to the older plastic IUDs (e.g., Lippes Loop), these coppers based framed IUDs still had room for improvement, due to the prevalence of abnormal and heavy menstrual bleeding, pain, and expulsion. It is for these reasons that the frameless and flexible copper-releasing IUDs (e.g., GyneFix®) were developed. The frameless standard IUD consists of six copper sleeves or four copper sleeves (small version) (See Fig 11.4), each 5 mm long and 2.2 mm in diameter, threaded on a length of polypropylene suture material. The sleeves are prevented from sliding off the material by crimping the upper and lower sleeves onto the thread. The proximal end of the thread is provided with a knot, which is inserted and anchored in place in the fundal myometrium using a specially designed inserter. The total, effective surface of copper, including the inner and outer surfaces, is 330 mm^2 for the standard version and 200 mm^2 for the small version. With no plastic body, this implant device is completely flexible.

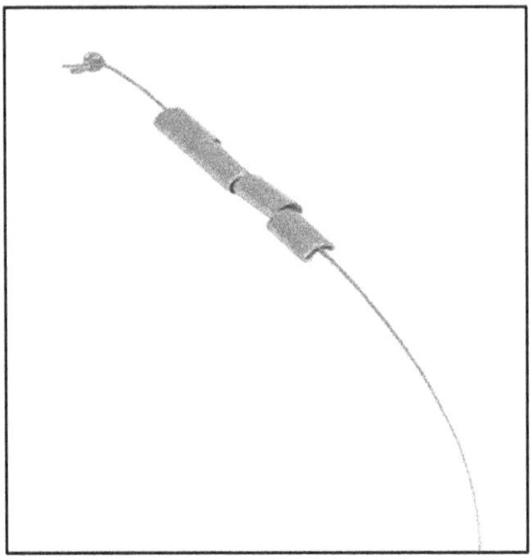

Fig.11.4 Schematic representation of frameless copper IUD.

It should be noted that the frameless IUDs, which consist only of copper sleeves, differ from conventional copper IUDs, which have a copper wire wound around the stem, in terms of their effective copper surface area. Only in the case of sleeves, unattached to a plastic frame, is the nominal and the effective copper surface area the same. When copper wire or copper sleeves fixed to a plastic body are used, that part of the wire or sleeve lying against the plastic body is ineffective and should not be calculated as a part of the effective surface area. The abnormal bleeding and pain incidences are significantly lower with this type of IUDs. The high efficacy of these tiny devices is due to exposure of inner and outer surface areas of the hollow copper cylinders to the uterine environment.

(iii) Framed hormone releasing IUDs: The first hormonal framed IUD was a "T-shaped" device releasing progesterone and was marketed in 1976. The device had a one-year life span and was not very popular. Subsequently, levonorgestrel releasing IUDs were developed which released the hormone for five years. Currently used hormonal IUDs are also called as intrauterine systems that release a specific dose of levonorgestrel. The primary mechanism of action is making the inside of the uterus uninhabitable for sperm. They can also thin the endometrial lining and potentially impair implantation but this is not their usual function. Because they thin the endometrial lining, they can also reduce or even prevent menstrual bleeding. As a result, they are used to treat menorrhagia (heavy menses), once pathologic causes of menorrhagia (such as uterine polyps) have been ruled out.

The commercial brands of levonorgestrel (LNG) releasing framed IUD includes Mirena®, Levosert®, etc. Each of these IUDs is composed of a T-shaped polyethylene radiopaque frame measuring 32 mm × 32 mm (See Fig 11.5). Encircling the stem is a hormone cylinder composed of a mixture of 52 mg levonorgestrel and silicone (polydimethylsiloxane). A semi-opaque silicone (polydimethylsiloxane) membrane controls the drug delivery rate from the reservoir. A polyethylene thread is attached to a hook at the end of the vertical stem creating two tail-strings that are useful to reassure the woman of the IUD's continued presence and to facilitate removal. Levonorgestrel is released during the first year at a rate of 20 μg/d. After early equilibration, plasma levels average 150–200 pg/ml. The average levels over the first 3 years were 218 ng/l.

(iv) **Frameless hormone releasing IUDs:** The FibroPlant® is a LNG releasing anchored frameless IUD in development stage not yet marketed. It is a multicomponent system consisting of a non-resorbable thread with a single knot on its proximal end (See Fig 11.6). Attached thereto is a 3-cm long and 1.2 mm wide (FibroPlant1 14) or 3.5 cm long and 1.6 mm wide (FibroPlant120) fibrous delivery system, releasing 14 mg or 20 mg of LNG per day, respectively. The fiber consists of a levonorgestrel-ethylene vinyl acetate (EVA) core and an EVA rate-controlling membrane. Both systems have a lifespan of 5 years. The fiber is fixed to the anchoring thread by means of a stainless steel clip located 1 cm from the anchoring knot. The anchoring knot is implanted into the myometrium of the uterine fundus using the same insertion instrument as the frameless copper releasing IUD, which secures the implant in the uterine cavity. Since the system has no frame, it is completely flexible, adapting to cavities of every size and shape, in contrast with framed IUSs which sometimes do not fit properly in the uterine cavity.

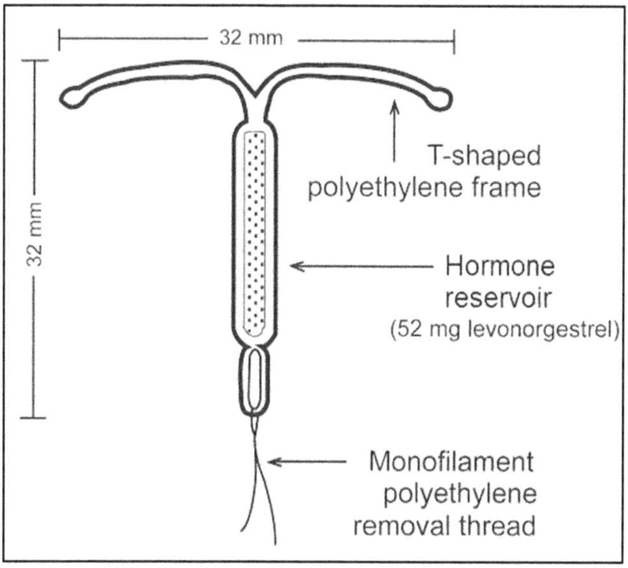

Fig.11.5 Framed hormone releasing IUD.

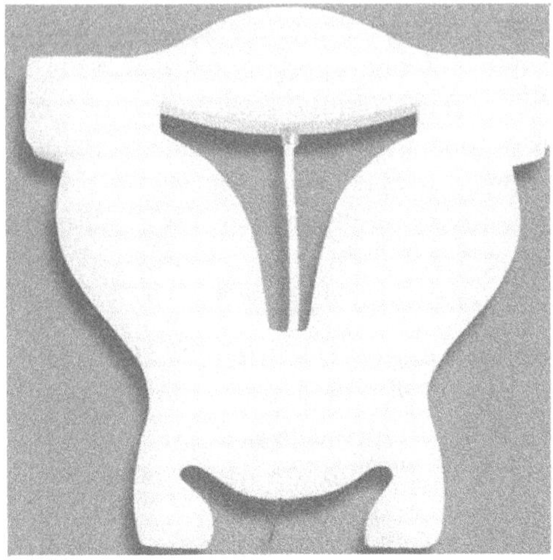

Fig.11.6 Frameless anchored hormone releasing IUD.

11.3 APPLICATIONS

However, several non-contraception applications of IUDs are also in existence. The various applications of IUDs are as follows.

- IUDs have been used for long acting reversible contraception in both, parous and nulliparous women.
- For immediate postpartum and postabortal contraception.
- For post-coital emergency contraception when fitted within the first 5 days following unprotected sex.
- As an alternative to female sterilization.
- Hormone releasing IUDs have been used in hormone replacement therapy.
- Levonorgestrel releasing IUDs have been used for treatment of dysmenorrhea associated with endometriosis.
- The Levonorgestrel releasing IUDs have been used as an alternative to hysterectomy for treatment of excessive menstrual bleeding and medical treatments of idiopathic menorrhagia

11.4 TIME LINES

1909	The German physician Richard Richter developed the first IUD made of silkworm gut.
1962	Development of Lippes loop.

1968	Development of T-shaped inert non-medicated IUD.
1968	Evidence of copper as a contraceptive agent.
1968	Development of T-shaped copper based framed IUD.
1970	Progesterone releasing framed IUD.
1997	GyneFix®, the first frameless copper IUD was introduced.
2001	Levonorgestrel releasing framed IUD (Mirena®) was introduced.

11.5 CHAPTER AT A GLANCE

Term	Description
LARC	Long Acting reversible contraception
IUD	Intrauterine device
IUD Types	Non-medicated and medicated based on either absence or presence of any pharmacological agent, respectively. Framed and frameless based on either presence or absence of polymeric frame in the device.
Applications of IUDs	• long acting reversible contraception in both, parous and nulliparous women. • immediate postpartum and postabortal contraception. • post-coital emergency contraception. • As an alternative to female sterilization. • Treatment in hormone replacement therapy, dysmenorrhea, idiopathic menorrhagia, etc.

EXERCISES

Multiple choice Questions

1. Lippes loop is a-

   (a) Frameless IUD　　(b) Non-medicated IUD

   (c) Hormonal IUD　　(d) Copper based IUD

2. Which of the following is the major limitation of Lippes loop?

   (a) Large size and heavy bleeding

   (b) Tiny size and less bleeding

   (c) inefficient in birth control

   (d) Small surface area

3. Why are most framed IUDs "T-shaped"?

   (a) To honor the inventor of IUDs whose initial name started with "T".

   (b) The "T" shape is a symbol of holiness.

   (c) To easily conform to the shape and size of the endometrial cavity

   (d) To easily remove the IUD when needed.

4. The daily dose of copper for contraception in most women is about-

   (a) 0.5 µg (b) 300 mg

   (c) 30 mg (d) 9.8 µg

5. Which of the following is a framed copper based IUD?

   (a) Paragard (b) CuT 380A

   (c) Nova T (d) All of the above

6. Which of the following is a frameless copper based IUD?

   (a) GyneFix (b) Lippes loop

   (c) FibroPlant (c) Mirena

7. How many copper sleeves are usually present in frameless copper IUDs?

   (a) Four or six (b) Two or three

   (c) Single bilayered (d) About 100

8. What is the total effective surface area of copper in standard frameless copper based IUD exposed to the endometrial environment?

   (a) 330 mm^2 (b) 200 mm^2

   (c) 30 mm^2 (d) 3000 mm^2

9. What is the composition of drug reservoir of Mirena®?
   (a) 52 mg levonorgestrel in silicone
   (b) 20 μg levonorgestrel in silicone
   (c) 52 mg levonorgestrel in EVA
   (d) 20 μg levonorgestrel in EVA
10. Which of the following is a frameless hormone releasing IUD?
   (a) Mirena (b) Nova T
   (c) ParaGard (d) FibroPlant

Short Answer Questions

1. What are the advantages of intrauterine devices?
2. What are the limitations of IUDs?
3. Write a short note on the copper based IUDs.
4. Write a short note on frameless IUDs.
5. What are the applications of IUDs?

Long Answer Questions

1. What is the need of long acting reversible contraception? Classify the intrauterine devices with suitable examples.
2. What are the advantages of IUDs? Discuss in brief about the copper based IUDs.
3. Discuss in brief about the hormonal IUDs. What are the applications of IUDs?
4. What are the limitations of IUDs? Discuss in brief about frameless IUDs.
5. Present a detailed note on various types of intrauterine devices with suitable examples.

Answer Key MCQs

(1) – (b), (2) – (a), (3) – (c), (4) – (d), (5) – (d), (6) – (a), (7) – (a), (8) – (a), (9) – (a), (10) – (d)

BIBLIOGRAPHY

1. Wildemeersch D. New intrauterine technologies for contraception and treatment in nulliparous/adolescent and parous women. Facts Views Vis Obgyn. 2009; 1(3): 223–232.
2. Vyas SP and Khar RK. Controlled Drug Delivery -concepts and advances, Vallabh Prakashan, New Delhi, First edition 2002.
3. Nelson A, Massoudi N. New developments in intrauterine device use: focus on the US. Open Access J Contracept. 2016;7:127-141.

www.ingramcontent.com/pod-product-compliance
Lightning Source LLC
Chambersburg PA
CBHW071224230926
51849CB00001B/20
9789349562868